Political Science

COLLEGE OUTLINE SERIES

Political Science

G. A. JACOBSEN and M. H. LIPMAN

BARNES & NOBLE, INC., NEW YORK
PUBLISHERS • BOOKSELLERS • FOUNDED 1873

©

Reprinted, 1961

COPYRIGHT, 1937, 1939, 1955, 1956
BY BARNES & NOBLE, INC.
ALL RIGHTS RESERVED
L. C. CATALOGUE CARD NUMBER: 56-13335

PRINTED IN THE U.S.A.

Preface

The previous edition has been brought up to date, much new factual information has been added, and the most recent interpretations of political scientists have been included in most discussions. The subject matter has been so rearranged that it supplements the textbooks used in political science courses throughout the country.

This outline helps the student to comprehend political theory: first, by providing the structure of the course; second, by summarizing the descriptive material; and third, by emphasizing the analyses of theory and function. The Quick Reference Table to Standard Textbooks and the Tabulated Bibliography, which are features of most College Outlines, afford the reader ready reference to important topics in the textbooks.

Because of its simplicity and the use of explanatory captions and sideheads, *Political Science* is readable as well as instructive. The selected bibliographies for each chapter offer additional guidance for readers who wish to make an intensive study of one or any aspect of the field.

In addition, the outline should be helpful as a co-ordinate textbook for courses in American government, state and local government, contemporary European government, international relations, and international law. It is a useful complement to courses in history and economics, for which some knowledge of political theories is imperative.

We gratefully acknowledge the helpful comments of Professor Edward Conrad Smith (Chairman of Social Sciences, New York University) on both the revised manuscript and the proofs.

Table of Contents

Chapter

1—The Study of Political Science	1
2—The Historical Background	7
3—The Purposes and Functions of the State	15
4—Theories of State Functions	19
5—The Concept of Statehood	29
6—Sovereignty	35
7—Concepts of Law	41
8—Current Governmental Systems	50
9—The State and the Individual	60
10—Constitutions	68
11—Suffrage and Elections	80
12—Political Parties	90
13—Public Opinion and Influences Upon It	99
14—The Legislature	112
15—The Executive	124
16—The Judiciary	140
17—Public Administration	153
18—Public Finance	164
19—Local Government	177
20—International Relations and Associations	187
21—International Law	208
Selected References 217—Examination Questions 228—Index 238	

Charts

Federal System of the United States	53
Government of the United States	70
Government of Great Britain	73
Government of France	75
Government of the U.S.S.R	75
Territorial Subdivisions of France, Great Britain, and the United States	178
League of Nations	190
Organization of the United Nations	196-197

TABULATED BIBLIOGRAPHY OF STANDARD TEXTBOOKS

This College Outline is keyed to the standard textbooks in two ways: (1) If you are studying one of the following textbooks, consult the cross references listed here to find which pages in the Outline summarize the appropriate chapter of your text. (Roman numerals refer to textbook chapters; Arabic figures refer to corresponding Outline pages.) (2) If you are using the Outline as a basis for study and need a fuller treatment of a topic, consult any of the standard textbooks in the Quick Reference Table on pp. x-xi.

Corry, J. A. and Abraham, Henry J. *Elements of Democratic Government* (New York: Oxford University Press, 1958).
    I (1-14); II-III (19-28); IV (68-79); VI (51-56); VII (177-186); VIII (60-67); IX (90-98); X (99-111); XI (112-123); XII (124-139); XIII (112-123); XIV (127-130); XV (140-152); XVI (159-163); XVII (78, 153-163); XVIII-XIX (187-216).

De Grazia, A. *The Elements of Political Science* (New York: Alfred A. Knopf, Inc., 1952).
    I (1-6); II (1-6, 35-40); V (80-89); VI-VII (90-111); IX (41-49); X (112-123); XI (124-139); XII (153-163); XIII (140-152); XIV (50-59); XVI (187-207); XVII (50-59); XVIII (99-111).

Dillon, Conley H., Leiden, Carl, and Stewart, Paul D. *Introduction to Political Science* (Princeton: D. Van Nostrand Company, Inc., 1958).
    I-II (1-34); III (35-40); IV (24-26); V (80-98); VI-VII (26-28, 54); VIII (15-28); IX (112-123); X (124-139); XI (140-152); XII (124-152); XIII-XIV (153-163).

Finer, H. *The Theory and Practice of Modern Government* (New York: Henry Holt and Company, Inc., 1949).
    I (14-15); II (19-28, 50-55); III (1-14); V (19-28); VIII-IX (68-79); X-XI (50-59); XII-XIII (90-98); XIV (99-111); XV-XVI (90-98); XVII-XXII (112-123); XXIII-XXVI (124-139); XXVII, XXIX-XXX, XXXIII-XXXVI (153-163).

Flechtheim, O. K. *Fundamentals of Political Science* (New York: The Ronald Press Co., 1952).
    I (1-6); II (90-111); III-IV (7-14); V (7-14, 41-49); VI (7-14, 29-34);

VII (4); VIII (60-67); XI (41-49); XII-XIII (68-79); XIV (50-59); XV (60-67); XVI (99-111); XVII-XIX (90-98); XX (80-89); XXI (112-123); XXII (124-139); XXIII (140-152); XXIV-XXV, XXVII (187-207); XXVI (208-216).

Lipson, L. *The Great Issues of Politics; An Introduction to Political Science* (New York: Prentice-Hall, Inc., 2nd ed., 1960).
I (1–6); II (7–14); III (15–18, 29–34); IV–VII (19–28); IX (41–49, 60–98); X (50–59, 112–160); XI (50–59, 160–186); XII (187–216).

Ranney, Austin. *The Governing of Men* (New York: Henry Holt and Company, Inc., 1958).
I-II (1-15); III (15-28); IV (50-59); V (68-79); VI-VIII (60-67); IX (26-27); X-XI (99-111); XII-XIV (80-89); XV (90-98); XVI (99-111); XVII (112-123); XVIII (124-139); XIX (153-163); XX (140-152); XXI (177-186); XXII (187-207); XXIII (209-216).

Rienow, R. *Introduction to Government* (New York: Alfred A. Knopf, Inc., 1956).
I-II (1-6); III (7-18); IV-VII (19-28); IX-XI (29-34, 50-79); XIII (99-111); XIV-XVI (90-98); XVII (60-67); XVIII-XX (80-89); XXI-XXIII (112-123); XXIV (124-139); XXV (153-163); XXVI (164-176); XXVII (140-152); XXVIII (177-186); XXIX-XXX (187-207).

QUICK REFERENCE TABLE TO STANDARD TEXTBOOKS

Roman figures indicate pages; italic figures indicate chapters.

Chapter in this outline	Topic	Corry and Abraham	De Grazia	Dillon et al.	Finer	Flechtheim	Lipson	Ranney	Rienow
I	The Study of Political Science	*1*	*1*	*1*	3	*1*	*1*	*1*	5-8 169-189
II	The Historical Background	*1-2*	30-33 446-475	*2*	37-54	3-6	*2*		7-17
III	The Purposes and Functions of the State	*1-2*	30-33 46-47	110-122		40, 48	*3*	*3*	9-46
IV	Theories of State Functions	*2*	43-46	110-122	5 23-36	6	*4-7*	*3*	*4-7*
V	The Concept of Statehood		30-31	*3*		39-43	58-81	25-38	9-13
VI	Sovereignty	*9, 11*	*2*	*3*	14-15	5 100-106	176-178 293-296 378-381	176-178	20-23 553-558
VII	Concepts of Law		291-298 422-428	32-34		*11*	257-272	98-100 450-451	27-30 27
VIII	Current Governmental Systems	19-24	43-46 *15, 17*	*2*	*10-11*	*14*	324-340	*4*	*11*
IX	The State and the Individual	*8*	576-605	*4, 14*	78-83	121-141 *15*	254-261	6-8	13-19 *17*

		4	298-317	150-151 185-186	8-9	12-13	261-277	5	9
X	Constitutions								
XI	Suffrage and Elections	274-275 398-412	149-173	42-43 256-257	228-236	20	281-287	13	18-19
XII	Political Parties	9	174-206 476-487	252-258	12-13 15-16	2 17-19	277-281	15	14-16
XIII	Public Opinion and Influences Upon It	10	206-250 18	141-143 259-266 274	14 458-470	2, 16		16	13 428-438
XIV	The Legislature	11, 13	318-356	9	17-22	21	265-272 295-304 313-314	17	21-22 428-430 438-442
XV	The Executive	12	357-381	10, 12	23-26	385-392	297-305 308-313	18	24 75-79 96-99
XVI	The Judiciary	15	421-446	11-12	141-157	23	257-261 303-304 313-314	20	27 221-223
XVII	Public Administration	17	382-420	13	27 29-30 33-36	188-191 392-402	303-314 333-334	19	25 489-497
XVIII	Public Finance				508-523		333-335		497-505
XIX	Local Government	7	14			402-407	316-321	21	28
XX	International Relations and Associations	18-19	16			24-25 27	13	22	29-30 461-464
XXI	International Law	18-19	516-524			26	387-392	23	555-556

See pp. viii-ix for list of titles.

1 The Study of Political Science

Civilized man everywhere lives in some system of organized society, which is known as a "state." Under a democratic organization, the individual has a wide choice of what he will do and how he will do it; he participates in determining his own and his neighbor's rights and duties, in selecting the officials who will govern him and his neighbor, and in defining the powers which those officials may exercise. Under a totalitarian organization, the individual has a much narrower choice; he is a worker, or soldier of industry, who must fall into place wherever the state most needs him.

The function of political science is to discover the principles that should be adhered to in public affairs and to study the operations of governments in order to demonstrate what is good, to criticize what is bad or inefficient, and to suggest improvements. Its findings and conclusions may be of immense practical use to constitution-makers, legislators, executives, and judges who need models or norms that can be applied to immediate situations. Again, they may be of immense practical use to individuals who seek to understand the states in which they live. The study of political science deals with problems of social welfare, governmental economic programs, international co-operation, and a wide range of other matters that are urgent concern to public officials and to private citizens. However, practical applications are only one aspect of political science.

If the term *science* means "accumulated knowledge which has been systemized and formulated with reference to the discovery of general truths or the operation of general laws,"[1] *political*

---

[1] *Webster's New International Dictionary*, 2nd ed. (Springfield: G. & C. Merriam Co., 1945).

science is correctly designated "the science of the state": objectively gathering and classifying facts about the state is the main purpose of this branch of learning. These facts pertain to the essential nature of statehood, the forms in which states have existed and do exist, the extent of state authority, and the instrumentalities and procedures through which that authority is exercised; furthermore, they pertain to the relationships among individuals within the state, between individuals and the state, and between state and state.

Obviously, so comprehensive a science will have many subdivisions and many points of common interest with other social studies.

SCOPE

Some colleges have no departments of "political science" as such, but instead have departments of "government" or of "politics" which include substantially the same subject matter in the courses they offer. Nearly every department provides one or more courses during which the various topics brought together in this College Outline are surveyed. Its curriculum is almost certain to include courses in political theory, in public law, and in public administration as well as in various more specialized subjects.[2]

Political Theory. The entire body of doctrines relating to the origin, form, behavior and purposes of the state are dealt with in the study of political theory. Some doctrines are purely speculative, as in More's *Utopia;* others are based upon empirical observations of political phenomena.

Public Law. The organization of governments, the limitations upon governmental authority, the powers and duties of governmental offices and officers, and the obligations of one state to another are handled in the study of public law. This area is so specialized that separate courses are commonly offered in each of its subdivisions—"constitutional," "administrative," and "international" law.

---

[2] Courses are frequently offered in the following subjects: local government, party organization, elections, public opinion, civil rights, public finance, government and business, and international relations and international organization.

Public Administration. In the study of public administration attention is focused upon the methods and techniques used in the actual management of state affairs by executive, legislative, and judicial branches of government. As the complexity of government grows and the social responsibility of the state increases, the traditional distinctions among the managerial powers of the separate branches become ever less clear-cut. Today, for example, the Congress of the United States often delegates sublegislative, subexecutive, and quasi-judicial powers to "administrative" experts. Hence, administration is sometimes referred to as a "fourth branch" of government.

INTER-RELATIONSHIP WITH OTHER BRANCHES OF LEARNING

The beginner in any social study soon realizes that there are no walls between sciences and that even the most minute researches in one may contribute importantly to the advancement of all. In similar fashion, the student of political theory quickly becomes aware that competence in his chosen field depends to an extent upon an acquaintance with more than a half-dozen other branches of learning: (1) The bond between the political scientist and the historian is obvious in the observation that "history is past politics and politics present history." If political science furnishes direction and meaning to many historical studies, so the study of history provides to political science accurate data on the past experiences of states and their governments. The political scientist, therefore, frequently adopts a "historical approach" and employs knowledge of the past when he seeks to interpret present and probable developments in political phenomena. (2) Until late in the nineteenth century, political science and economics (the study of the production, distribution, conservation, and consumption of wealth) were coupled under the name "political economy."[3] Today, these fields are jointly concerned with the fact that economic conditions affect the organization, development, and activities of states, which in turn modify or even prescribe economic conditions. The political scientist regularly adopts an "economic approach" when seeking to in-

---

[3] See "political economy" in H. S. Sloan and A. J. Zurcher, *A Dictionary of Economics,* an Everyday Handbook (New York: Barnes & Noble, Inc., 1953).

terpret such matters as "welfare states," public financial policies, and the relationships between government and business. (3) Strategic frontiers, population pressures, colonial expansion, spheres of influence, and sources of raw materials are fundamental concerns to the political scientist and the geographer. *Geopolitics*[4] indicates one approach which a political scientist frequently must adopt to help explain such problems as the early growth of democracy in Great Britain and the United States and its retarded growth in certain Continental European states; it is significant that, among other factors, the former have enjoyed the protection of strong natural defenses and the latter have not. (4) The political scientist, the sociologist (who specializes in the study of "society as a whole"), and the anthropologist (who studies "mankind" in relation to physical, social, and cultural development) all are deeply concerned with the origins and nature of social control and governmental authority, with the abiding influences of race and culture upon society, and with the patterns of collective human behavior. (5) The political scientist as well as the psychologist promotes studies of the mental and emotional processes motivating the political behavior of individuals and groups. One of the many topics which the political theorist handles from a "psychological approach" is that of public opinion, group pressure, and propaganda. (6) The concepts and doctrines of Plato, Aristotle, and Locke (and other universal thinkers about the state) are important to the specialist in academic philosophy and also to the political theorist; these concepts are the underlying forces in the framing of constitutions and laws. The political scientist considers the branch of philosophy called "ethics," too, when he contemplates the moral background of proposed changes in social legislation. (7) To maintain a full understanding of the facts of political life, the political scientist has to combine the legal with the extralegal viewpoints. A comprehension of the nature of law (and of statutes enacted by legislatures) is indispensable to the political theorist. He should, however, be cautioned against overemphasizing the "juristic" approach—as many authorities do when they regard the state purely as a "legal person" and the political society

---

[4] "A science concerned with the dependence of domestic and foreign politics of a people upon the physical environment."—*Webster's New International Dictionary* (Springfield: G. & C. Merriam Co., 1945).

merely as a collection of legal rights and obligations. (8) The political theorist must possess a broad scientific background and a knowledge of current political problems, and he must employ scientific methods in gathering and evaluating data and in drawing conclusions. These involve a proper application of statistical procedures for the quantitative measurement of social phenomena and of logical procedures for the analysis of reasoning.

METHODS

No one today pretends that political science is an "exact science" like chemistry and physics: its subject matter is too closely associated with human nature and emotions to permit certainty of conclusion or prediction, its experiments are not capable of laboratory control, and its terminology is not precise.[5] Yet all true sciences, whether social or natural, are brothers with a common ancestry in ancient and medieval philosophy and modern empirical thinking.

Prior to the Renaissance, formal reasoning followed the methods of *deductive logic* (that is, the drawing of specific conclusions from premises preassumed to be infallible). So long as accredited thinkers in all fields grounded their theories upon premises taken from Holy Scriptures, from the works of Aristotle, or from other supposedly supreme authorities, political philosophers were not overly concerned with assembling and analyzing facts about actual states, governments, and laws. During the Renaissance, and particularly as a result of new discoveries in such fields as astronomy, geography, and medicine, the trend in methods of reasoning turned towards *inductive logic* (that is, the establishing of general truths upon the basis of known facts before such truths were to be used as premises for specific application). With the general advance of experimental science, which draws working hypotheses from demonstrable facts and which continuously checks and revises its hypotheses in the light of new discoveries,

---

[5] Attempts have been made to couple political science with the exact sciences. For example, after the announcement of the Darwinian theory, a few enthusiasts propounded an "organismic theory" of political society which regarded states as organisms and men and women as cells within those organisms; but their exclusively "biological approach" was soon discredited because the laws of growth and change that apply to living organisms simply do not apply to states. Again, some writers have sought to show that the institution of checks and balances in modern democratic government is an application of the Newtonian theory of the universe.

political science became the objective factual study which it is today.[6]

After precisely defining his immediate problem for investigation, the political scientist must observe four rules. (1) He must take care to assemble all available pertinent data. (2) He must be critical of his sources of information and evaluate each in the light of the circumstances behind it. (3) He must avoid superficial analyses and hasty conclusions. (4) He must regard the results of his own investigations as hypotheses to be tested (for accuracy and applicability) by other specialists in his field.

His methods of collecting and analyzing data are sometimes called "observational" ("experimental") "historical," or "comparative." Usually they are all three.

Observational (Experimental) Method. Although the political scientist can not, like the laboratory researcher, arrange experiments to order, he can observe the workings of political processes under a vast variety of circumstances. His "laboratory" consists of the some seventy national states in today's world; their separate component political divisions (such as states or provinces); their thousands of counties, cities, and other local governmental units; and their colonies and dependencies. To the political theorist, every change in governmental structure, law, or policy has significance.

Historical and Comparative Methods. If he could depend upon the evidence of the past experiences of states to explain the present and probable future development of political institutions, the political scientist would employ a purely historical method. Actually, however, he must correlate economic, geographical, psychological, or other scientific approaches and even conduct supplementary researches in related fields before he attempts to draw conclusions of general validity.

---

[6] "Political thought" is as old as the first human attempts at co-operation and "political philosophy" is as old as the first attempts to formulate doctrines about human co-operation; but "political science," as we use the term today, is no older than modern experimental science. Although individual kings and statesmen may have used trial-and-error methods in formulating policies from time immemorial, a landmark in the development of political science is sometimes recognized in the writings of the Renaissance statesman Niccolo Machiavelli (1469-1527), and particularly in his book *The Prince*. At all events, Machiavelli derived his theories of government and statecraft from acute observations of human nature and of conditions in the Italian principalities of his day.

2 The Historical Background

Man's subjection to political and social authority began untold centuries before recorded history. Once established political and social authority continued to increase in scope and complexity. The earliest written records contain accounts of the activities of rulers during peace and war, often with trenchant observations about good and bad management. The attitudes of theorists in many eras have been similarly varied: some have supported an existing order, some have taken the lead in bringing about changes, and some have provided a restraining influence.

STAGES IN THE DEVELOPMENT OF THE MODERN STATE

A short summary of political evolution from preliterary times to the mid-twentieth century will provide a frame of reference for the discussion of contemporary states and contemporary political theories.

Primitive Social Units. Despite a lack of written records, sociologists and anthropologists generally agree that the first social unit was the *family* headed by a parent, that a later and larger unit was the *clan* of related families headed by a single chieftain or by a council, and that a still broader unit was the *tribe* of families connected by ancestry, by friendship, and by a realization of advantages to be obtained through co-operation under some common head.[1]

It is safe for the political scientist to assume that important bonds of cohesion within primitive social units were a sense of common ancestry, common language, and common religion, a

---

[1] Sometimes tribes formed *leagues,* such as that which existed among the twelve tribes of Israel.

7

realization of common military and economic interests, and a geographic proximity. As in various tribal civilizations that exist today, the sense of kinship was probably so strong that candidates for chieftainship, in the absence of blood connection, resorted to fictitious adoption into some leading family before assuming authority. It is generally assumed that prehistoric religions included both ancestor worship and nature worship and that religious rites were carried out by family or tribal heads until a special priestly class arose to officiate and to proclaim supernatural justification of tribal customs and acts. Common needs in times of war certainly encouraged co-operation under unified leadership. Economic needs, even in the hunting-and-fishing stage of society, required leaders to organize projects and to oversee division of spoils; in pastoral stages, they required recognition of property rights and a greater division of labor; and in handicraft and commercial stages, they required trade agreements. Finally, geographic proximity must have led to claims of territory by individuals and by tribes and to the use of force in coercing some individuals and tribes into the service of others.

The political scientist can say positively, then, that laws and governmental structures arose long before the time writings existed and that man at an early stage surrendered much individual freedom to the will of society. Upon the bases of sociology and anthropology, he can premise that the roots of contemporary cultural, economic, geographic, and military bonds and antagonisms are very old, however much these bonds and antagonisms may have become distorted in the course of written history. The political scientist must regard as pure hypotheses any conceptions of the benevolence or selfishness of man in a "state of nature," of the "natural rights" of mankind, or of "social contracts" between primitive subjects and primitive rulers; but he must study such hypotheses and recognize their influence in the formation of modern state constitutions.

The States and Empires of the Ancient World. A transition from unrecorded to early recorded history brings successively into focus the empires which existed in Asia Minor and the Far East (*c.* 4500-500 B.C.), the Greek city-states (*c.* 800-363 B.C.) and the Roman Empire (*c.* 27 B.C.-476 A.D.). Original bonds of kinship were complicated by a division of society into classes—noblemen, freemen, and slaves; simple bonds of religion were complicated by the fact that an official state religion was sometimes superimposed upon the beliefs of divergent private groups. However, bonds of common military and economic welfare had become stronger in holding societies together than they had been in primitive eras.

EASTERN EMPIRES. People congregated in those regions of the world which nature had favored with warm climates, fertile soils, abundance of water, and unbroken plains. These conditions permitted men to accumulate wealth and to develop and to expand their lands. Such were the geographical conditions in the valleys of the Nile, the Tigris-Euphrates, the Ganges, the Yangtze, and the Yellow rivers where the Eastern empires sprang up in ancient times. These Oriental empires did not accomplish the adjustment necessary for successful government. They emphasized the exaltation of and fear of the ruler, and the people saw the empires as tax-burdens and tax-collectors and themselves as slaves. None of the empires had any real cohesion because they were based on despotism. Under such circumstances, political and cultural unity was impossible and the empires disintegrated under weak rulers.

In these Eastern empires, the ocean was considered a handicap, not an opportunity for promoting commercial or cultural enterprises. The cultural centers of these empires lay in their valleys, for they were mainly agricultural powers. As such, they increased the yields of their lands by developing the first-known irrigation systems.

GREEK CITY-STATES. The islands of the Aegean Sea and the deeply indented coasts and secluded valleys of the Greek mainland encouraged the development of maritime city-states and eventually led to the colonization of areas with which they had commercial dealings. On the other hand, the natural barriers within the region made a union of city-states impossible or unsatisfactory.

The course of political evolution varied in place and time among the Greek city-states, but in general the pattern followed the Aristotelian cycle of monarchy, tyranny, aristocracy, oligarchy, and democracy. The small size of the city, with its active and changing life, was conducive to the development of individual enterprise and democratic government. On this basis was built a short and brilliant civilization. At that time, however, democracy functioned well only in states with very small areas and the rest of the then-known world was unprepared for it.

Lack of unity was the main deficiency of the political system of the Greek city-states. It was an important factor in their conquest by Philip of Macedon (4 c. b.c.) and, afterwards, in their control by Rome.

THE ROMAN EMPIRE. The origins of the Italian city-states were similar to those in Greece, except that in Italy the small city-states were set up as centers of agricultural communities. Eventually, the Italian city-states were united (usually by force) with Rome at the head. Since there were fewer geographical barriers in Italy than in Greece, unification was more easily attained. At this point, Rome began the process of extending citizenship to selected inhabitants of conquered lands.

Italy's subsequent career of conquest and expansion rendered her city-state constitution inapplicable to a world empire. Consequently, she developed another type of state: an imperial system with emphasis on authority (which was vested in the hands of the Roman aristocracy), centralized organization, and uniformity of law. With these innovations emperor worship became a patriotic duty.

The Roman Empire contributed importantly to many modern systems of law (see Chapter 7), colonial administration, and ideas of world unity. Its influence may be seen in the development of international law (see Chapter 21) and world organization (see Chapter 20).

But there were also inherent weaknesses in the system. It provided no laboratory in which individual liberty could be nurtured. Local self-government languished even in the city of Rome, and the result was a steady degeneration of Roman patriotism and the ultimate collapse of the empire. The Teutonic tribes, who had not been conquered, invaded the empire in the fifth century, dividing the land among themselves and starting the feudal system.

Kingdoms of Medieval Europe. Although the Teutonic tribes overran the Roman Empire in the west, the empire in the east with its capital at Constantinople continued to exist. After the rise of Mohammedanism, it was severely limited in both its territory and its power.

THE HISTORICAL BACKGROUND

It is doubtful whether the feudal kingdoms of Europe would be considered "states," if they existed today. Each kingdom was divided into sections controlled by dukes, counts, and other members of the nobility, who, although they had sworn allegiance to a titular king, were accustomed to act independently.

With control of the land—which became important after the decay of Roman commerce—came political power. The Teutonic concepts of individualism, freedom, and local autonomy conflicted with the Roman system which emphasized centralized authority. The results were confusion, conflicts in law and authority, and absence of both unity and liberty.

The Church retained its unity, adopted a modified form of imperialism, strengthened and consolidated its power, and enlarged the scope of its control. However, its influence started to diminish in the fourteenth century when the Renaissance, with its reaction against authority and its interest in many cultures, swept over Europe. During the period of the Reformation, which followed, much of Europe embraced Protestantism. Furthermore, the Crusades had revived commerce, which in turn increased the wealth and power of the cities.

During this period many forces were interacting to develop nationalistic feelings: the growth of the mercantile and commercial classes (which were hostile to the feudal system), the growth of cities, the decline of the power of the Church, the impact of other cultures, and the consequent formation of new cultures and common interests. As a result, a new form of political life gradually unfolded.

Modern States and Empires. National cultural ties, strengthened by natural boundaries, proved a foundation for combining feudal territories into larger political divisions. Following the restoration of order within national states, there resulted a new social stratification and a subsequent change of emphasis in political society. Moreover, as in other eras, the renewed strength of nations made many of them ambitious to acquire more territory.

NATIONAL STATES. The great enemies of centralized authority had been the feudal lords, against whom the kings and the people united. The advent of national states, organized according to cultural ties, destroyed the power of the local lords and gave rise to the theory of legal equality of states in international law.

National states emerged as absolute monarchies, with national armies and national systems of taxation, which replaced old feudal levies. Among these states were France, Spain, England, Switzerland, The Netherlands, and Russia, and later, Germany and Italy.

DEMOCRATIC STATES. As commerce and industry progressed the number of industrial workers increased greatly, and many serfs became tenants, establishing a new class of small landholders. As the masses of people acquired wealth and education, they demanded additional political rights and privileges. Representative assemblies developed in England, for example, making possible a gradual transition from absolute monarchy of the national state to a limited monarchy or a democracy. Concepts of limited governmental authority and of individual rights grew as these institutional changes occurred.

Some political theorists consider the modern democratic state as the most advanced form of state evolution. Its combination of local self-government with national representation they believe makes possible an adjustment of liberty and sovereignty which may serve the interests of individuals and of society. Many problems of the relationship of the state to individuals and to associations within the state still remain to be solved. At one extreme, there are those who demand strong governments to provide for efficient administration even at the expense of democracy, and, at the other extreme, there are those who insist on economic and political control of the state by the working class. Obviously, there are many viewpoints between these extremes.

COLONIAL EMPIRES. Despite the emphasis which the countries of modern Europe have placed on ethnic unity and on natural boundaries, there has been a marked tendency toward the development of overseas empires. Large sections of Africa and Asia are claimed by one or another European power. Competition for these colonial lands has been a major element in conflicts among states.

Subjection of dependent peoples to the great powers is considered incompatible with the theory of democracy and of self-determination of peoples. It is sometimes argued, contrariwise, that economic interdependence today is so great that the subjected people as well as the rulers benefit from the relationship of empire. However, with the increase in trade, education, and industry in overseas possessions, there have come insistent demands for self-determination and independence. Within the present century, the British Empire has become an "empire-commonwealth" held together by loose political arrangements and by economic interests, traditions of co-operation, and kinship. Most of the rich Dutch colonial empire was lost when the Republic of Indonesia became independent. Other empires are feeling the same stresses.

It is obvious, then, that nationalism and internationalism are powerful influences which often pull in opposite directions. They may be, however, only two phases of the same movement toward an ultimate world federation based on national units.

STAGES IN THE DEVELOPMENT OF POLITICAL SCIENCE

Those who trace the origins and growth of political science as a branch of modern learning frequently point out three chronologically overlapping stages in the development of political thought.

In an early "religious stage" the state was regarded as an instrument for establishing order and justice as laid down in God's law; political (as well as other) phenomena were attributed to supernatural causes. This stage began well before the advent of recorded history and persisted as long as the divine right of kings was supported—that is, it persisted until relatively recent times.

In a "metaphysical stage," the state was regarded as the most perfect of human institutions. Plato and Aristotle thought of it as the means by which the individual could obtain his highest development. Scholastic writers of the Middle Ages attempted to reconcile this viewpoint with religious theories. Some influential nineteenth-century idealists (notably Hegel, 1770-1831) glorified the state at the expense of the individuals who compose it and laid the foundations of a new absolutism in the form of totalitarianism.

In a "positive stage" the state was and still is regarded as a human institution which can be assessed and improved by empirical observation and experimentation. This stage is considered to have been ushered in by the Renaissance thinker Niccolo Machiavelli (1469-1527).

It is with the positive stage that political thought first becomes a "science" based upon "inductive" conclusions, for political thought during the religious and metaphysical stages was almost wholly "deductive"—i.e., based upon *a priori* application of what were accepted as truths established by a god or at least by nature.

3 The Purposes and Functions of the State

For what purposes does the state exist? This question has been asked many times in every age from the beginning of political society. It is indeed the fundamental question of politics. Should the state do a certain thing, or refrain from doing it? Different answers have been given by patricians and plebeians, cavaliers and puritans, and individualists and socialists as each group has urged that the adoption of its own ideas would best subserve the interests of society as a whole. The building of irrigation works in ancient Mesopotamia, the protection of commerce in Carthage, the development of the cultured man in Athens—all must have appeared to be essential functions of the state along with protection from invasion and maintenance of order. In more recent times, state action for the enhancement of resources, for the proper distribution of wealth, and for social services have seemed important. There is no single best theory concerning the purposes of the state that will be valid at all times and for all societies. The political scientist should consider how far advanced in civilization a society is, the stage of its political development, the nature of the problems that it faces, and its needs and aspirations. Changes in social conditions beget altered concepts of the purposes of the state.

THE PURPOSES OF THE STATE

A brief analysis of purposes provides a useful frame of reference for evaluating theories of state functions. The purposes or ends of the state are the ultimate aims for which it exists.

Establishment of Order. A primary end of the state is to insure freedom from invasion and to secure domestic tranquility and justice for its people. The existence of the state can hardly be justified unless it succeeds reasonably well in achieving this end. The attainment of all other objectives depends on the success of the state in securing the highest degree of order consistent with the liberties of individuals and of groups in the society.

Promotion of Individual Welfare. Nearly all modern theory stresses the importance of the individual. The very existence of the state creates a condition in which individual progress can be realized. Whether the individual fares best through decisions "made for him" or through decisions "made by him" constitutes an essential difference between totalitarian and democratic theory. Democratic theory recognizes the inherent worth of the individual and seeks to provide the most favorable conditions, consistent with the interests of society as a whole, under which he may complete the fulfillment of his personality. Among these conditions are the protection of personal rights and effective participation in government.

Promotion of General Welfare. A third end of the state is the development of public capacities. This involves care for the common interests of the society and provision for united action in achieving goals which individuals or associations can not achieve by themselves. It involves the reconciliation of interests among groups and between individuals or groups and the society as a whole.

Promotion of Morality. One of the oldest and most persistent theories declares that an essential purpose of the state is to promote morality among its people. Applications of the theory in various ages have usually been attempts to impose upon a citizenry one standard of morality, one code of conduct, or one religion. There is something incongruous in the use of force to establish morals, for force begets physical resistance to force, with resulting loss in the maintenance of order (moral action depends upon voluntary behavior). However, the state is not obliged to remain neutral on such matters. It may punish vicious and criminal conduct by criminal laws and it may encourage good conduct by means of various rewards.

THE FUNCTIONS OF THE STATE

Theorists may be in substantial agreement concerning the purposes of the state and yet be poles apart in their ideas of state functions. The *functions* of the state may be defined in terms of the particular activities in which it engages. Inevitably, any debate over the propriety or impropriety of the state's exercising a function soon becomes involved with the question of ultimate aims. Whether or not a particular state should undertake a given function must be considered with reference to the questions: (1) Is the end desirable? (2) Will the means to be used actually accomplish the end? (3) Is the cost of attaining the end commensurate with the good to be obtained? Obviously, the answers will vary widely from place to place, from time to time, and according to the underlying philosophy of state functions.

In surveying the functions carried on in any particular state, it is necessary to include those delegated to governments of provinces, cities, and other subdivisions, as well as those undertaken by the central government. Functions may be classified as (1) *essential,* those which are necessary to the existence of the state; (2) *service,* those which the state may perform or not perform according to the needs and desires of the society at a given time; and (3) *business,* those in which the state sells services or goods.

Essential Functions. The state must exercise those functions which are necessary to uphold its power and to safeguard its existence. *Essential functions* include the following: the maintenance of such armed forces as are necessary for defense against foreign invasion or domestic violence; the maintenance of such police forces as are essential for the suppression of crime and the prosecution of criminals; the maintenance of courts for the punishment of offenses, for the protection of the rights of individuals, and for the settlement of controversies by legal means; the maintenance of a foreign service for the conduct of relations with other states; the maintenance of tax-collecting and record-keeping systems for the implementation of other functions.

Service Functions. *Service functions* include many activities conducive to the attainment of general welfare or other ends of the state. (It is sometimes difficult to determine the exact boundary between these and essential functions. For example, the building of railways and highways seems at first thought to be a service function; however, strategic considerations may dictate the building of such works for purposes of national defense.)

Service functions include many activities which might not exist at all unless the state engaged in them. Among these are the care of the poor and the incapacitated; the building of roads, canals, docks, bridges, harbors, and the like; provision for education, public parks, and recreation centers; maintenance of sanitation and other assets to public health; the regulation of business "clothed with a public interest" and the establishment of basic rules for the conduct of other business enterprises; and the dissemination of information.

Business Functions. The *business functions* include acts which might be carried out for profit by individuals or private corporations if the state did not exercise them. Sometimes the state engages in them because private capital is not available at all or is available only in insufficient amounts. Sometimes, as in the postal service, the state desires to extend service throughout its whole territory to many places where private enterprise could not make a profit. Other motives are related to inadequacy of the services or to excessive charges of private enterprises. Business functions include social security, unemployment and workmen's compensation, insurance, protection of bank deposits, and the maintenance of employment offices. In many countries, railways, telephones, and radio stations are owned and operated by the state.

4 Theories of State Functions

Theories of state functions are numerous and varied, ranging from the extreme of the *anarchist* who denies the necessity of any government to the extreme of the *communist* who would have the state take over all the instruments of production and distribution and, in addition, regulate minutely many details in the private lives of individuals. However, for our discussion the major theories of state functions may be classified according to their relationships to economic systems and according to their prominence in the contemporary scene. In considering these theories, the student should keep in mind the chief purposes for which the state exists.

POLITICO-ECONOMIC THEORIES OF STATE FUNCTIONS

The emphasis which most of the following theories place upon economics might almost suggest that there is a struggle today between political and economic power. Actually, they can not be divorced; they constantly react against each other and are dynamic and forever changing. The problem of politics is to find a proper adjustment among the economic forces of modern life—an adjustment that will benefit the whole society and avoid disruptive and wasteful conflicts.

Anarchism. Generally basing their conclusions upon a faith in the innate goodness and reasonableness of human nature, anarchists deny any need for the existence of states. They believe that law and order could be maintained without force. Anarchists would replace coercive government with voluntary associations which would perform those few state functions considered necessary. Followers of this theory would replace private ownership with collective ownership. There is a difference of opinion among the leading advocates of anarchism as to the precise nature of the social and economic order which would prevail after the dissolution of the state, and there is disagreement as to the means to be used for abolishing the state. Some (like Mikhail Bakunin in midnineteenth-century Russia) have advocated a general program of violence, but others believe that the desired ends can best be reached by means of peaceful co-operation.

Opponents of anarchism deny that voluntary associations would be sufficient to prevent the strong from encroaching upon the weak; they assert that the associations themselves would soon develop the characteristics of statehood. However, anarchists have made substantial contributions to political thought through their criticisms of the faults of coercive government.

Individualism. Individualist theories today are supported by strange bedfellows: among them are those who for selfish ends desire to escape governmental control and those who on principle object to interference with private lives and habits.

The extreme individualist is not an anarchist, for he considers the state to be necessary. It is needed to protect life, liberty, and property; but its powers should be limited to these essential (as opposed to service and business) functions. The state should interfere in human activities only to prevent encroachment of the strong upon the liberties of the weak; it is not justified in taking positive action merely for the sake of general welfare, since any extension of state power is always made at the expense of individual freedom. The more moderate individualist, however, feels that state regulation and, in some instances, even state services are necessary to the realization of true individual freedom. Those of this viewpoint insist essentially that the exercise of each function of the state must be determined by the degree to which it promotes the best interests of society and of the individual.

Theories of individualism have been supported on various ethical, political, and economic grounds. Conceptions of "natural law" derived from reason and from the immutable principles of morality and justice have been advanced as justification, on the ground that only through the greatest degree of personal freedom can man develop his faculties and achieve a truly advanced culture.

Individualists believe that many duties now undertaken by the state could be better performed by private organizations: they hold that the state is not equipped to perform certain services, that government is extravagant and inefficient whereas private initiative would provide better service at less cost.

Some individualists have held that in economics there is a "natural order," which would work itself out to the advantage of all concerned if there were no interference by governmental laws and regulations. If each individual would pursue his own best interests, both private and public welfare, it has been thought, would be achieved. Unrestricted competition would provide the proper balance between wages and prices, keep interest at a reasonable rate, stimulate production, and promote the general good.

Critics of individualist theories point to the error of assuming that the general welfare is necessarily the sum of individual welfares. Also, they point to those who through chance or through lack of opportunity or capacity are unable to provide for themselves in an enormously complicated economic system.

Socialism. The term *socialist* may be applied to those doctrines which stand for a relatively rapid and sweeping economic collectivism. The bases of socialism are (1) collective control of at least the means of production and (2) a wide extension of state activity. In a socialist society the organized community would own and manage the land, capital, and the productive mechanism; its activities would extend to the distribution of the products of industry and to everything that is necessary for the promotion of the general welfare.

Advocates of socialism hold that it would remedy the injustices and wastefulness of the capitalist system. Subject to intelligent regulation, the community's economic requirements could be more closely judged and an efficient program could be initiated to meet the demand. Duplication, waste, spoilage, unnecessary competition, and unproductive competitive advertising and selling could be eliminated; great inequalities of wealth and opportunity could be reduced.

Socialists are not agreed as to the method of distributing income in their ideal state. Some feel that the abundance of wealth would be such that there would be plenty for all, with no real problem of distribution. Others say, "from each according to his capacity; to each according to his need." Still others advocate a wage system, some arguing for equality of wages and some for differentiation according to performance.

Opponents of socialism maintain that socialists overemphasize the state's capacity for effective operation. They insist that a socialist regime would promote deterioration, subterfuge, and the power of individual influence. Governmental managers, they assert, would be content to do things in a bureaucratic way. Socialism and democracy could not go hand in hand because regimentation would preclude individual liberty. They deny that socialism would provide incentive to individual initiative, arguing that men do not work effectively without a profit motive and that the result of socialism would be general poverty instead of general wealth.

Communism. Both communism and socialism were developed from the theories of Karl Marx. One of the main differences is in the means to be employed: socialists emphasize the possibility of attaining their objectives through peaceful democratic processes; communists rely implicitly on those portions of Marxian theory which preach the necessity for catastrophic revolution. This, communists believe, will be followed by a concentrated coercive rule with ruthless use of force to crush opposition until all but the proletarian class shall have disappeared. Then there will follow a transition period in which the state will "wither away" because the reason for its existence—the suppression of workers in the interest of the capitalist class—will have ceased to exist.

Communism, in theory as well as in practice, goes further than socialism in advocating the abolition of private property. Such freedom of enterprise as exists is restricted to the small trader and the cultivator of a small plot of ground not included in a collective farm. Marx rejected democratic ideals of freedom, justice, and equality because these terms seemed to have no real meaning in a society in which masses were exploited.

Syndicalism. The doctrines of *syndicalism* have been drawn from Marxian socialism, anarchism, and pluralism.[1] The goal

---

[1] *Pluralism* is "the doctrine that government authority within a community should be distributed among various functional groups and neither monopolized nor—according to some writers—shared by a sovereign power in the state."—E. C. Smith and A. J. Zurcher (eds.), *Dictionary of American Politics*, an Everyday Handbook (New York: Barnes & Noble, Inc., 1955).

of the syndicalists is to place ownership of the means of production and exchange into the hands of the workers. The characteristic feature of the proposed syndicalist society is extreme decentralization. Local workers would form syndicates according to their trades; these syndicates, affiliated through labor exchanges, would perform local police and judicial services. National federations of syndicates would collectively own the capital of society. In its organization, syndicalism would resemble closely the soviet system.

Guild Socialism. *Guild socialism* derives its theory from both socialism and syndicalism; its theory has in turn had much influence with socialists and syndicalists and also with fascists. The goal of guild socialism is the attainment of democracy in economic life as well as in political life. Its advocates would organize society into guilds or unions with the shop unit as an important basis of representation. Economic functions would be performed through guild organizations; all political functions would be exercised by the state, which, among other things, would be the supreme arbiter in conflicts among guilds.

Fascism. *Fascism* is an opportunistic philosophy hastily composed after Mussolini's seizure of power in Italy in 1922. Its elements are derived from idealism, nationalism, socialism, syndicalism, and even republicanism. The basic concept of fascism is that the state has a life, unity, and will of its own apart from, superior to, and not necessarily identical with, the wills of the individuals who compose it. The discretion of the rulers determines both the character and extent of the state's power. The role of the people is obedience and subjection to discipline, from which they are supposed to achieve their moral and cultural destiny. The government of the state may control every kind of human endeavor. Labor and capital must work together, under state compulsion if necessary. The fascist regime was both authoritarian and totalitarian.

Empirical Collectivism. The general attitude toward the functions of government which prevails in the United States and many other industrialized states may be called, for want of a better term, *empirical collectivism*. It is empirical because it is based on experience rather than on any well-defined theory. It is collectivist because it represents an attempt to promote the general welfare by supplying services which could not be provided, or be provided so well or so inexpensively, by private enterprise. Factors contributing to the growth of the movement have been scientific and technological developments, the concentration of industry, urbanization, and the consequent dependence of the individual on others for social services. Advocates of collectivism have included populists, radicals, liberals, progressives, New Dealers, and moderate conservatives.

They reject the doctrines of extreme individualism because they regard them as inefficient in the conservation of social values. They reject also the socialist doctrines of economic determinism and class warfare. They recognize, however, the existence of groupings in society whose social, cultural, and economic opportunities are unequal because of differences in wealth and productive power. They emphasize the interdependence of all groups and seek proper adjustments in their relations to one another. Typical proposals deal with public ownership or rigid regulation of public services such as electric power and light, telephones, water supplies, and transportation; labor legislation for the protection of all workers; the suppression of monopolistic power in industry; the use of the taxing power to control economic enterprise and in some degree to redistribute wealth; conservation and other policies to insure the proper use of natural resources; social security against old age and unemployment; and facilities for recreation. Under the National Industrial Recovery Act (1933-1935), the United States sponsored self-government in industry; but the act was declared unconstitutional, mainly because Congress had not fixed precisely enough the limits within which the code authorities for each industry should operate.

CONTEMPORARY THEORIES OF STATE FUNCTIONS

By the end of World War I, it was apparent that the traditional classification of governments—as absolute and limited monarchies, aristocracies, and republics—was of little practical value in differentiating among existing governments. Many new constitutions had been drawn up, all creating governments of popular form. However, all were untried and some proved unstable. Lord Bryce in his *Modern Democracies* (1921) made a partial classification of governments based, as he said, upon political "facts." Of the twenty-one "republics" in the Western Hemisphere, he classified only two as ostensible "democracies";

furthermore, he found that nine European "monarchies" and three British "dominions," which gave allegiance to a king met his tests for democracies because their governments were responsible to electoral majorities.

As dictators appeared in governments with republican forms, many observers carried Bryce's classification to its logical conclusion; that is, governments began to be classified as "democracies" or "dictatorships."

Democracy. By 1921, the word "democracy" had long been in general use as an expression of a broad social ideal. The slogan of the French Revolution (1789), "Liberty, Equality, and Fraternity," expresses this ideal. It is impossible to achieve complete liberty for the individual without the development of a condition of inequality. On the other hand, if complete equality is enforced, the liberty of the individual to develop his own intellectual and other resources is impaired. Equality and liberty, therefore, at first glance appear to be antithetical concepts. Through the application of the third principle, fraternity, a reconciliation between liberty and equality may be achieved. The modern idea of *democracy* includes all three concepts applied in harmonious adjustment with one another.

Democracy connotes equality of participation in the power to determine the major issues of public policy—in other words, universal suffrage. But equality in suffrage is meaningless unless it is accompanied by the liberty to exercise a genuine choice, by secret ballot, among candidates or measures. This liberty implies free access by the voter to sources of information and therefore includes freedom of speech and of the press, freedom of petition and of assembly, and freedom from arrest for political opinions. Inasmuch as one man acting alone can exert little influence, democracy signifies freedom to organize political parties. It expresses further the parties' freedom to criticize and oppose the policy of the government; to convince others, if they can, that the government's policy is unwise; and to offer both alternative policies and alternative slates of candidates for the government. Democracy implies fairly frequent elections and the acceptance of majority decisions. Without those freedoms, equality in voting is a mockery. Equality and freedom of the suffrage are of little value unless the representative body is also free. The traditional frequency of legislative sessions and the exemptions of members from arrest and from being called to account by the executive for words spoken in debate must be observed.

For the protection of equality and liberty, democracy also implies that there must be a constitution which actually limits the powers of government officials. It does not matter whether the constitution be written or unwritten. It is essential that the limitations of the constitution should be enforced either by the legislature (as in Great Britain and France) or by the courts (as in the United States). Democracy includes also the principle of equality before the law and the liberties that must be safeguarded by due process of law. The individual's rights must be protected from encroachments by officers of the government (through administrative courts as in France or through what the British call the "rule of law" and Americans call "due process"). The basic concepts of democracy are that the individual is an end in himself and that government is a means of achieving the fullest development for all individuals.

Not everyone would agree with the foregoing analysis. Some would include references to economic and social democracy or would emphasize equality of opportunity and the absence of distinctions not based on merit. Others would object that "liberty" is not sufficiently emphasized. Especially violent objections would come from those who interpret "democracy" solely in terms of equality, as do all communists when they claim that true democracy exists only in the U.S.S.R. It may be freely admitted that the tenets of democracy are not always fully realized in "democratic" states. No state has fully enforced the criminal code or fully abolished poverty. But many governments have striven toward the ends of democracy and have met with pronounced success.

Dictatorship. In times of acute national crises, the ancient Romans sometimes appointed one or two dictators for strictly limited periods. The modern dictator probably derived his title from this source, but there the resemblance ceases. The modern dictator, self-called to his position, never returns to his plow. Aristotle might have classified him as a "tyrant" from his methods both of gaining and exercising power. Some modern observers have called him an "absolute monarch, twentieth-century style." He is not a hereditary monarch, and he refrains from taking any monarchial title, but he does resemble historical monarchs in some respects. It is precisely because his methods are modern that dictatorship must be classified as a special kind of government.

THE OVER-ALL PATTERN OF DICTATORSHIPS. To begin with, the dictator utilizes all the discoveries of modern psychology concerning methods of influencing the human mind. He identifies himself with the people by taking a title like "Leader." He stages great spectacles full of color, music, symbolism, and hypnotic suggestion. He disposes of real or potential opposition by endlessly repeating lies, by finding scapegoats, and by employing other propagandist methods—by using force if he must. He stirs the popular imagination by portraying the brilliant destiny toward which he is leading his people. He speaks much of "duty," "service," "equality," and "democracy." He maintains constitutional and popular forms of government except such as he says may be utilized by "enemies of the state"—meaning enemies of his own regime—to weaken or destroy it. The suffrage is widely extended and elections are frequent; but there is no opportunity to cast a really secret ballot. Nominations are monopolized by one party, leaving the voter no choice but to ratify the official slate. Under such circumstances the election becomes an empty form, a ritual in which the voter reaffirms his loyalty to the regime. The almost unbelievably high percentage of participation in elections is asserted to be "proof positive" of popular support. Actually, legislative bodies become mere sounding boards for official statements, and judges become subject to political control.

TOTALITARIANISM IN THE U.S.S.R. The foregoing statement of the characteristics of dictatorship applies to the Soviet dictatorship as well as to others. Communism is totalitarian in scope. Actual power in the U.S.S.R. is in the hands of the *Politburo,* an organization of the Communist party, which determines the orthodox party line and keeps a watchful eye over the various ministries. It also controls the M.V.D. (*Ministerstvo Vnutrennikh Del,* The Soviet Ministry of Internal Affairs) which is essentially a secret police force. Government is elaborate in structure. The Constitution of 1936—with its bill of rights guaranteeing, among other things, the freedom to work, the right to rest, the right to education, and the right to social security—seems to have been made for propaganda purposes at home and abroad. Some of its original provisions have been altered by decree without observance of a simple amending procedure. The individual as such is submerged. In the later development of communist theory, the worth of man appears to depend on the class to which he belongs. Communists have no patience with doubters or willful obstructionists. The consequence is a strong tendency to ruthless suppression. Individual freedom is not for the present, but for the future when all opposition to communism or deviation from its orthodox doctrines has ceased to exist. In practice, inequalities that rest on birth and possession of private property have been suppressed, but the equality that has emerged has consisted of equal subjection to an autocratic government.

All industry is operated by the state, and the kinds and quantities of goods to be produced are determined through orders issued by the government. Labor unions have been reduced to a minor role, and the individual workman finds it difficult to change jobs. Wages are fixed by the state, but not with absolute uniformity; the worker who exceeds his quota may receive additional rewards.

Reports of an improved psychological climate since Stalin's death have emanated from the U.S.S.R. Although the regime in power has relaxed many restrictions, there is no indication that the supposedly "temporary dictatorship" will come to an end.

Unstable Governments. The classification into "democracies" and "dictatorships" omits many existing governments. Generally these governments are republican in form, but they are also unstable. Their outstanding characteristic is their inability to achieve an orderly and peaceful succession of heads of state. Frequently, they are subjected to revolutionary upheavals engineered by persons such as army officers and ambitious politicians. High death rates attest to the lack of public services; administration is inefficient; public credit is low; and rights of citizens are not well protected.

5 The Concept of Statehood

Definitions of the state are almost as numerous as the authors who write about it. In part, the confusion is due to the differences in approach to political science: historians may regard the state as a concrete reality, philosophers may regard it as an abstraction, and lawyers may regard it as a juristic person. In part, the confusion is due to the difficulty of formulating any single definition that would fit both a tiny republic and a great federal union, both a state with simple governmental structure and one with a huge bureaucracy, both a state that barely maintains internal order and a police state, and both a state whose foreign policies are swayed by powerful neighbors and one which is numbered among the greatest in world diplomacy.

Formally, the modern *state* has been defined as "a politically organized body of people occupying a definite territory and living under a government entirely or almost entirely free from external control and competent to secure habitual obedience from all persons within it."[1] Other definitions have emphasized the sovereignty and independence of the state by specifying that it must have ability to use force in compelling internal obedience and in repelling outside interference. Some have included an explanation of its functions—which are to establish justice, to mitigate conflicts, to defend the social body from external and internal violence, and to promote the general welfare.

THE ATTRIBUTES OF STATEHOOD

However generalized or however detailed a political scientist's definition may be, it recognizes five essential attributes of

---

[1] E. C. Smith and A. J. Zurcher (eds.), *Dictionary of American Politics, an Everyday Handbook* (New York: Barnes & Noble, Inc., 1955).

statehood[2]—population, territory, government, sovereignty, and independence.

Population. The first essential is people: no minimum number is required to constitute the population of a state, but the number must certainly be great enough to place the relationship between governor and governed upon a larger scale than that of a mere family or tribal group. The *population* of a state is defined as including the following elements insofar as they may exist: (1) *citizens* or *subjects,* who enjoy full civil rights and who owe full allegiance; (2) *nationals,* or natives of the dependencies of a state; (3) persons of such subordinate status as *slaves,* who are bound to the service of masters, *peons,* who are bound to the service of creditors, and *serfs,* who are bound to the service of the owner of the soil on which they live; and (4) *aliens,* or citizens and subjects of other states who reside within the territory of a given state, participate in its civil benefits, and are required in turn to pay taxes and perform various services.[3]

Territory. A second essential of modern statehood is a definite portion of the earth's surface marked off from the portions occupied by population of other states. The broad term *territory* (for which some writers prefer to substitute the phrase "physical basis of the state") embraces not merely the land itself, but also the air above the land, the waters extending outward from its coast for a distance of at least three miles, the lakes and mountains and all other features that comprise the topographical contour of the land, the natural resources pertaining to the land, and the climate.

Government. A third essential is the possession of agencies that are sufficient to maintain order, to perform required services, and to carry out international obligations. *Government* includes the legislative, executive, and judicial bodies and also the ad-

---

[2] Inasmuch as political science is concerned with historical development, it should be noted that these attributes do not necessarily pertain to all the so-called "states" that have existed within the period of recorded history. Some of these have lacked exact populations from whom allegiance could be claimed, some have lacked exact territorial limits, some have lacked exact governmental agencies, and some have lacked definite seats of internal authority or complete independence of outside powers. Various writers concede statehood to the Huns and to the wandering conquerors of the Middle Ages; few if any, however, concede it to nomadic tribes which exist today.

[3] See Chapter 9 for a fuller discussion of the relationship between populational groups and the state.

ministrative agencies which secure the ends of the state. Governments may change frequently both in personnel and in form, whereas states have continuous existence.

Sovereignty and Independence. A fourth essential of modern statehood is *sovereignty* (or supreme authority over population, territory, and government within its confines), and a fifth is *independence* (or freedom from control by outside states). Both may be called "theories," "concepts," "fictions," or "doctrines" inasmuch as their reality depends upon recognition by organized society; usually recognition of the two is simultaneous, and frequently both are indicated by the single word "sovereignty."[4] Yet for the purpose of analyzing the attributes of statehood, they require at least temporary distinction: the first refers to the ability to exercise power, and the second to immunity from power. Such varied political units as "townships" and "provinces"—though they do have population, territory, and government—are not states because they lack sovereignty; that is, they are not centers of supreme authority. Such units as "protectorates"—though they possess most of the attributes—fail to be full-fledged states because they are not recognized in the international community as independent.

STATEHOOD IN FEDERAL UNIONS

The United States, Switzerland, and Canada are examples of *federal unions,* which parcel the exercise of political powers among a general government and component units (respectively called, in these instances, "states," "cantons," and "provinces")[5] Statehood in federal unions belongs to the political society as a whole, because that alone has the essential attributes of sovereignty and independence. The component units are not states because (despite their possession of population and territory and of governmental powers of lawmaking and law-enforcing) they may not ignore federal constitutions, nullify the laws of the federal government, or conduct foreign affairs.

---

[4] Some textbooks distinguish them as "internal" and "external" sovereignty; the present Outline will frequently couple both under the word "sovereignty."
[5] See Chapter 8, for a distinction between *federal unions* like the three mentioned here and *unitary states* like Great Britain and France which accumulate political powers within an over-all structure.

STATES AS DISTINGUISHED FROM INTERNAL ASSOCIATIONS

The state is only one of the many associations that exist in society. Members of the state are born into it and are unable to withdraw from it except through expatriation; but the same people may be born into or may voluntarily join religious, financial, labor, political, or other public and private associations. These associations may operate on a state-wide or even worldwide scale, and they may exercise powerful influence upon governments. Yet unlike the state (which seeks to comprehend the complete interests of a society), each is devoted to the accomplishment of relatively few purposes; all are subject to the supremacy of the state—whether they be created, encouraged, protected, tolerated, or repressed by it. On the other hand, the state is not subject to any other organized group. It alone may legitimately use force to carry out its orders.

STATES AS DISTINGUISHED FROM CULTURAL GROUPS

Although the words *state* and *nation* are commonly used as synonymous even in the literature of political science, the former properly connotes political unity and the latter cultural unity—two types of social bond that must be recognized as essentially different. *Political unity* depends upon the ties which hold together a whole (and usually economically and culturally varied) population that occupies a common territory, employs a common government, and enjoys in common the sovereignty and independence of statehood. *Cultural unity,* on the other hand, depends upon the ties within a single populational group; and if these ties include a sense of common race, common language, common religion, and common historical experiences and traditions, the group is technically to be termed a "nation" or "nationality." Such a culturally unified group may constitute the majority in the population of a given state, it may constitute a minority, or it may be diffused in various degrees of concentration throughout many states.

Since political and cultural unity are fundamentally distinct, peoples of diverse nationalities can and do live peaceably as fellow members of the same states and enrich one another's existence so long as governments do not interfere unduly with cultural heritages and so long as members of nationalities do not form political factions subversive to social orders. Obviously in today's world they must live together, for any general attempt to rearrange political boundaries on a cultural basis would be impossible even if it were demonstrated to be socially desirable.[6] Yet when economic or other types of tension develop within a society, cultural differences may easily become confused in the popular mind with the political incompatibility. The political scientist should discriminate between matters that pertain to the state and matters that pertain to racial, linguistic, religious, and other cultural interests.

Race. Physical resemblances and supposed ancestral kinship constitute one of the bonds of nationalism. In times of tension, real or imagined differences in complexion and descent are sometimes seized upon as signs of "racial" superiority or inferiority; even differences in educational opportunity are sometimes mistaken for "racial" differences in mental ability. However, the findings of anthropologists indicate that there are no pure races in Europe and that there are probably none in the world; the investigations of psychologists show no possible connection between race and political thinking.

Language. The preservation of an ancestral tongue enables a cultural group to maintain its literature and customs and provides a powerful nationalistic force. In times of unrest, it becomes an object of suspicion to other cultural groups which can not understand the tongue. Still the only possible linguistic barrier to political unity would be the lack of a state-wide language through which all groups could communicate.[7]

---

[6] Nevertheless, in recent history nationalistic aspirations for unified statehood sometimes have affected the drawing of interstate boundaries. For example, in the nineteenth century, they brought about the unification of Germany and of Italy, both of which had previously been composed of many small states; at the close of World War I, they contributed to the dismemberment of the Austro-Hungarian and the Turkish empires; and after World War II, they brought about other changes (including the recognition of Israel as a state). Such attempts to make state and national boundaries coincide prove permanent only insofar as they satisfy both the political and the cultural needs of the populations.

[7] Even this barrier is not insurmountable. Switzerland, for example, has retained its political unity for many centuries though its population has four national languages; some large Eastern states seem to have achieved political unity despite many local differences in language.

Religion. Religious customs and rites are influential in the maintenance of cultural bonds and frequently are an object of suspicion among different population groups; but again they have no fundamental connection with statehood. In the course of world history, many governments have confused religious with secular allegiance; in modern times, however, the tendency among states has been to permit freedom of belief and to recognize religious life as something apart from political life.

Historical Experience and Tradition. The fact that a nationality may once have constituted a political community and that it retains legendary memories of military valor and cultural accomplishments is another element of nationalism. In itself, it raises no political problems; but not infrequently, through confusion or purposeful distortion, it has been used as a basis for political hostility. That is, zealous nationalistic groups headed by aggressive political leaders sometimes demand a redrawing of interstate boundaries, not because the disputed territories are currently occupied by their members, but because they were once possessed by their forefathers.

6 *Sovereignty*

The fundamental attribute of the present-day state is *sovereignty*—that is, supremacy of will and power over its subjects. The essence of the state is power, which results from its conceded monopoly in the legitimate use of force; but power must be directed by conscious will. In every state there must be a person, or a group of persons, having the final authority to determine what the law shall be and to command the obedience of the people to the will thus expressed. There can be no legal limit to the exercise of sovereignty, for a limitation would imply some authority higher than the supreme power. Although, by allowing freedom of action to individuals and groups, the state ordinarily refrains from exercising some of its authority, it can at its discretion recall grants of power or interfere in matters with which it has not previously concerned itself. Several recent writers emphasize the legitimacy of its exercise by defining *sovereignty* as a claim to power when that claim is authorized by the established order.

DEVELOPMENT OF THE THEORY OF SOVEREIGNTY

The word *sovereignty* seems to have been first used in 1576 by Jean Bodin, a partisan of the King of France in the struggle to obtain more power for the throne and thus to decrease that of the Church and that of the feudal lords. Bodin, in his *Six Books concerning the State,* developed the theory that sovereignty is an essential element of the state, and that the legitimate holder of power (in this case, the king) has absolute supremacy that is not to be shared with others. The sovereign's power, however, was admitted to be subject to the laws of God, of nature, and of nations.

In the seventeenth century in England, Thomas Hobbes, a partisan of Charles I during the Puritan Revolution, went further and in his *Leviathan* declared that the exercise of power by a single will was subject to no restraints whatever. After the English Revolution (1688), John Locke, in his *Second Treatise of Civil Government* (1690), expressed a somewhat more limited idea of sovereignty by denying it to the king and assigning it to a supreme legislative body. Society retained the authority to change governments if it felt that it was being deprived of its civil rights. Locke's theories established the principle that sovereignty should be controlled, at least in part, by the people.

It is noteworthy that all these theories were brought forth during periods of stress when political authority needed strengthening.

CHARACTERISTICS OF SOVEREIGNTY

Hardly any brief definition of sovereignty is sufficient to convey the meaning of this complex concept. Definitions may be clarified by a consideration of the principal characteristics of sovereignty: (1) absoluteness, (2) comprehensiveness, (3) permanence, and (4) indivisibility.

Absoluteness. Sovereignty can not be restricted, for the power that imposed restrictions would then become sovereign. Although morality, prudence, or considerations of policy may cause the sovereign to refrain from a course of action, his power is legally unlimited.

Comprehensiveness. The power of the sovereign extends without exception over every person and association within the state. The apparent immunity of diplomatic representatives and of officials from other states is merely an international courtesy.

Permanence. Heads of state may die, governments may succeed one another, the state itself may even be reorganized, but sovereignty continues without interruption as long as the state exists.

Indivisibility. Today the majority of jurists and political scientists hold that sovereignty can not be divided; it is impossible to have two or more co-ordinate supreme powers in the same state. The state may delegate powers of government to its subdivisions, but what it grants it may take away. In a federal system of government (for example, the United States), the authority to govern is shared, but not the supreme power. There is but one true state, one sovereignty.[1]

TYPES OF SOVEREIGNTY

In states with simple governmental structure it is fairly easy to determine the person or public body that actually has the supreme power. In complex modern states the location of sovereignty is often difficult to determine, especially during periods of revolutionary activity.

Legal Sovereignty. The English jurist, John Austin, in his *Lectures on Jurisprudence* (1832), defined the sovereign as a determinate human superior, not in the habit of obeying a like superior, who receives habitual obedience from the people of a political society. As a lawyer, Austin undoubtedly had in mind the fact that when courts are enforcing a law, they look only to the legislature or other authority which is competent under the constitution to express the commands of the state in legal form. They do not ask whether the law is supported by public opinion.

In Great Britain, Parliament is the legal sovereign. In the United States, the legal sovereign is difficult to locate. It is not Congress, for laws may be declared unconstitutional by the Supreme Court. It is not the Supreme Court, because amendments to the Constitution may make constitutional what the Supreme Court has declared unconstitutional. It is not the forty-eight states, for their powers may be limited by amendments to the Constitution. The legal sovereign then consists of the combinations of authorities that have power to amend the Constitution —conventions or two-thirds of each house of Congress which may propose amendments, and state legislatures or state conventions which may ratify them.

Political Sovereignty. Behind the legal sovereign in a democracy is another power, the electorate, which is ordinarily not able to express its commands in legal form, but it is the body to which final appeal is made when issues arise. The electorate constitutes the *political sovereign*.

---

[1] Some writers attribute a portion of sovereignty to each. According to this argument, sovereignty is divisible: (1) if the component members are sovereign, the result of the union is a mere confederation; but (2) if the central government is sovereign, and the component members are not sovereign, the result is a unitary state; therefore (3) the component members are partly sovereign, party nonsovereign, to make possible a federal union.

The concept of political sovereignty is less exact than the concept of legal sovereignty. Some writers have considered these two concepts to be in conflict; actually, they are different aspects of the same concept. In any well-ordered state the will of the legal sovereign corresponds closely to the will of the political sovereign.

Popular Sovereignty. In the United States, the term *popular sovereignty* is often encountered, particularly in journalistic and unspecialized writings. Its use is inexact: usually it refers, not to the electorate, but to the great unorganized mass of people. This mass has no means of expressing its will in legal form. At best, popular sovereignty means action through the duly constituted electorate; at worst, it connotes the so-called "right" to revolt.

De Facto **Sovereignty.** When a legitimate sovereign has been displaced as a result of revolution or invasion, the person (or body of people) who can enforce obedience to his will is called the *de facto sovereign*. If this person (or body) succeeds in keeping power over a considerable period of time, he is recognized usually as a legitimate sovereign. During the American Revolution the legislatures of the American states were *de facto* sovereigns in the areas not occupied by British troops.

De Jure **Sovereignty.** *De jure sovereignty* is based on law rather than on physical power. The law assumes that obedience is enforceable—even if the rightful sovereign is temporarily unable to enforce obedience or is actually displaced. Whoever possesses legal sovereignty has a great advantage during a revolutionary period, for people tend to oppose a power which rests on force alone.

External Sovereignty. The term *external sovereignty* presupposes freedom from subjection to foreign states. When the term is extended to include powers to conduct international relations and to declare or to end war, it is correct. Since the term "external sovereignty" implies that the state has power outside its own territory, there would be less confusion if the term "independence" were substituted and if the word *sovereignty* were used only to denote internal supremacy.

OPPONENTS OF THE THEORY OF SOVEREIGNTY

There are at least four schools of thought which believe either that sovereignty is not an essential quality of the state or that it may be divided or limited. Critics of this theory (1) point out that political life has changed radically since the concept of sovereignty was first developed; and (2) formulate new theories (based on present conditions) which take into consideration the vast powers actually exercised by other organizations. However, should there occur a period of stress in which some interest or section within a state becomes dominant and uses its power to aggrandize itself at the expense of other interests or sections, it is likely that the doctrine of sovereignty will be reasserted.

At all events, even if we discarded the idea of sovereignty of the state, we should have to admit the supreme will of some other association which would override all other wills in case of conflict.

Pluralists. Pluralists insist that groups in which men are organized, such as the church, the labor union, and the farmers' association, are as important as the state insofar as they may have a claim equal to or superior to the state's claim to the loyalty of individuals. Some pluralists argue that self-government in industrial and other organizations would ensure better performance of essential functions now allocated to the state. Some would retain the state as a specialized agency, but reduce it to equality with other associations. Still others would retain it, with curtailed powers, as a co-ordinating agency if specialized associations could not function peacefully together.

Federalists or Dualists. Another attack on the theory of sovereignty comes from partisans of member states in federal unions, who insist either that sovereignty may be divided or that it is not an essential attribute of the state. The federalist (or dualist) viewpoint is familiar to Americans in the doctrine of "states' rights."

Internationalists. Internationalists hold that the state is not really free to do as it pleases, but that it is bound by a true international law. The real sentiments which unite or divide men, they say, are independent of geographical, political, or other national boundaries; they are economic or intellectual.

They urge that, in the interest of international good, it is undesirable that each state should interpret its own international obligations or set its own standards of conduct. If the present tendency is really toward the development of an international organization with power to create and to enforce law, national sovereignty will cease to exist. We shall then have the unified will of a world state.

Sociological Jurists. Another attack comes from those who believe that law is anterior to or superior to the state. This belief directly challenges the assertion that the state makes law or that law is the will of an inherently authoritative sovereign. It asserts instead that law is the sense of right of the community, and that the state itself is the creature of law, subject to legal limitations. Therefore, if we have a sovereign at all, law is sovereign.

7   *Concepts of Law*

The theory and practice of law are closely intertwined with all other phases of government and politics. Law is a means of special control which helps to establish order, peace, and justice in private business and public affairs. This chapter will summarize briefly the nature, origins, and sources of law and indicate the main types of law within and among states.

A single *law* may be defined as "a general rule for the conduct of members of the community either emanating from the governing authority by positive command or approved by it and habitually enforced by some public authority by the imposition of sanctions or penalties for its violation."[1] *Law* in a broad sense is "the whole body of such rules . . . together with the principles of justice and right commonly applied in their enforcement."[1] Law which creates, discovers, or defines rights is called *substantive law;* law which provides a method for protecting rights is called *adjective* or *procedural law*.

Law exists for the maintenance of rights and of their corresponding obligations. The struggle for "a government of law, not of men" is part of the history of democratic peoples. The significance of this struggle lies in its presumption of uniformity of judicial action: (1) the law should apply generally to all persons within a category; (2) the law should apply equally to all within the scope of its provisions; and (3) the administration of justice should be certain to all who seek the protection of the law. These are the basic principles which legal systems and courts strive to effect, but sometimes fall short of effecting in the actual application of law to concrete situations. A poor legal system may become at least acceptable if administered by

---
[1] E. C. Smith and A. J. Zurcher (eds.), *Dictionary of American Politics*, an Everyday Handbook (New York: Barnes & Noble, Inc., 1955).

able judges and practiced by honest attorneys, but the best system yields poor results if it is in the hands of incompetent or politically dependent judges and unscrupulous lawyers (see Chapter 16).

THE NATURE OF LAW

In *jurisprudence* (the science of law), all schools of thought agree upon the need for uniformity of law. Differences in viewpoints among the various schools center upon controversies over definitions. In political science, law is sometimes taken to mean only *positive law*—that is, to mean only the commands issued by the state and enforced by its sovereign political authority. However, if this definition were generally accepted, there could be no legal restriction on the lawmaking power of the state and no authority other than the state could make laws. Many jurists, therefore, deny that law is always created by a definite sovereign body and assert that philosophy, custom, and popular consent also play important roles in its creation. Some emphasize philosophic concepts of justice, some stress social need as the source and end of law, some emphasize the importance of social custom as revealed in the history of legal development, and some seek to correlate historical systems with the knowledge that may be gained from the study of social sciences. These jurists have all contributed to the field of political science.

The Philosophical Concept. Philosophical jurists are concerned with the formation of an ideal system of law that will be based upon ethical principles of justice. Currently, social interests and the creation of theories of social justice are of ethical concern to this group.

The Sociological Concept. Sociological jurists hold that law is the product of social needs which existed prior to the commands issued or the enactments promulgated by states. It is possible, they point out, to conceive of a condition of society in which there is law and no state, but it is not possible to conceive of a state in which there is no form of law. The purpose of law is to serve society, and the purpose of the state is to enact and administer rulings which will result in the achievement of socially desirable ends.

The Analytical Concept. Analytical jurists are concerned with positive law; they search for the fundamental principles and theories underlying the deliberate conscious demands or regulations enforced by existent states. Although rigid, use of this method has removed uncertain and ambiguous elements from the law. Moreover, recognition of the utilitarian goal[2] of these jurists has resulted in an emphasis upon the general welfare in law.

The Historical Concept. Historical jurists are primarily interested in the origin and development of law and in the causes of its change and its growth. They view law less as a matter of deliberate legislation than as a slow evolution within the social body. Adherents of the historical concept tend to be conservative because of their reverence for the past, they stress legal history rather than legal philosophy, and they valuably supplement the analyses of the positive school.

The Comparative Concept. Comparative jurists attempt to reach sound statements of principle through the study of all historical and current legal systems and of all pertinent sciences, including biology and anthropology. Although relatively new, this school has contributed useful information about the nature of law.

BASIC SYSTEMS OF LAW

There are, of course, many legal systems in the world today. Almost every society has developed a distinct legal system, usually closely related to its customs (traditional rules which are constantly being qualified and expanded). In primitive cultures, numerous rules and elaborate rites are observed and it is almost impossible, at this stage, to separate the laws from the customs.

Throughout history, as tribes have become welded into states, there has been a tendency towards coalescence of legal systems; however, there remain some states in which different laws are enforced in different regions. Other states, profiting from the existence of strong governments and the conscientious efforts of able judges and legal theorists over a long period, have created national systems of law (see Chapter 2). These systems derive from two great roots: Roman law, which is basic in most of the

---

[2] Utilitarianism is "the ethical doctrine that the good of any action is tested by its contribution to results, especially to human happiness."—Albert E. Avey, *Handbook in the History of Philosophy*, College Outline Series (New York: Barnes & Noble, Inc., 1954), p. 292.

states of Western Europe and of Latin America; and common law, which (supplemented by equity) is generally basic in Great Britain, in the parts of the British Commonwealth colonized by Englishmen, and in the United States.

The Roman System. What we call "Roman law" today is really a fusion of Roman and Teutonic laws. The term "Roman law" originally meant the commands of the state issued through state officials such as the emperor, the senate, and judges. "Teutonic law" originally consisted of accepted custom handed down from one generation to another. Roman law was enforced uniformly over the entire empire; Teutonic law was tribal and based on personal allegiance to leaders. Roman law early came to be written (and finally in the sixth century to be systematized in the Justinian code); on the other hand, Teutonic law was transmitted orally. After the barbarian invasions in the fifth century, the contact between these two entirely different legal systems brought temporary confusion, but order gradually came out of chaos. Teutonic customs modified the Roman system, but Roman uniformity did prevail over Teutonic multiplicity. In the Middle Ages, church (or canon) law and admiralty law helped to preserve spirit and organization of Roman law. More recently, Roman and Teutonic law were successfully integrated and systematized in great codes of law.

The British System. The sources of English law lay in the customs of people living in various parts of the land—customs which eventually became common to the realm through the regular conferences of judges and the writings of commentators. This development was possible because of the geographical separation from Continental Europe and because of the centralization of authority which came with the Norman Conquest of 1066.

COMMON LAW. Common law is essentially *case* (as opposed to *statutory*) law, developed by precedent from decisions first of local courts and later, as the judicial system became centralized, of "king's courts" such as the Court of Common Pleas and the King's Bench, established in the twelfth and thirteenth centuries, respectively. Disorder came to be regarded as a breach of the "king's peace" and an offense against the state which had assumed the duties of maintaining order and of punishing crime. Each new decision became a precedent for the settlement of similar cases in the future—this is the principle of *stare decisis*. In contrast to the Roman method (used in Europe) where each case was decided through the application of the rules of a written code, the common law of England allowed judges wider powers in interpretation of customs and the application of justice. Gradually these case decisions and the commentaries on them came to constitute a great body of law, highly revered in England and transmitted in time to the territories overseas settled by the English. Though common law may be modified or repealed by statutes, it continues to be developed by decisions; in cases of conflict, however, the statute governs.

EQUITY. Because the common law was not always sufficiently elastic to insure justice, a branch of remedial justice known as *equity* began to develop perhaps as early as the twelfth or thirteenth century. Although common law provided for redress in the form of damages for an injury, it provided no adequate means for prevention of an impending injury. In such cases, suitors began to appeal directly to the king as "the fountain of justice"; he in turn referred them to the lord chancellor. Since the chancellor was usually a churchman trained in canon law (which is based on Roman law), equity became strongly tinctured with Roman law. In time equity, which had at first been easy to apply, developed its own rules and precedents and became as formal as common law. Today it is used primarily to compel performance or to prevent performance of a specific deed: the best-known modern form of action in equity is the injunction. Like common law, equity had been amplified by statutory law and on many points superseded by it; in current practice, the statute governs when a conflict arises.

SOURCES OF LAW

The development of law long antedates the separation of powers and the specialization of governmental functions; the agencies responsible for its development are many.

The following discussion presents the sources of various kinds of law and the forces responsible for their development and modification. Generally, nine different sources of law are considered: ethical belief, custom, judicial decision, legislation, constitutions, treaties, executive proclamations and decrees, commentaries, and codifications.

Ethical Belief. During periods when there is strong disaffection toward the enforcement of unpopular laws, it is usual to find appeals to a supposedly "natural" law—a law alleged to be higher than the decrees and statutes of any earthly authority. Natural law is sometimes derived from "right reason," sometimes from immutable principles of morality and justice embedded in the human heart, sometimes from ancient customs, and sometimes from the Bible. It must be strongly emphasized that the so-called "natural law" does not constitute any part of law as that term is defined in this chapter. Nevertheless, philosophical, religious, and ethical concepts have at times exerted a profound influence on the people and on the various agencies charged with the making of law.

Custom. The various schools of jurisprudence are in substantial agreement upon the importance of custom as a source of law. Even conquerors who impose new legal systems upon defeated countries tend to honor many of the traditional local rules. Early in the development of the modern state, kings (personally or through their advisers) found it necessary to declare which local customs should be accepted among the many varying ones existing in different parts of their domains. From the time of their declarations, such customs have continued to be law.

Judicial Decision. In England, prior to the rise of Parliament, royal judges traveling on circuit were responsible for evolving uniformity in the law: by comparing decisions and by basing new decisions on preceding ones, they developed the common law. Since the establishment of statutes and written constitutions, judges have continued to so change the law through expansion and interpretation as to accomplish, in reality, the making of new law.

Legislation. In addition to selecting customary usages for enforcement, kings had to issue general decrees concerning new matters. This practice was the source of legislation, which came to be for a time shared with parliamentary assemblies; eventually it was to become the special province of those bodies subject to the king's formal approval. In most parts of the world today, statutes made by Parliament, by Congress, or by other legislative bodies constitute a great portion of the law of states.

Constitutions. The desirability of creating a superior law to limit the activities of legislatures and other organs of government and to establish norms for their guidance led, in many states, to the writing of constitutions. In order that the constitutions might have greater authority than statutes, special constituent organs called *conventions* were set up to express the will of the states concerning the organization and powers of their governments. Amendments to a constitution usually require a more difficult procedure than statute lawmaking.

Treaties. Generally speaking, treaties become law upon their proclamation. Treaty-making is usually within the province of the executive, though the United States and some other states require approval by the senate or the legislature as a whole before a treaty is proclaimed.

Executive Proclamations and Decrees. Because of the complexity of the governments of modern states, legislative bodies have tended to delegate some of their authority to executive officers. Proclamations and orders issued within the specific limitations of such grants of power are known as *decree law* or *administrative law*.

Commentaries. Concurrently with the development of law by governmental organs, jurists began to analyze and comment upon what had been done and upon what should be done. Over several centuries, a succession of able English commentators— Glanville, Bracton, Littleton, Coke, and Blackstone—influenced judges and legislators to such an extent that actual commentaries may be included within the sources of law.

Codifications. As the volume of law grew, attempts were made both in ancient and modern times to codify it—that is, to arrange the law systematically and reconcile inconsistencies. In this process changes were made, so that codification, too, is an important source of law. The Justinian Code of the sixth century A.D. consolidated existing Roman law. The most famous modern code is the Code Napoleon, which is largely a restatement of the Justinian Code as that body of law had been modified through many centuries of use. It was prepared (1804-1807) by a group of French jurists and was promulgated by the Emperor Napoleon I. It was later adopted by other countries of Western Europe and Latin America, and it is the basic law in the American state of Louisiana and the Canadian Province of Quebec to cite two examples in this hemisphere.

INTERNATIONAL AND MUNICIPAL LAW

Classified on the basis of the geographical areas to which it applies, law consists of two types: (1) *International law* is an inchoate body of rules concerning states in their relations with one another (e.g., rules of peace, neutrality, and war) and concerning parts of the world, such as the open sea, which are not within the boundaries of any state. (2) *Municipal law* (or *national law*) governs the people within particular states.

International Law. International law is derived from Roman law. *International public law* applies when states, as such, are parties; *international private law* applies when individuals residing in one state claim rights acquired under the laws of another state. (See Chapter 21, *International Law*.)

Analytical jurists, who recognize only positive law, hold that international law is not "law" at all inasmuch as it lacks a sovereign enforcing agent. Other jurists, using a broader definition, admit international law as true law though of a kind different from municipal law.

Municipal (National) Law. *Municipal (national) law* is an ancient term which means the law of a particular state; it must not be confused with laws governing cities or other "municipal corporations." Municipal law results from the internal sovereignty of the state and is the law in the "positive" sense. It also may be subdivided into *public law* and *private law:* if the relation of the state as an entity is affected, a law is public; if the relation is that of an individual or group to another individual or group, the law is private.

Public Law. Public law includes the whole field of law through which a government is set up and maintained and through which its various branches and officers are defined and regulated. It also includes the relations of the individual to the state.

The meaning of *constitutional law* varies in different countries. It may be limited to the bare particulars of the organization and functions of the principal branches of government. It may, in addition, embrace guarantees of individual liberties. It may be further extended to include detailed substantive and procedural limitations and grants of power. In the United States, constitutional law is enforced by courts exercising the power of judicial review.

ADMINISTRATIVE LAW. On the Continent of Europe that part of public law which regulates the conduct of officials and determines the rights of individuals in dealing with these officials is referred to as *administrative law;* it also includes the remedies which are provided to the individual for the protection of these rights. (In some states, as in France, special administrative tribunals enforce administrative law.) In the United States and Great Britain, administrative law is the law created through the rules, orders, and decisions of administrative agencies acting under the authority of statutes and enforced by administrative agencies subject to appeals to the courts.

CRIMINAL LAW. *Criminal law* deals with offenses which affect the safety and order of the state and which are hence considered to be offenses against the state itself, not merely against the persons injured. Such offenses are called *felonies* (if they reach a certain magnitude) and *misdemeanors* or *petty offenses* (if they are of lesser gravity). The state prosecutes crimes, and any fine imposed is paid into the state treasury. Criminal law defines and forbids acts which infringe upon the rights of the state and designates in general terms the penalties for infringement; specific penalties are determined by the judges in individual cases. *Criminal procedure* is the body of rules which defines the method by which offenders shall be brought to trial and punished.

PRIVATE LAW. *Private* or *civil law* governs the relations of one person to another. It provides a means by which an individual may maintain his rights against infringement by other individuals. The field of private law is increasingly regulated by statute because of the complexity of modern industrial organization.

8 Current Governmental Systems

Many factors have contributed to the growth and survival of states. The two most important factors seem to have been the strength that results from internal unity and the strength that results from internal and external co-operation. The great national states that arose at the beginning of the Modern Era pursued a consistent policy of welding together their territorial components under governments of unitary structure. Other states have sought strength through confederation or through the establishment of federal unions. However, most of the states of the world are organized under unitary systems. The United States, the Bonn (West German) Republic, Switzerland, Canada, and Australia are true federal states. Some others, though federal in form, are unitary in fact. A clear understanding of these systems of government is essential.

UNITARY SYSTEM

In unitary governments there is only one source of authority. Whatever local governments exist are merely agencies of the central government established for its convenience in local administration. They owe their legal existence to it. All provisions for local home rule are authorized by the central government, continue during its pleasure, and may be legally voided at its will. At the discretion of the central government, counties, municipal corporations, and other territorial units of government may be created out of other divisions, or their boundaries may be altered, or their powers may be increased or diminished, or their legal existence may be ended.

Variations among the Unitary Systems. Unitary government does not necessarily mean highly centralized government. The degree of local autonomy may vary widely from state to state—

as in the governments of Great Britain and France. In Great Britain, the statutes of Parliament have created local governments so that local affairs may be managed by local people; the actions of local councils are not interfered with unless they overstep the bounds of legal authority. In France, on the other hand, councils of departments and communes are subject to constant detailed supervision by central authority; in most other states of the Continent of Europe, this same attitude towards local government applies. Between these widely varying systems there may seem to be nothing in common; but both are unitary governments and in each case the central government has final authority to command and to control.

Advantages. Unitary government is more advantageous to a country with a relatively small area and homogeneous population than to a large country with widely different economic and social interests and with widely different standards of political conduct. The advantages of this system are that its organization is relatively simple; that conflicts of jurisdiction are avoided; that duplications of officers and services are comparatively rare; and that, even though a large degree of local autonomy is conceded, uniformity of law, policy, and administration can be maintained throughout the whole state.

Disadvantages. The disadvantages of unitary government are many. A unitary system overburdens the national legislature with numerous local matters to the detriment of both national and local legislation. It may cause unnecessary delay when local authorities can not act promptly. It leaves to distant authorities, who may lack adequate knowledge of local conditions, the determination of policies and the regulation of matters which may be of concern only to the localities affected. It tends to repress local initiative and interest in public affairs, and it impairs the vitality of local government. Finally, it facilitates the development of a central bureaucracy.

Future of Unitary Systems. Because of popular demands for state services on an ever-increasing scale, the present trend is strongly toward the unitary organization of the state.

FEDERAL SYSTEM

Federal government is the direct antithesis of unitary government; instead of one government which controls all others, a federal system provides for an actual division of powers between two or more nearly independent governments each of which exercises control, within its scope of authority, over the same people. The component parts of a federal system are (1) a number of political communities (variously called "cantons," "provinces," "states," or "Laender"), each of which has its own government that is supreme with respect to matters of *particular* importance to it as a unit; and (2) a central government that is supreme with respect to all matters of *common* importance to the whole federal state. The line of division between what is of particular and what is of common importance is always drawn.

In a federal system of government it is essential that there be a written constitution which defines the relation between the union and its component parts, marks out the sphere of each, and is paramount to the individual constitutions of its members. It is also essential that there be a tribunal empowered to interpret the constitution, judge the limits of the spheres of action of the central and local government, restrain the central authority from encroaching on the local governments, and prevent the component units from interfering with or usurping the powers of the general government.

Variations among Federal Systems. Federal systems may be created by the voluntary agreement of independent states; after a preliminary experience with confederation, as in Switzerland, the United States, and Germany; through the influence of the mother country when a number of separate colonies are federally united, as in Canada and Australia; or by the division of previously unitary states, as in Brazil and the post-World War II republic of West Germany.[1] Hardly any two federal systems

---

[1] Of merely historical importance are the personal and real unions, in both of which two or more states have the same king. In *personal unions,* each state is wholly independent of the other and has its own body of laws, political organization, citizenship, and local institutions. The acts of the common sovereign in relation to one state have no effect in the other. A *real union* results when two or more states with the same king enter into constitutional or international arrangements for the administration of certain common affairs, usually including the conduct of foreign relations. For other matters each state retains its own separate institutions and laws. (The most notable example of a real union was Austria-Hungary from 1867 to 1917).

A real union should be carefully distinguished from a *merger* of two states to form a new state, such as occurred in 1707 when the personal union of England and Scotland was merged into the Kingdom of Great Britain

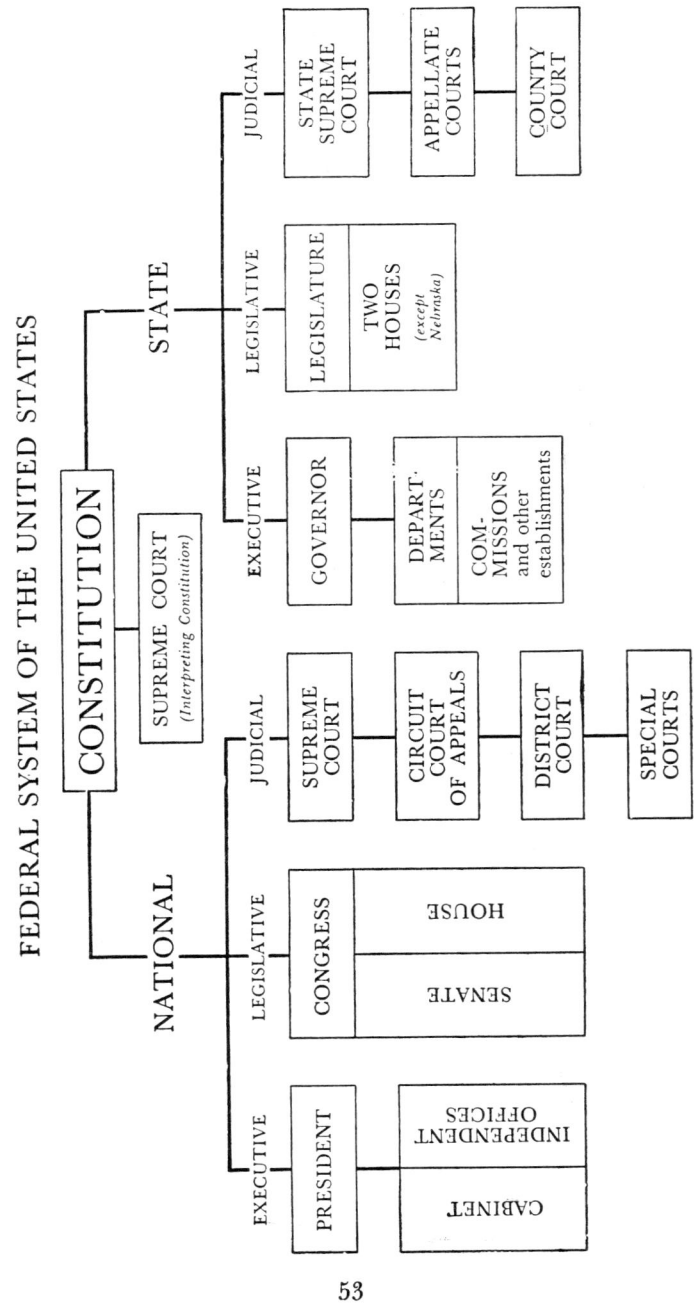

FEDERAL SYSTEM OF THE UNITED STATES

CONSTITUTION

SUPREME COURT
(Interpreting Constitution)

NATIONAL

EXECUTIVE
- PRESIDENT
  - CABINET
  - INDEPENDENT OFFICES

LEGISLATIVE
- CONGRESS
  - SENATE
  - HOUSE

JUDICIAL
- SUPREME COURT
- CIRCUIT COURT OF APPEALS
- DISTRICT COURT
- SPECIAL COURTS

STATE

EXECUTIVE
- GOVERNOR
  - DEPARTMENTS
  - COMMISSIONS and other establishments

LEGISLATIVE
- LEGISLATURE
  - TWO HOUSES *(except Nebraska)*

JUDICIAL
- STATE SUPREME COURT
- APPELLATE COURTS
- COUNTY COURT

53

agree as to the extent of powers assigned to the general government or as to the exact line of division between the powers of the general government and those of governments of the component units. In Canada, for instance, both the powers of the provinces and those of the general government of the Dominion are enumerated, and all not mentioned are assigned to the general government. In the United States, only the powers assigned to the federal government are enumerated, and all others are reserved to the states. Again, there are variations in administration. In the United States, laws of the general government are enforced by its own complete administrative and judicial establishments. In Germany, most of the laws of the general government are enforced by officers of the separate *Laender*.

Governments that are federal in form but not in fact have been created in unstable states or in dictatorships. In the U.S.S.R. the Constitution of 1936 provides that the autonomous republics may control education and foreign and military affairs, and may even secede; obviously, none of them has attempted secession, for the penalties for "nationalist deviation" are severe. Federal government is so delicately balanced internally, and the balance is so dependent on the existence of independent judicial safeguards, that it can not operate under dictatorship or in states subject to violent revolutionary movements.

Advantages. Federalism is the essential compromise without which the formation of many large states would have been impossible. It affords a means by which petty states may be united into a more powerful commonwealth, obtaining the advantages of union without wholly sacrificing their separate existences. It combines the advantages of national unity with those of local autonomy and the rights of self-government. It is the means of maintaining a balance between the centrifugal and the centripetal forces in a state. Where uniformity is essential, federalism accomplishes it in legislation, policy, and administration; yet it leaves wide diversity in matters of primarily local concern. It permits experiments to be tried in autonomous districts, such as could not be attempted on a state-wide scale in a unitary system. It stimulates interest in government by leaving the determination of local policy in the hands of local officers and assemblies that are responsible in greater or less degree to local electorates. It relieves the central legislature and the central administrative authorities from the necessity of devoting time and energy to the solution of local problems.

Disadvantages. The organization of federal government is necessarily complex. There are two sets of legislatures and other offices, and two sets of laws. In periods of stress, disputes are likely to arise over the proper construction of the constitution. Under the best conditions, there is some duplication of activities and services—with resulting increase in expense. It is not always easy to determine which government has the power to deal with a specific situation. Division of power may lead to conflicts of jurisdiction between national and local officers or else to a sort of "no man's land" in which neither authority takes decisive action. Crime prevention, for example, becomes unusually difficult on this account. Fugitives from justice often cross state lines and can not be returned to states where they are wanted, except through troublesome extradition procedures. Unwilling witnesses sometimes leave the states where their testimonies are needed. In the conduct of foreign relations, a federal government is handicapped as compared to a unitary state. Members of a federal union, by the exercise of their right to legislate, and by failure to administer their own or national laws with sufficient diligence, may seriously embarrass the general government in carrying out its treaty obligations. (In the United States, for example, the policies of some Western states to discriminate against Orientals to whom certain rights have been guaranteed by treaty have caused the central government great difficulty.) As regards domestic affairs, federal governments sometimes find it difficult to keep up with the times because of relatively cumbersome procedures for amending federal constitutions (in which both the general government and the component units share).

The Future of Federalism. Not all the weaknesses pointed out in the preceding paragraph are due to inherent defects of federalism. Many of them are due to the existing division of powers. The rapid growth of transportation, communication, and industrial development has caused many matters which were formerly of purely local concern to become national problems. Demands for greater governmental services have caused pressures to be brought on that particular government which had the most resources—financial and otherwise—to meet them. Often constitutional obstacles stand in the way of accomplishment. Not only has technological progress made local problems national, it has also decreased the importance of the component units of a federal system. In the United States, there have sometimes been proposals for establishing a new federalism that would be based on regions—each of which would include several of the existing states—rather than on historical state borders. There is no reason other than tradition why the interests of North and South Carolina or North and South Dakota, for instance, should vary enough to require four separate governments; there is, however, a real difference between the needs of the Carolinas and those of the Dakotas.

Some observers feel that federalism is a transitional stage from the independence of a small state or the relative freedom of a confederation to a unitary government. They believe that the advantages of federalism might be as well achieved through a system of home rule granted by a unitary state to districts organized to meet the needs of a particular time. As conditions changed, alterations might be made in the boundaries of such districts. Other observers, somewhat more utopian in their outlook, believe that federalism has been so successful in obtaining co-operation among formerly independent states that entire continents might be federalized—with complete world federation as the ultimate goal.

TYPES OF IMPERIAL ORGANIZATION

Colonization and imperialism have generally made use of the unitary pattern of organization, with the home government exercising direct control. However, several governmental relations have developed and should be considered briefly.

The British Commonwealth. British colonies planted in under-populated areas tended to develop sentiments of nationality which led to demands for either complete independence or freedom from all but nominal control by the mother country. (The same demands were echoed by India and other areas as they developed culturally.) The present members of the British Commonwealth are definitely states. Quite as definitely, the commonwealth possesses a high degree of unity. In spite of the fact that there is little formal governmental structure, common allegiance to the British king or queen is acknowledged, except in India. There are numerous agencies for co-ordination, but there is no formal organization such as a league. The unity of the Commonwealth seems to be based on the willing co-operation of legally equal member states which results from long traditions of former political association, ties of kinship, and a realization of common interests.

Protectorates. One result of imperialism has been the recognition of a peculiar relationship between states, known as the *protectorate,* in which the protected state retains nominal independence and is generally free to manage its domestic affairs, yet concedes the right of the protector to dictate its foreign policies, to represent it in international affairs, and in some instances to intervene in internal matters, often financial. Such relationship may rest on treaty in which the protected state gives its explicit consent or on the assertion of control by the would-be protector.

Satellite States. *Satellite states* have all the characteristics of states except freedom to determine their own foreign or domestic policies. They are obliged to pursue policies determined by another stronger state or face the possibility of restrictions on their trade or even of armed intervention.

Mandates and Trust Territories. At the close of World War I a new type of dependent territory, the *mandate,* came into existence. Former possessions of the German and Turkish empires which had not yet reached a sufficiently high stage of development for complete independence were placed, by the League of Nations, under the administrative supervision of one of its members. The state to which such a mandate was given undertook to govern in the interest of the inhabitants and to render an account of its stewardship to the League. Some of these mandated territories were annexed by the mandatary state. At the close of World War II, some former possessions of Japan and Italy were made *trust territories,* and their administration was assigned temporarily to individual states under the supervision of the United Nations.

TYPES OF CO-OPERATIVE ORGANIZATIONS AMONG STATES

Even before the large national states began the development of their unitary forms of government, a group of small Swiss cantons had demonstrated the fact that strength may result from co-operation. At first there seem to have been more or less informal alliances, then there was a league, and by 1573 a confederation with fifteen member cantons. What is meant by "alliance," "league," and "confederation"?

Alliances. An *alliance* is an agreement concluded by treaty between two or more sovereign states for mutual defense against actual or potential enemies. Its terms may include provisions for mutual consultation in matters of foreign policy affecting the signatory states; for mutual assistance in preparation against enemy attack; and for the use of all military, naval, and other forces against common enemies when the need arises. Sometimes an alliance results in the pooling of all forces under the direction of a single commander; but the over-all direction of military policy is likely to be determined by means of conferences held from time to time as the occasion warrants. Treaties of alliance made in anticipation of war at some future date have often proved of no value. At the outbreak of war an allied state may declare that the conditions anticipated by the treaty do not actually exist.

Leagues. A *league* is an association of states, usually created by a formal treaty. Unlike an alliance, a league has at least a rudimentary governmental structure, with organs for consultation with and recommendation to the member states. It ordinarily has a treasury to which members contribute. Most leagues have been created for the accomplishment of only one or a few objectives, and ordinarily they do not wield powers of government. The best-known example in recent times is the League of Nations.

Confederations. A *confederation* is an association of states which rests upon the common agreement of its members expressed in an elaborate document. It differs from an alliance in that it has a fixed central organ through which the common will of its members may be expressed and in the intention that it will be perpetual. It differs from a league in the greater variety of objectives it is designed to achieve. These objectives always include external security. In addition, they may include promotion of cultural unity through the establishment of uniform weights and measures, through a uniform currency, and through the operation of a postal service. The scope of a confederation, in short, may include any activity that the member states choose to confer on it. In actual practice, both the scope and extent of its authority are often limited or nullified by the action of member states in collectively or individually refusing to carry out the resolutions of the confederation government or to contribute their quotas toward its financial support. Each member of a confederation retains its own sovereignty and governmental autonomy except insofar as it expressly surrenders and delegates governmental powers to the confederation government. Although it is often stated that the confederation is "perpetual," the member states may withdraw whenever they choose to do so.

The chief organ of a confederation is a congress. Delegates to a confederation congress vote by states, subject to the instructions given them by their state authorities. The orders of the confederation apply only to the member states. They do not reach down to individuals. For that reason, executive and judicial organs are not well developed. The confederation itself is not a true state. Outstanding examples of confederations are the Swiss confederation which lasted until 1848, and the United States under the Articles of Confederation from 1781 to 1788.

9 *The State and the Individual*

The exercise of the state's power strikes at the foundations of life, liberty, property, and the pursuit of happiness. The fundamental problem in any constitution is to reconcile the freedom of the individual with the necessary restraint which must be imposed upon him in the interest of the political society as a whole. Almost equally fundamental is the necessity for protecting individuals from their rulers' greed for power. The principal theories concerning a proper relationship between state and individual have been presented in Chapter 4: these range from the complete individual freedom advocated by the anarchist to the regimentation upheld by the totalitarian doctrinaire. Here we are concerned with the actual position of the individual in political society and with the rights and liberties which he may enjoy.

CITIZENSHIP

The relationship of the individual to the state varies in accordance with his legal status. He may be a *citizen*—that is, a member in full standing of his state—or he may be a subordinate member. Slaves and serfs, national minorities, conquered peoples, and alien residents all have been subjected to various degrees of subordination. Slaves have been bound to masters, serfs to the soil. Individuals in Nazi Germany and elsewhere have been deprived of citizenship for racial, political, or religious reasons. Inhabitants of conquered or annexed territories have been given the subordinate status of "nationals." Alien residents are compelled to pay taxes and perform obligations determined by the laws of the states in which they reside; they enjoy protection and many civil rights, but not all the privileges of citizens—and at any time, they may be expelled from the states.

The modern tendency is for states to confer citizenship on practically their whole populations. A citizen owes *allegiance* to the state—that is, fidelity, the duty of compulsory military service, and the faithful performance of such other duties as the state imposes on its members. When traveling or residing abroad, he may call upon the protection of his own state if he is subjected to oppression or indignities. Within his state he may or may not enjoy greater immunity from legal regulation than is accorded to other residents. The citizen alone is entitled to hold office and, with rare exceptions, to exercise suffrage. Laws of the state usually discriminate in his favor in admission to public employment and to the professions and in the enjoyment of economic and other privileges. Citizenship may be acquired either by birth or by naturalization.

Citizenship by Birth. The vast majority of the citizens of every state are citizens by birth. As long as a citizen remains within the state of his birth he has no choice but to be a citizen and to perform all the obligations which citizenship entails.[1] Laws of states vary, but two main principles (which sometimes conflict) are followed in determining citizenship by birth: *jus sanguinis* and *jus soli*.

THE PRINCIPLE OF JUS SANGUINIS. On the Continent the general principle is that citizenship is determined by the law of blood relationship—that is, according to the citizenship of the parents. No matter where a child is born, he is considered to be a citizen of the state of which his parents are citizens. The laws of the United States recognize *jus sanguinis* to a limited degree—for example, granting citizenship when the child is born in an American embassy or when both parents and the child have by their conduct or by affidavit proved that their residence abroad is only temporary.

THE PRINCIPLE OF JUS SOLI. The opposite principle, that citizenship is determined by the place of birth, is fundamental in the laws of Great Britain and the United States. A child is held to be a citizen of the country in which he is born, even though his

---

[1] "Most contemporary states permit their citizens or subjects to expatriate themselves (the action of an individual in renouncing his allegiance) and become the naturalized citizens of other states."—E. C. Smith and A. J. Zurcher, *Dictionary of American Politics*, an Everyday Handbook (New York: Barnes & Noble, Inc., 1955).

parents are aliens, and as such, ineligible for naturalization.

CONFLICTS OF PRINCIPLE. Conflicts in the two principles of *jus soli* and *jus sanguinis* may result in dual citizenship when a child is born in a state recognizing *jus soli* of parents whose citizenship is in a state which recognizes *jus sanguinis*. A child may be without any citizenship at all if the opposite circumstance exists.

Citizenship by Naturalization. Citizenship conferred by naturalization is a gratuitous concession on the part of the state. The conditions under which it is conferred vary greatly from state to state and are rigid or lenient according to the desire of the state to obtain additional citizens at a particular time. Naturalization may be either collective or individual.

COLLECTIVE NATURALIZATION. By passing a general law, a state may admit to citizenship a class of persons who have previously had a subordinate status. In the process of acquiring new territory, a state may collectively naturalize the inhabitants by treaty, or it may prefer to wait until they have become sufficiently indoctrinated with its principles of government when it may collectively naturalize them by statute.

INDIVIDUAL NATURALIZATION. The laws for the naturalization of individual aliens are often detailed and specific.[2] They refuse naturalization altogether to persons who are opposed to fundamental principles of government of the state and to persons who do not possess good moral character. They grant naturalization usually only after an extended period of residence. Usually, the citizenship of naturalized aliens may be revoked if they show by their subsequent conduct that they did not intend to fulfill the obligations of citizenship at the time they took the oath of allegiance.

RIGHTS AND LIBERTIES

A *right* is a privilege or prerogative conferred by usage or law upon a person or a group. Since a state which recognizes a right

---

[2] An alien who wishes to become a naturalized citizen of the United States must present a certificate of arrival to prove that he entered the country legally, must renounce his past citizenship, and must declare that he intends to reside permanently in the United States. The declarent alien, after a thorough investigation by administrative officers, is given a final hearing in court. If he prove himself worthy of citizenship, he takes an oath of allegiance to the United States and receives a certificate of naturalization. His naturalization carries with it the naturalization of his children under the age of eighteen. His spouse, if an alien, must be separately naturalized.

is under obligation to forbear from the exercise of power which would annul it, a right can be defended in the courts. A *liberty* is a less specific immunity from restriction and is presupposed to exist unless curtailed by law; it involves no corresponding obligation on the part of the state.

Natural Rights and Liberties. In the seventeenth and eighteenth centuries insistent demands arose for the recognition of rights and liberties which individuals were supposed to possess under "natural law," and for their protection under positive guarantees by law. The ideas that natural law exists and that it is discoverable by human reason have continued to exert a profound influence on political thinking. The basic principles of *natural law* are (1) that justice is part of man's nature, not merely a product of his desires; (2) that the law of nature is the law of reason, so that what is unreasonable or arbitrary can not be just; (3) that the law of nature is universal, not limited to any one time or place; and (4) that men are by nature equal and that the decisions of the majority, though not infallible, should govern because they provide the only practical way of deciding what is just and for the best interests of society. The content of natural law has been often drawn from the Bible, from prevailing custom, or from a condition supposed to exist in a state of nature before the creation of government. It is often cavalierly pointed out that the individual in a state of nature could not have had any "rights" at all—such an individual was at the mercy of individuals and groups stronger than he; there has been a tendency to dismiss the idea of natural rights and liberties and to insist that true freedom can exist only when it is guaranteed by law and backed by the strength of government. When a government is in the firm grip of a dictator or of a corrupt oligarchy, what is the force of paper guarantees? Under such circumstances, a fundamental belief in natural rights is a potent force in support of active or passive resistance.

Civil Rights and Liberties. When a privilege or immunity is expressed in the constitution or laws of a state, it becomes a *civil right*. Within the limits set down by law, each individual may act as he chooses. If his rights are invaded by other individuals or organizations or by the officers of the government, he may secure the enforcement of his civil rights through the courts. Civil rights in England were guaranteed by Magna Charta (1215),

Petition of Right (1628) and Bill of Rights (1689). During and after the American Revolution, bills of rights were incorporated into state and federal constitutions. In 1789, the French Assembly adopted the Declaration of the Rights of Man. These examples were followed when new constitutions were adopted in other countries. At present no constitution would be considered complete without a bill of rights. In 1948, the United Nations adopted a Universal Declaration of Human Rights, including most of the customarily guaranteed rights and, in addition, the rights to an adequate standard of living and to a social and international order in which rights and freedoms can be fully realized.

Too frequently in the past, governments have failed to properly observe bills of rights—sometimes because the provisions have not been formally incorporated into the text of a constitution, but more often because the provisions have been so broad in statement as to need specific interpretation (and, hence, to permit misconstruction). If a bill of rights is placed merely in the preamble and not incorporated in the constitution itself, courts will have no jurisdiction to enforce it. If, as is customary, the provisions assert the absolute right of individuals to freedom of speech, possession of property, and the like, definitions will be needed in actual practice—for rights are relative, not absolute. Obviously, the individual who slanders his neighbor, shouts "fire" in a crowded theater, or conveys secret information to his country's enemy can not claim valid defense under the "right" to freedom of speech. Obviously, individual rights can not be permitted to imperil the safety of the state or to stand in the way of the best interests of all: thus through taxation, through zoning ordinances, and through exercise of its power of eminent domain, the state may curtail an individual's "right" to hold property. There is an ever-present danger, however, that governments may overstep the bounds of their legitimate functions. Unless there is a rule of law applied by independent judges who are immune to the commands of dictators or the influence of politicians and pressure groups or the excitement of the crowd, civil rights will not be preserved.

Until recently, the contents of bills of rights indicated by their surprising similarity that they had been derived principally from the English Bill of Rights (1689). That document placed restrictions on the government's action; but the contemporary tendency is to state the guarantees of rights in the form of positive obligations of the government. In many new constitutions, the number of rights has also been expanded to include economic and social benefits, as well as some freedoms (such as freedom to choose one's place of residence and one's occupation) which are desirable and which exist in America without any constitutional protection at all.

FREEDOM OF SPEECH AND PRESS. Democratic states usually permit free expression of opinion orally or in writing so long as statements are not obscene, libelous, or slanderous. In time of war, freedom of speech may be curtailed to maintain unity and to avoid giving aid to the enemy by direct or indirect means. Traditionally, Anglo-Saxon people have valued freedom of expression highly because they believe that the best antidote for subversive ideas is to allow the ideas full hearing. In Russia and its satellites, rigid censorship of the press (and other means of communication) exists.

FREEDOM OF RELIGION. Frequently in history, only the religion and worship officially approved by the state have been permitted. The modern tendency is to permit religious freedom and to keep the church and the state separate. Freedom of belief, however, does not necessarily mean that the individual may refuse to obey the laws which are in conflict with his personal opinions of right and wrong; nor does it permit a religious sect to engage in rites which are contrary to the state's ordinarily accepted standard of morals.

FREEDOM OF ASSOCIATION. The state permits wide freedom in the formation of associations for various purposes, such as religious associations, labor associations, social clubs, scientific organizations, and commercial corporations (see Chapter 13). Such organizations must serve legal ends and are subject to control in order to safeguard the general welfare. The right of the people to assemble peaceably and petition for redress of grievances is basic, along with freedom of speech and press, for the operation of a democratic government.

FREEDOM OF CONTRACT. The state permits only contracts that are not in conflict with the general welfare. The rights and obligations growing out of such contracts become the subject of laws regulating them in detail. The state prohibits contracts establishing a monopoly of goods or services and refuses to enforce contracts involving the personal servitude of an individual. Sometimes legislation for the social welfare has been opposed or prevented on the ground that it interferes unduly with freedom of contract.

PROPERTY RIGHTS. Except in a communist state, the right of the individual to property is generally recognized. The state protects personal property against theft and usually provides for protection against damage of various sorts through its code of civil law. However, it interferes with property rights—by power of eminent domain and, in emergencies, by martial law—whenever the social good demands it. There is much controversy over the degree of public regulation which should be permitted, and the degree to which the state itself should own the means of providing public services.

PERSONAL FREEDOM. An individual should have the right to determine his profession or calling and to go where he chooses, insofar as he does not interfere with equal liberties of others. Marriage and divorce, and the major obligations in the relationship between husband and wife, parent and child, are regulated by law. Most states permit the family unit a large degree of freedom to regulate its own affairs; and most permit its members to arrange inheritance of property as they choose, though there is more interference in this field than formerly. Children were at one time at the mercy of their fathers; today most states would take a child from parents who were judged to be improper guardians because of their failure to provide adequately for his physical or moral care.

PROCEDURAL RIGHTS. In both civil and criminal actions, the individual is entitled to uniform procedure at the hands of the state. These rights vary according to the judicial code of the state, but in any event they include trial according to the law of the land. The Bill of Rights in the Constitution of the United States affords liberal treatment to the individual, guaranteeing, among other things, that he shall have the right to speedy and fair trial and the right to trial by jury, and that he shall never be deprived of life, liberty, or property without due process of law. In theory, the modern state enforces the same law for rich and poor alike and gives all persons equal legal rights, privileges, obligations, and protection. In practice, however, the rich, able to afford counsel and the expenses and delays involved in appeals to higher courts are frequently said to obtain better treatment (justice) than those with less financial means.

10 Constitutions

A *constitution* may be defined as a collection of norms or standards regulating the legal relations of the government to its subjects. Every state that ever existed has had a constitution of some kind, though in early political societies it may have consisted only of rules determining the succession to the throne and of customs concerning the way in which the monarch's power should be exercised. In some modern states the constitution is an elaborate document in which the organization of the government, its powers, the limitations on the exercise of its powers, and its relations to individuals are all carefully set down. It is inconceivable that any state could exist without a written or unwritten constitution, defining the relationship between governors and governed.

THE CREATION OF CONSTITUTIONS

Constitutions have been classified as *written* or *unwritten* Written constitutions consist of single documents in which the whole structure of government is described and rules for its conduct are presented in orderly sequence. Unwritten constitutions consist of customs reinforced by historical precedents. This classification is not exclusive. Some written constitutions do not include all the fundamental standards; they leave any number of standards to custom. Unwritten constitutions, except those of states where complete illiteracy exists, include much written material in the form of laws.

Evolutionary Development. The best-known example of an unwritten constitution is that of Great Britain. In her case power passed gradually (sometimes by almost imperceptible stages) from monarchs and finally, after many centuries, became **vested in Parliament.** Factors contributing to this trend were the common law; the rights and obligations established under feudal systems; the policy of the kings, when they wanted additional revenue, of asking Parliament to levy taxes; and Parliament's habitual requests for redress of grievances before making financial grants. Later on these principles were established: the acts of a king must be countersigned by a minister and the ministers collectively must resign when one of their important policies is not approved by a majority of the House of Commons. Important landmarks in the development of the constitution were Magna Charta, 1215; Petition of Right, 1628; Bill of Rights, 1689; Act of Settlement, 1701; various acts for the reform of the suffrage in the nineteenth and twentieth centuries; and the Parliament Acts of 1911 and 1949 limiting the power of the House of Lords. These written documents together with the principles maintained through a series of precedents comprise the complete constitution of the British state.

The Constitutional Convention. The written constitution is an American invention; but, like most inventions, it began as a combination of previously existing elements.[1] In the course of the American Revolution the states established written constitutions combining the principles of freedom which had developed in Great Britain and the colonies with the principle of a limited government which was contained in the colonial charters. The instrument for drawing up the state constitution was based on English precedents, for Parliament had declared itself a "convention"[2] when it called Charles II to the throne after the Puritan Revolution and again when it installed William and Mary as sovereigns after the abdication of James II. In many states, the legislatures turned themselves into conventions for the purpose of writing and promulgating constitutions; in other states, conventions were especially chosen for the purpose. In either case the implication was that the convention was a higher authority than a legislature—that it was not an ordinary representative body, but somehow a solemn convocation of the people.

---

[1] "The Americans were used to being governed by written instruments, beginning with feudal land grants and company charters."—M. Smelser, *American Colonial and Revolutionary History*, College Outline Series (New York, Barnes & Noble, Inc., 1950), p. 213.

[2] That is, an extraordinary body which possesses full powers of sovereignty and is convoked to effect constitutional changes.

THE GOVERNMENT OF THE UNITED STATES

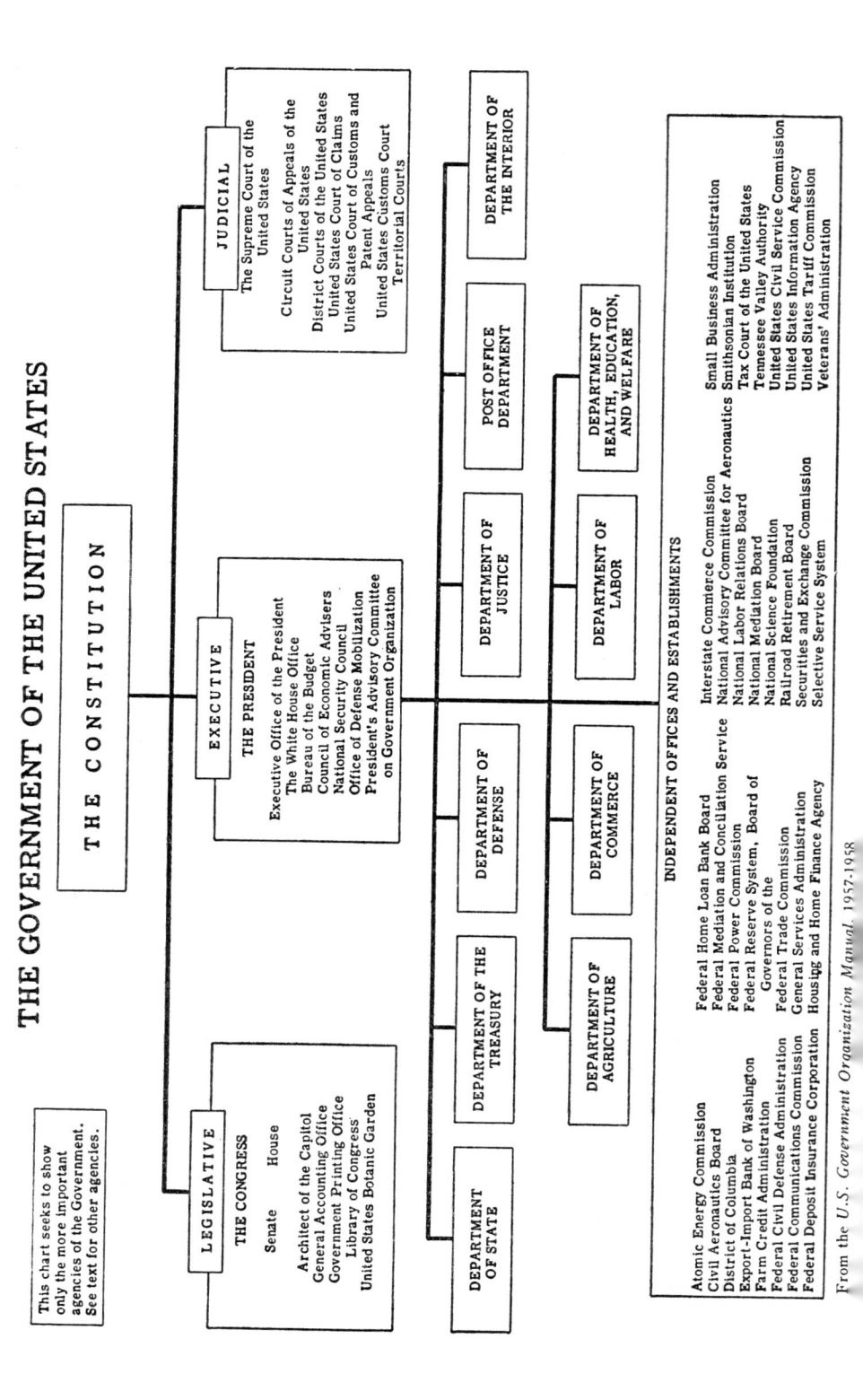

This chart seeks to show only the more important agencies of the Government. See text for other agencies.

THE CONSTITUTION

LEGISLATIVE

THE CONGRESS

Senate House

Architect of the Capitol
General Accounting Office
Government Printing Office
Library of Congress
United States Botanic Garden

EXECUTIVE

THE PRESIDENT

Executive Office of the President
The White House Office
Bureau of the Budget
Council of Economic Advisers
National Security Council
Office of Defense Mobilization
President's Advisory Committee on Government Organization

JUDICIAL

The Supreme Court of the United States

Circuit Courts of Appeals of the United States
District Courts of the United States
United States Court of Claims
United States Court of Customs and Patent Appeals
United States Customs Court
Territorial Courts

DEPARTMENT OF STATE

DEPARTMENT OF THE TREASURY

DEPARTMENT OF DEFENSE

DEPARTMENT OF JUSTICE

POST OFFICE DEPARTMENT

DEPARTMENT OF THE INTERIOR

DEPARTMENT OF AGRICULTURE

DEPARTMENT OF COMMERCE

DEPARTMENT OF LABOR

DEPARTMENT OF HEALTH, EDUCATION, AND WELFARE

INDEPENDENT OFFICES AND ESTABLISHMENTS

Atomic Energy Commission
Civil Aeronautics Board
District of Columbia
Export-Import Bank of Washington
Farm Credit Administration
Federal Civil Defense Administration
Federal Communications Commission
Federal Deposit Insurance Corporation
Federal Home Loan Bank Board
Federal Mediation and Conciliation Service
Federal Power Commission
Federal Reserve System, Board of Governors of the
Federal Trade Commission
General Services Administration
Housing and Home Finance Agency
Interstate Commerce Commission
National Advisory Committee for Aeronautics
National Labor Relations Board
National Mediation Board
National Science Foundation
Railroad Retirement Board
Securities and Exchange Commission
Selective Service System
Small Business Administration
Smithsonian Institution
Tax Court of the United States
Tennessee Valley Authority
United States Civil Service Commission
United States Information Agency
United States Tariff Commission
Veterans' Administration

From the *U.S. Government Organization Manual*, 1957-1958

CONSTITUTIONS

This theory of the convention continued in most of the Southern states until after the Civil War and is still apparent in Louisiana. (In some foreign countries, constitutions have been drafted and promulgated by successful revolutionary organizations.)

Popular Ratification. Before the end of the Revolution an opposing theory developed in Massachusetts and spread to other Northern states. It was that the convention was not a sovereign body but merely a drafting body whose proposed constitution was of no value until accepted by vote of the electorate. A sort of compromise between the two theories occurred when the Constitution of the United States was submitted for ratification to conventions in the separate states. In most of the world today, constitutions are submitted to popular vote after being drafted by conventions assembled for the purpose. This is now the normal method of constitution-making.

Royal Grant. During the numerous revolutions that occurred on the Continent of Europe in the nineteenth century, many kings were forced to grant written constitutions guaranteeing liberties which had been denied under the customs and precedents of the existing unwritten constitutions. These constitutions depended on the good faith of the monarch for their future observance. Obviously if the monarch had power to grant them, he had power to negate or recall them. Only a few were observed after the revolutionary crises had passed.

REQUISITES OF CONSTITUTIONS

The reader should familiarize himself with the nature of a constitution by studying the Constitution of the United States and the constitution of his own state. He should then compare his state constitution both with the written constitutions of foreign states and with the Model State Constitution prepared by a committee of experts for the National Municipal League.[3] (This model is made up from the best provisions now contained in our state constitutions and includes concise provisions concerning certain subjects based on the experiences of many states. The Model State Constitution as a whole would probably not fit the needs of any one state, but its provisions could be adapted to meet particular needs anywhere.)

---
[3] The Model State Constitution may be obtained from the National Municipal League, 299 Broadway, New York, N. Y.

A constitution helps to reduce the uncertainties of political life to a minimum. Such questions as how officers shall be chosen, which officers shall exercise certain powers, how far their powers extend, and what right the people may legally claim against the actions of the executive, the legislatures, and the courts should be clearly set forth in terms as definite as possible. A written constitution should be concise and yet comprehensive. It should cover the whole field of government and make provision for the exercise of all political power. It should not include minute details. Many constitutions now in existence are too long, too verbose, and too full of minor matters better fitted for enactment as statutes; detailed provisions make a constitution inadaptable to changing conditions. It should always be kept in mind that a constitution must be carried out by men in governing other men—therefore, the provisions should incorporate the best experience of the nation for which the constitution is made. Few constitutions based on ideal concepts or copied from the constitutions of other nations have been successful in practice.

Provisions for Governmental Organization. The constitution should set forth the functions to be performed by each of the important divisions or departments of the government. For a federal state, it is proper to define the powers which shall be exercised by each division and its chief officers; for a unitary state, it is probably better not to grant powers but to fix definite and clear limitations on the powers to be exercised and the procedures to be followed. Concerning the officers of each division, there must be statements determining their qualifications, the person or groups who choose them, the procedures to be followed in making the choice, and the length of their continuance in office. The groups who exercise the suffrage should be clearly defined, and their freedom to act according to democratic principles should be guaranteed. A section should be devoted to the organization, powers, and immunities of local governments.

Separation of Powers and Checks and Balances. The doctrine of *separation of powers* was advanced by Montesquieu in his *Spirit of the Laws* (1748) and was incorporated into the federal and state constitutions in the United States. It is based on the idea that those who hold power are likely to extend it as far as they can and thus to encroach on the liberties of the people. By separating the powers of government into executive, legisla-

GOVERNMENT OF GREAT BRITAIN

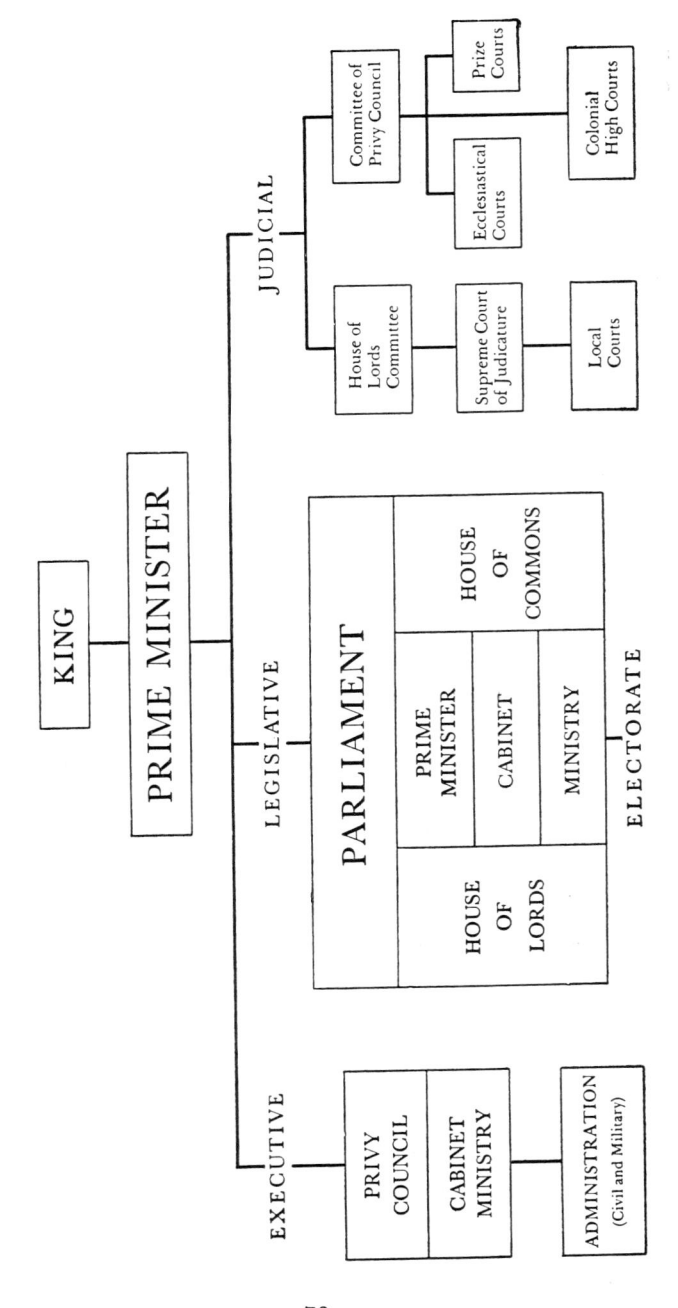

KING — PRIME MINISTER

EXECUTIVE
- PRIVY COUNCIL
- CABINET MINISTRY
  - ADMINISTRATION (Civil and Military)

LEGISLATIVE
- PARLIAMENT
  - HOUSE OF LORDS
  - PRIME MINISTER / CABINET / MINISTRY
  - HOUSE OF COMMONS
- ELECTORATE

JUDICIAL
- House of Lords Committee
  - Supreme Court of Judicature
    - Local Courts
- Committee of Privy Council
  - Prize Courts
  - Ecclesiastical Courts
  - Colonial High Courts

73

tive, and judicial departments and by making each department supreme within its own sphere it was thought that a constitution could be preserved, for no single department would possess sufficient power to overthrow it. It was recognized, however, that the departments were unequal in strength, and so a number of additional internal *checks* were applied: thus the president's treaty-making and appointive powers were made to depend on senatorial approval, and congressional legislation was subjected to a suspensive veto by the president. European constitutions have generally not observed a clear separation of power between the executive and the legislature, though they have made the judiciary independent. Before the development of dictatorships, the theory of separation of powers was much criticized in the United States and abroad because it seemed to result in useless friction, indecision, and delay. Recently, however, there has been a renewed respect for separation of powers.

Bill of Rights. Practically every constitution in the world today contains an elaborate statement of the rights which individuals may claim against officers of the government. (A discussion of the rights of individuals is presented in Chapter 9.) It is necessary to note here that when the statement of rights is inserted only in the preamble of a constitution, it is not enforceable—the preamble being merely introductory and not an actual part of the constitution. Rights must be carefully defined, not left to general statement. If rights are to be suspended for reasons of emergency, the nature of the emergency and the officers who are empowered to suspend rights must be clearly identified.

FLEXIBLE AND RIGID CONSTITUTIONS

Constitutions have been classified as *flexible* or as *rigid* according to the relative ease or difficulty of the amending process. At one extreme is the British constitution which can be changed by an ordinary act of Parliament following a general election in which the proposed change was an issue. At the other extreme are constitutions which do not provide a means of amendment. However, their rigidity is more apparent than real, for in practice such constitutions are usually dispensed with or circumvented. Such actions tend to destroy the faith of a people in

GOVERNMENT OF FRANCE*

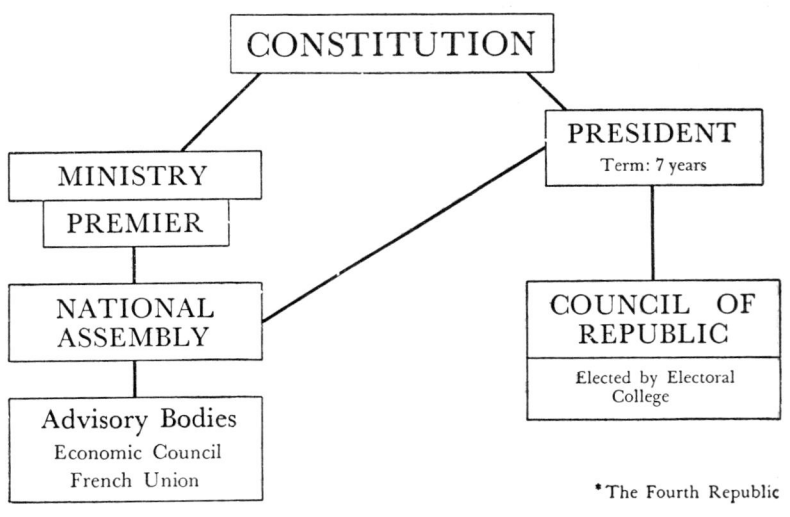

- **CONSTITUTION**
  - **MINISTRY / PREMIER**
    - **NATIONAL ASSEMBLY**
      - Advisory Bodies
        - Economic Council
        - French Union
  - **PRESIDENT** — Term: 7 years
    - **COUNCIL OF REPUBLIC** — Elected by Electoral College
    - National Assembly

*The Fourth Republic

GOVERNMENT OF THE U.S.S.R.

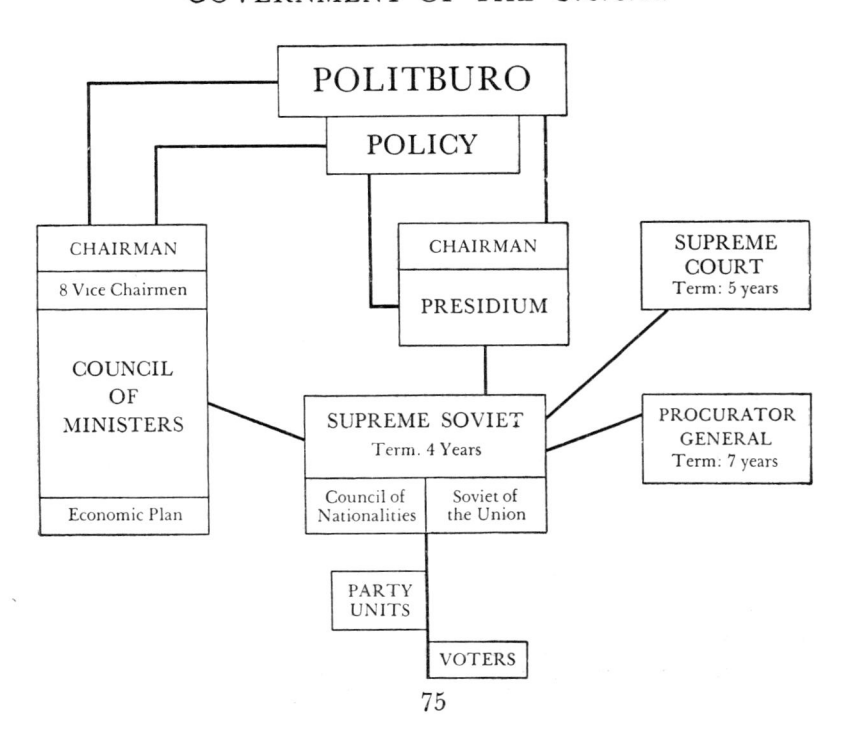

- **POLITBURO**
  - **POLICY**
    - **CHAIRMAN** — 8 Vice Chairmen
      - **COUNCIL OF MINISTERS**
        - Economic Plan
    - **CHAIRMAN**
      - **PRESIDIUM**
    - **SUPREME COURT** — Term: 5 years
    - **SUPREME SOVIET** — Term: 4 Years
      - Council of Nationalities
      - Soviet of the Union
    - **PROCURATOR GENERAL** — Term: 7 years
  - PARTY UNITS
    - VOTERS

75

their constitution and thus to lessen the constitution's usefulness as fundamental law. If, on the other hand, the process of amendment is too easy, lack of stability will result; amendment will be piled on amendment until the constitution takes on the character of a bundle of statutes. A few constitutions attempt a compromise by stating that certain provisions are not subject to amendment at all or that these require an unusually difficult amendment procedure. It is the general opinion that statements of this kind are of no value, because the amendment procedure, which is an exercise of sovereignty, is unlimited. At present, the tendency in constitution-making is to strike a balance between too great flexibility on the one hand and too great rigidity on the other hand.

Formal Amendment. The methods of amending a constitution give the strongest of all possible clues as to the location of sovereignty in a state. They provide a means for estimating the vitality of a constitution and its adjustability to new and unforeseen conditions. They have been aptly called "the safety valves of the governmental engine." The usual processes of amendment provide for action by the legislature alone, by the convocation of conventions created for the purpose, and by popular vote through the initiative or the referendum.

LEGISLATIVE AMENDMENT. Few states possess the internal stability of Great Britain, in which amendments are passed under the procedure of making statutes. In the Third French Republic (1870-1940) amendment was by an absolute majority of both houses sitting together, but the constitution of the Fourth Republic (adopted 1946) provides for a more complicated procedure. Under it, a resolution may be adopted by an absolute majority of the National Assembly stating the nature and purpose of a proposed amendment, followed after three months by balloting upon the actual text. If the amendment is adopted by two-thirds of the National Assembly or by three-fifths of each house, it is promulgated. If passed by only a simple majority of the National Assembly, the amendment must be submitted to a referendum. The time of promulgation may be shortened if the Council of the Republic adopts the resolution for an amendment by an absolute majority. In Germany, the constitution of the Bonn Republic may be amended by a two-thirds vote of each house, but the bill of rights and the existence of the *Laender* are not subject to amendment. In Russia, a two-thirds vote of each chamber is required, though amendments have actually been promulgated by sole action of the executive. In the United States, the usual method of amendment has been proposal by a two-thirds vote in each house of Congress and ratification by three-fourths of the state legislatures.

ELECTORAL PARTICIPATION. In Switzerland, amendments to the federal constitution may be proposed by the two chambers or by a petition of 50,000 voters, and they may go into effect if approved by a majority of the voters and a majority of the cantons. In nearly all the states of the United States, amendments to state constitutions may be proposed by the legislatures, usually by extraordinary majorities, and adopted by the electorates. A few states have made provision for popular initiative in proposing amendments. In Japan's post-war constitution, amendments may be proposed by a two-thirds vote of all the members of each of the chambers and adopted by a majority of the voters in a referendum. Italy's constitution of 1948 requires a referendum on the demand of one-fifth of either chamber, or of five regional councils, or of 500,000 voters. The latter provisions make it a simple matter to obtain a referendum.

CONSTITUENT ASSEMBLIES. In nearly all states of the United States, entirely new constitutions may be drafted or amendments may be proposed by constitutional conventions. They become effective when approved by the electorate. Conventions may also be used for proposing or ratifying amendments to the federal Constitution. Several Latin American countries require ratification of amendments by conventions.

Expansion of Constitutions. Few constitutions exist over a long period of time without undergoing change. The gradual erosion of custom may weaken or destroy the force of certain provisions and build up others. It is sometimes discovered that unintentionally or deliberately the framers of a constitution have left some fundamental questions unsettled. Without waiting for the procedure of amendment, the legislature fills in the empty spaces by statute. Technological and other developments may compel a redefinition and expansion through judicial interpretation of the meaning of the terms used in a constitution. Written constitutions are never considered finished; they constantly continue to grow.

THE ENFORCEMENT OF CONSTITUTIONS

With the exception of documents granted by autocratic rulers through revolutionary duress or for purposes of propaganda, every constitution was meant to be observed. But there is a wide difference of opinion between Americans and most Europeans as to the methods of enforcement. The American regards his Constitution as law to be enforced, like other kinds of law, by the courts. The European regards his constitution as fundamental, but can not understand why the courts, more than other branches of government, should be its special guardians. To him, a legislature which is representative of the electorate seems better fitted for the task: if the legislature should err, then the electorate may elect different members to the next legislature. The people know what rights are being infringed upon when a constitution is reduced to written form.

Judicial Review. The basis for the American doctrine of judicial review, which applies in the states as well as in the federal system, was laid by Chief Justice John Marshall in the famous case of *Marbury* v. *Madison* (1803). *Judicial review* means in effect that courts, when asked to enforce statutes, must compare them with the Constitution: if they find a conflict, or if they find that the legislature lacked power to make a statute, the courts must resolve the conflict in favor of the Constitution because it is the supreme law of the land. There is no such thing as an unconstitutional law, for such a statute could never have had legal existence. The same rule is applied when acts of executive officers are in question. The decision of the Supreme Court as to the meaning of the Constitution is final in a particular case, though in later cases it may sometimes find reasons for refusing to follow the precedent. Of course, a Constitutional amendment which grants power where the Court has denied its exercise may be passed. Judicial review has often been criticized because of the conservatism which many judges have shown.

Review of Statutes in France. The constitution of the Fourth French Republic (1946) provides for a Constitutional Committee to determine whether or not laws passed by the National Assembly imply amendment to the constitution. The committee consists of the President of the Republic, the presidents of the two chambers, seven members chosen by the National Assembly, and three members chosen by the Council. Whenever the Council by an absolute majority so requests, the Constitutional Committee examines the law, strives to bring about an agreement between the chambers, and if no agreement is reached may send the statute back to the National Assembly for reconsideration. If the legislature adheres to its original vote, the law may not be promulgated until the constitution has been amended.

11 Suffrage and Elections

The function of the electorate in a democratic state is to exercise general supervision over the conduct of the government by periodically choosing the principal officers. Thus, the electorate directly or indirectly determines the personnel of the government and the general policies to be followed. In some states, an electorate may be asked to consider recalling a given officer, to determine whether or not a given statute passed by the legislature may go into effect, or to approve or to reject a proposed bond issue or city charter. It may be asked to adopt a new constitution or to amend an old one; by means of such a decision it exercises powers of legal sovereignty.

SUFFRAGE

Suffrage is a privilege or a right granted by the state to an expressly designated group of persons which entitles them to participate in the choice of officers and in the decision of questions submitted to them. The process of admission to the suffrage is called *enfranchisement;* the process of depriving persons of the suffrage is called *disenfranchisement*.

Theories of Suffrage. There are many theories as to the nature of the suffrage. Those following have been extremely important in the history of legislation regulating enfranchisement or disenfranchisement: (1) The theory that suffrage is an attribute of citizenship and a necessary and natural outgrowth of the citizen's membership in a city or tribe was fundamental in the political organization of Greek, Roman, and Germanic peoples. (2) In feudal times, suffrage was considered to be a privilege associated with a certain social status: enfranchisement was usually determined by land ownership but might also result from a person's position in a guild. Traces of this theory, which developed in the Middle Ages, may still be found where a property qualification for suffrage exists. (3) The "natural-rights" theory of the suffrage is based on the principle of the natural equality of men and of their equal interest in public affairs. (4) The ethical theory holds that participation in government is essential to the opportunity for full development of the individual in society. (5) The legal theory—upon which governments now act—states that the suffrage is a political privilege conferred by law and that the electorate is an organ of government whose composition and powers are determined by the laws of the state.

EXTENSION OF THE SUFFRAGE. Property qualifications for the suffrage remained in effect until long after the American and French revolutions. They were defended on the ground that property owners alone possessed a stake in society and the requisite responsibility for the proper exercise of the suffrage. In protest against this idea, the natural-rights and ethical theories of the suffrage were advanced; the argument was presented that those who paid taxes or rendered military service had a stake in a particular political society equal with that of property owners. Moreover, it was maintained that if suffrage is a public trust, education rather than property should be made the test. The old order gave way grudgingly.

In France, the property qualification was supplanted by a taxpaying qualification in 1814, and that in turn gave way to manhood suffrage in 1848. In the United States, where suffrage was determined by the individual states, the same general pattern was followed. In Great Britain, property qualifications were relaxed in the reform acts of 1867 and 1884 and finally disappeared in 1918. Elsewhere in Europe, when suffrage was granted, the laws usually provided for property qualifications or for plural voting, or at least they weighted representation in favor of property holders. By the end of the nineteenth century, manhood suffrage had been achieved in many nations of the Western world.

Woman suffrage existed hardly anywhere until well into the twentieth century. It was argued that women's participation in public affairs would destroy their qualities as wives and mothers; that in voting they would follow their emotions rather than reason; that women's interest in public affairs was slight and would last only until the novelty had worn off; or that, if they voted at all, women would vote as their husbands or fathers did.

These arguments, however, could not stand up under the cold facts of universal education, the economic independence of women, and their valiant services on the home front in wartime. In 1918 Great Britain granted suffrage to women over thirty years of age, and ten years later to all adult women. The United States, by constitutional amendment in 1920 forbade discriminations in the suffrage on account of sex. The U.S.S.R. early granted suffrage to women workers and, in 1936, extended the right to all women. After the close of World War II, France and Italy and nearly all other countries made the suffrage universal.

Qualifications for the Suffrage. Today the principal qualifications for the exercise of the suffrage are based on age, citizenship, residence, and literacy.

AGE. Obviously there must be some minimum age limit for voting. Usually the minimum is twenty-one years, which is generally the age of legal majority. In Germany the minimum age is twenty, and in the U.S.S.R. it is eighteen. In the United States, the minimum is twenty-one; only the states of Georgia and Kentucky have fixed the minimum age at eighteen.

CITIZENSHIP. With the exception of the U.S.S.R., most states restrict the suffrage to citizens. In the past, as an inducement to rapid settlement, several states in the United States enfranchised aliens who declared their intention to become citizens. Citizenship of itself does not necessarily carry with it the privilege of the suffrage; many citizens are not permitted to vote because they do not meet other requirements.

RESIDENCE. Nearly every state in the United States requires that each voter must establish a legal residence in a particular place for a stipulated period and may vote only in the district in which he resides. This requirement is desirable in order that registration lists may be prepared and checked in ample time to prevent fraud.

LITERACY. Literacy tests have been justified on the ground that a person who can not read is unable to obtain proper information concerning public affairs or to mark a ballot properly. They are not justified when used as a subterfuge to debar persons from the suffrage on racial or other grounds. If used, their administration should be confided to permanent educational authorities rather than to the temporary precinct boards which in the United States usually administer them.

OTHER QUALIFICATIONS. Miscellaneous mental and moral qualifications are enforced. Lunacy and idiocy are grounds for disqualification everywhere; so also in most states is conviction of a felony or of an offense against election laws, especially of bribery. In Great Britain, peers are disqualified on the ground that they may vote on legislation in the House of Lords. In certain Latin-American countries, priests and members of monastic orders may not vote. Property and taxpaying qualifications still exist in a number of Southern states of the United States.

Freedom of the Suffrage. In the movement for suffrage extension, great emphasis was placed on equality of the suffrage and relatively less emphasis was placed on freedom of the suffrage. The existence of democracy depends on political liberty as well as equality. In other words, it rests upon the freedom of an equal electorate to choose officers of the government and at intervals to have the opportunity to replace them. If the electorate is not free to make a real choice, or if the officers to be voted for have no real control over the government, freedom of the suffrage is a delusion. The substance of both equality and liberty is lacking if the result is determined through duress or fraud. With an equality of the suffrage now prevailing throughout the world, the real distinction between democracy and dictatorship depends on whether or not the suffrage is free. In a dictatorship, the exercise of suffrage is little more than mass participation in a ritual through which from time to time the voters are called upon to reaffirm their faith in the regime.

ELECTIONS

An *election* is a choice, by persons qualified to vote, among candidates for a public office. (There is general agreement that elections should be held on a Sunday or else on a holiday and that polling places should be convenient to the homes of voters.) The laws of various countries differ concerning the extent of direct participation by the electorate, the number of officers to be chosen at one time, the actual range of choice, the secrecy of voting, the frequency of elections, and the administrative procedures for the conduct of elections.

Direct and Indirect Elections. At the beginning of the democratic movement, the opinion was often expressed that an electorate if left to itself could not make the best choice among candidates. Such a choice, it was thought, should be confided to an intermediate body of able and responsible persons. Thus, the Constitution of the United States provided that an electoral college should choose the president. Many nations having either unitary or federal governments required that the upper house of the legislature be elected indirectly; and a few nations chose even the supposedly popular house in the same way. The development of party systems has tended to reduce electoral colleges and like bodies merely to formal positions. The actual choice among candidates by the party for President of the United States is made directly by the electorate, voting by states.

At present, France is conspicuous for its provision for the indirect election of the president and members of the Council of the Republic. Wherever the cabinet system prevails, the legislature or one of its chambers chooses the actual executive. In Great Britain, the voters know in advance of an election the probable composition of a cabinet, and this fact has had an effect in increasing the cabinet's powers relative to those of the Parliament.

Types of Offices. In judging an electoral system, an essential consideration is whether the electorate chooses officers who exercise real power, or whether it fritters away its efforts in meaningless choices of officers with little or no authority. In Great Britain, the ballot for a Parliamentary election contains the names of only two or three persons who are candidates for a single vacant seat; but the successful candidate becomes a member of the body that exercises sovereignty in the British state. In Russia, the ballot contains the names of candidates for election to the Supreme Soviet and to other offices; but real power is in a little group in the Kremlin who are responsible to no one. In the United States, the voter is presented on election day with a long list of candidates for national, state, and local offices, most of whom—like state treasurers, county clerks, and coroners—hope to fill routine positions. The present "long ballot" is a relic of the first half of the nineteenth century, when it was believed that democracy meant the election of all officers. It has often been pointed out that voters have no real basis for choice in the filling of little-publicized positions, and that in most instances their votes are cast for a party's nominee whoever he may be. Political scientists generally agree that such offices should be filled through appointment by responsible executive officers.

Number of Candidates. Democratic states hesitate to place artificial limits on the number of candidates for a particular office. It sometimes happens that so many candidates enter the field that none of them can obtain a majority. Experiments with a preferential vote in which the voter is asked to name first, second, and third choices have not been successful. The same is true when a second election is required to choose between the two highest candidates, because it burdens the voters with too many elections. The other extreme is found in totalitarian states, where there is one official party which monopolizes the ballot. In Fascist Italy and Nazi Germany opposition candidates were almost unknown; the form of the ballot, the surveillance of the police and party militia, and dread of reprisals caused voters to give these candidates negligible support. In the U.S.S.R., anyone theoretically may be nominated for office, but all nominees except the one approved by the local Communist party organization almost universally withdraw before the election. What better means can be found for autocratic control than to restrict the voter to the approval of a single candidate for an office that does not count?

The Ballot. Secrecy of elections is a comparatively modern innovation. The general practice at the beginning of the nineteenth century was for voters to call out the names of candidates of their choice. The so-called "open vote" was often justified on the ground that, inasmuch as the suffrage is a public function, it ought to be exercised in public. But by the 1870's the ballot was required in elections in the United States and Great Britain in order to prevent employers and others from intimidating voters. The *Australian ballot,* which was adopted in the United States in 1888, contains the names of all regularly nominated candidates, is prepared by public authority, is given to the voter inside the polling place, and must be marked by him and deposited in the ballot box before he leaves. The two principal forms of this ballot are the *Indiana ballot,* in which the names of candidates are arranged in columns under the name and sometimes the emblem of the party, and the *Massachusetts ballot,* in which the names of candidates are grouped under various offices. Many states now use voting machines. Today, practically every country in the world requires the secret ballot, though no other lists so many candidates as the United States.

Frequency and Time of Elections. Elections should be held often enough for the electorate to exercise effective control, but not so often as to impair governmental efficiency by overfrequent changes of officers and policies. Terms in office of four or five years are generally recognized as proper. Great Britain and several other countries provide for dissolutions of the legislative body and the holding of new elections whenever the legislature refuses to adopt policies recommended by the ministry. In such cases, the time allowed for the election campaign is short.

Administration of Elections. Generally speaking, in Europe the administration of elections is centralized. The registration of voters, the polling and counting of votes, and the certifying of results are in the hands of persons appointed by national authority. In the United States, such matters are left to county or other local authorities. The American method is conducive to irregularities and fraud. The registration of voters should be on a permanent basis maintained by full-time civil service employees—not, as too often at present, by temporary employees appointed just before an election. The responsibility for allowing or refusing to allow a registered voter to vote and for an accurate counting of the ballots is too great to be confided to persons recruited on a partisan basis to serve for a single election day.

Prevention of Corrupt Practices. Offenses against the purity of elections such as bribery, intimidation, "repeating" (the casting of more than one ballot), and "personation" (voting in the name of another person) are everywhere prohibited by law. Those guilty of offenses—whether candidates, voters, or election officers—may be subject to penalties ranging in various countries from fine or imprisonment to disfranchisement and disqualification from holding office. The problem of enforcing such laws is especially difficult, where there is lax or partisan administration of elections.

Problems of Nonvoting. The percentage of participants in voting varies greatly from state to state. It is very high in the Scandinavian countries and in Great Britain and relatively low in the United States, where sometimes the number of votes cast in a presidential election is less than half that of the adult population. The reasons for nonvoting here are partly attributable to the electoral system which gives weight to votes according to states (in some states minority voters feel that their votes would carry no weight); where the result is a foregone conclusion, many members of the electorate neglect to vote. Nonvoting is also due to illness, absence from home, and general inertia caused sometimes by the feeling that there are too many elections and too many officers to be chosen. Participation increases in direct proportion to the degree of education among the electorate, to the amount of property or income, and to age. It tends to increase during economic crises and when the general conduct of political affairs has been unsatisfactory. This phenomenon has led to the theory that the suffrage may be regarded as a right of protest on the part of a voter against the conduct of government.

EXPERIMENTS WITH COMPULSORY VOTING. A number of states have enacted laws imposing penalties on voters who failed to vote. The results have varied. Belgian experience with a small fine indicated that although there was some increase in participation many blank ballots were cast and there was no appreciable improvement in the quality of the suffrage. By imposing a heavier fine, Australia succeeded in increasing participation from less than 60 to more than 90 per cent. In most countries, efforts to secure the enactment of compulsory voting laws have made little headway. Such laws would change the concept of the suffrage from a political privilege to a duty imposed by the state—a duty, moreover, that can be evaded by mere attendance at the polling place. There is no means of compelling a person to vote intelligently or to study the personalities and issues involved in an election.

DIRECT DEMOCRACY

The institutions of *direct democracy* are the initiative, the referendum, and the recall. The referendum was generally used from an early period by states of the United States for the ratification of new constitutions and constitutional amendments; the provision for recall was developed also in the United States. But the initiative and referendum for the enactment of legislation were developed in some of the more populous Swiss cantons as a substitute for personal attendance by the voters at the annual meetings of the cantonal assemblies. Their use for legislation spread to the United States beginning in 1898 and also to several European states. These institutions of direct democracy are unnecessary in states where dissolution of the legislative body and a new election may follow a vote of lack of confidence in the government. They seem to be useful elsewhere if invoked only occasionally when matters of general interest are involved; otherwise, their effectiveness is destroyed.

The Initiative. The *initiative* (which is permitted in some European states and in several states of the United States) is a means for overcoming the apathy or inertia of a legislative body or its refusal to enact legislation for which there is popular demand. In the *indirect initiative,* a private draft of a statute or a constitutional amendment is prepared and, if signed by the requisite number or percentage of voters, is submitted to the legislature; unless the legislature enacts it in complete form, it is then submitted to the electorate. In the *direct initiative,* the proposed law is submitted only to the electorate, not to the legislature. For the success of the initiative, it is necessary that the proposed statute or amendment should be carefully drafted and subjected to intensive private discussion and criticism before being submitted. The electorate should be on its guard against the proposals of selfish groups pretending to act in the public interest. Experience has shown that the electorate will not adopt intricate, technical, or other measures that they can not readily understand.

The Referendum. The *referendum* is a device whereby an unwise or unpopular law, or a law passed by a legislature dominated by some special interest, may be prevented from going into effect. Some states of the United States provide that if during the period between the passage and the promulgation of a statute 5 or 6 per cent of the people so petition, the law must be submitted to the electorate for acceptance or rejection. If rejected, the law never goes into effect. The referendum has sometimes been criticized because it seems to weaken the power and influence of the legislature, and because the electorate is less well prepared to vote on questions than on officers.

The Recall. On the analogy of the initiative and referendum for legislation, provision has been made (in several states and many cities in the United States) for a popular vote to dismiss an officer before the end of his term; this procedure is called *recall*. Usually after six months of his term have elapsed, a petition signed by a small percentage of the voters will compel the submission of the question for or against his recall to popular vote. The need for this device arose from the fact that no method except impeachment existed for removing an officer, and then only for high crimes and misdemeanors. The recall enables the electorate to remove an officer for incapacity, indolence, or any other cause. In practice, it has not proved completely successful —especially when it can be made to appear that the recall is invoked for merely partisan advantage.

12 Political Parties

A political party is an organized association of voters which seeks to control the personnel and policies of a government. Until a century and a half ago, parties were condemned because they were thought to threaten the internal security of the state. But actual experience in the United States and other democracies proved that parties might direct their efforts towards securing peaceful changes in the offices and policies of government without any intention of overthrowing the established order. Moreover, in the course of their competition with one another, it was observed that they performed services without which democracy could hardly exist. Parties organize the electorate so that it can function effectively. They nominate the candidates for office. They debate, discuss, and attempt to interest the electorate in the issues of a campaign. The parties in power attempt to conduct the government so as to win public approval, knowing that if they fail to do so they may lose office. The parties out of power point out defects in policies and make alternative proposals, hoping that the voters will entrust them with power.

PARTY SYSTEMS

The form and extent of party organization and activities depend greatly on the constitution of the state. A widespread suffrage requires more intensive organization than does a limited one. The greater the number of elective officers, the more involved are nominating procedures and campaign methods. The most striking difference in democratic party systems is that between the biparty system of English-speaking states and the multiparty system of Continental Europe.

The Biparty System. Normally the biparty system consists of two major parties, nearly equal in membership, and a few minor parties that are too small to have much influence on the result of an election though occasionally a third party may arise which threatens to, and sometimes does, supplant one of the two large parties. Of the major parties, the one in power, called the "majority party," assumes the responsibility for conducting public affairs. The other one, called the "minority party" or the "opposition," assumes the function of careful examination and criticism of the government's policies. Both parties compete for the approval of the majority of the electorate. Each seeks to avoid dissension within its own ranks and therefore makes adjustments and compromises to secure a united front. Frequently, neither of the major parties is willing to take up a new and untried issue lest it alienate part of its own following. New issues are often exploited and developed by the minor parties. If the innovations prove to be popular, they will be adopted by one or both of the major parties. Generally the major parties are on record in one way or another on a great many different issues. Voters, in attempting to choose between parties, may find the differences in principle confusing and therefore concentrate their attention on candidates.

The Multiparty System. In a multiparty system there are usually several parties of nearly equal strength. Each stands for a definite policy on one or a number of important issues, usually without equivocation or compromise. In a state with a multiparty system each voter supports the party which most nearly represents his own opinions. From the British and American points of view, the multiparty system is defective in that usually no one party can obtain a majority. Governments must rest on coalitions or blocs, and these are notoriously unstable. The voter, for all his freedom to choose among declarations of principles, can in practice do little more than choose the representatives who will make the compromises essential for the functioning of government. He can not approve or disapprove these compromises. Perhaps there is on the Continent a preference for indirect election which does not exist in English-speaking states. Voters in the United States and in Great Britain insist on participating in the final decisions.

The One-Party System. It is generally recognized that in countries with a one-party system the parties are in fact organs of government rather than voluntary associations of voters. The monopoly of political affairs by one party is a complete denial of everything for which democracy stands. Single parties in contemporary dictatorships have come to power by revolutionary means. They remain mobilized to prevent counterrevolution. Among other activities, they maintain discipline in the population, control nominations and elections, engage in espionage, enforce censorship, and propagate the official party faith among the people. Such activities more properly belong to governments than to parties.

PARTY ORGANIZATION

The extent of the party organization is always impressive on paper. In actual fact, it may range from a few volunteer workers hastily recruited for a single campaign to a permanent staff employed on a year-round basis. At best, it is only a fraction of what a business organization would consider adequate for the job: there are nominations to be made, campaigns to be conducted among millions of voters, factional misunderstandings to be rectified, research to be completed, and information to be supplied to newspapers and various other channels of communication.

Socialist Organization. Socialist, communist, and other left-wing parties are permanently organized on the basis of a carefully selected dues-paying membership. Dues are paid to a local unit, which retains a portion and transmits the remainder to the provincial and national offices of the party. Permanent national headquarters are maintained. Theoretically an annual meeting determines the true party doctrine and the principles to be followed in dealing with issues of the day, but in practice it is the permanent secretary who plays a dominant part in such matters. He often attempts to dictate to editors of party newspapers what they shall write and to the party members in the legislature how they shall vote. The support of nonmembers is welcomed at elections, but such voters are carefully excluded from any share in determining party policy. On the Continent, the socialist organization has profoundly influenced the organization of other than socialist parties. Parties there tend to be "close corporations" with doctrinaire attitudes determined in each instance either by the secretary and other members of the national organization or by the party membership in the legislative body.

British Party Organization. In Great Britain, party organization is well integrated. National and local party bodies act in close co-operation with one another, though each plays a different part in determining party policies, nominating candidates, and conducting election campaigns.

THE PARTY ORGANIZATION IN PARLIAMENT. All members of Parliament who belong to a particular party constitute what the British call the "parliamentary party." This body chooses directly or indirectly a group of leaders who constitute the *cabinet,* if the party has a majority in the House of Commons, or the *opposition bench,* if the party is in the minority. The cabinet and the opposition bench effectively determine the policies of their respective parties. Other organs of each parliamentary party are *whips,* who maintain communication between the leaders and the rank and file of members of Parliament; and a central office which is the point of contact between parliamentary leaders and party associations in the country.

PARTY ORGANIZATION OUTSIDE OF PARLIAMENT. In each constituency electing a member of Parliament, there is a representative party committee which nominates the candidate (subject to the prior approval of the central office) and assists him in conducting his campaign. Local associations also send delegates to a *national party conference,* which is usually held every year. In theory, the conference has the right to change the constitution of the party, to determine its organization and policies, and, through its executive committee, to supervise party activities at all times. Practically, its sessions are nearly always dominated by the parliamentary leaders of the party. The party conference is useful chiefly in bringing together the parliamentary leaders and the delegates from the local associations and in generating enthusiasm for the party cause. When the conference adopts policies contrary to those of the parliamentary leaders, the party is divided and weakened.

American Party Organization. In contrast to the British system, American party organization emphasizes local rather than national interests. In each township or ward, sometimes in each election precinct, there is a party committeeman or captain who is usually responsible to a county organization. The latter exists mainly to assist in electing county officers, but it is also an important instrument for the choosing of delegates to the congressional district and state party organizations. These, in turn, look after the interests of the party in their particular areas and contribute to the strength of the national party organization. In other words, there is a hierarchy of conventions and committees beginning near the "grass roots" and extending to the field of national politics. There is nothing remotely suggestive of the central control exercised in a British party, except for a weak conference or caucus in each house of Congress and for informal presidential repasts with congressional leaders.

THE CONVENTION. The fundamental unit of party organization is the convention—which has power to determine the rules of the party, nominate candidates, adopt the platform, and choose committees to carry on the campaign and manage party affairs during the intervals between its meetings. Conventions at the state and local levels have lost a good deal of their importance since the enactment of primary-election laws by state legislatures, but the national convention has been scarcely affected by such laws. Some of its delegates are chosen under presidential primary laws, but for the most part delegates are chosen by state or congressional district conventions of the party, which may be only indirectly representative of the party voters. The national convention contains few of the national leaders of the party and a great many persons with local reputations and local outlooks. There are more than one thousand delegates and an equal number of alternates in each national convention. Such a large body is entirely unfitted for deliberation. Its committees, composed of one member from each state and territorial delegation, are too cumbersome for effective work. The convention has little choice but to accept ready-made a platform drafted in advance. In nominating a presidential candidate, it is subject to being carried away by enthusiasm or to being manipulated by a few leaders of state delegations gathered in a "smoke-filled room." As yet, no adequate substitute for the national convention has been suggested.

PRIMARY ELECTIONS. Abuses of the convention system in counties and states led to a movement for the nomination of party candidates in a procedure similar to that of a general election. At first, primary-election laws were optional; that is, a party had the option to make use of or to refuse the state's help in conducting primary polling. With the general adoption of the Australian ballot, however, such laws became mandatory—that is, they required parties to conduct their nominations through primary elections. Today, a person who wishes to become a candidate for nomination by a political party must file a statement to that effect with an appropriate public officer. Usually he must at the same time pay a fee or submit a petition bearing the names of a certain number of voters. In nearly every state, separate ballots for each party are prepared by public authority and distributed at the polling places. In a few states which use the *open primary,* the voter receives the ballots of all the parties, marks one which he deposits in the ballot box, and discards the others in a waste receptacle. The open primary enables the voter to assist in nominating candidates of the party of his choice and to preserve the secret of his party preference. Most states use the *closed primary*—that is, a primary that is closed to all but members of one party. A voter who is registered in advance as a member of a party or who passes a simple test of party allegiance receives and marks the primary ballot of his own party. Ordinarily the candidate who receives a plurality of the votes cast for each office is nominated, although nearly all the states of the "solid South" require a second, or "run-off," primary between the two highest candidates if no one has received a majority.

What have been the results of the movement to restore the control of the political party to its members? The primary election provides a means by which a determined majority of the party members can break the power of a machine or boss. To do so, however, they must be well organized, for bosses' organizational facilities are extensive and ordinarily sufficient for the success at a primary election of persons whom they designate.

The primary election has several disadvantages. It is expensive to the candidate. It is resented or ignored by many voters, requiring, as it does, an additional attendance at the polls. It sometimes leads to factional contests which weaken parties internally. Sectional or factional majorities sometimes nominate badly balanced tickets which place a party at a disadvantage in the competition. The open primary often invites interference by the organization of a rival party which instructs its followers to vote for the weakest candidate. In spite of all these disadvantages, however, the primary election is a useful instrument of democracy, particularly in states and their subdivisions in which the preponderance of one party is so great that voters can not hope to correct an unfavorable political situation by electing candidates of the opposition party.

PARTY COMMITTEES. Each party has three independent committees at the national level: a *national committee* whose functions are to assist in the campaign of the party's nominee for the presidency and to arrange for the next national convention, a *congressional campaign committee* to help elect party members to the House of Representatives, and a *senatorial campaign committee* to assist party nominees for the United States Senate. At every lower level of government there is at least one committee for each party. Such committees nearly always have large memberships in order to honor persons who perform voluntary services or contribute liberally to the party campaign fund. In several states, the laws provide that party committeemen shall be elected at the primary election. Party committees have little influence in party affairs except when factional struggles occur. Most of the functions conferred on a committee are actually exercised by its chairman, who in many cases is chosen by the principal nominee of the party.

THE LEGISLATIVE CAUCUS. All the members of a party in each house of Congress (and of a state legislature) constitute a *legislative caucus*. At the beginning of each new legislature this caucus chooses the party candidates for the speakership and other offices. It may determine the party's stand on any legislative proposal and bind its membership to support a proposal under threat of loss of committee assignments and of party support for re-election. Usually, however, the caucus leaves party leadership to the executives or to speakers, floor leaders, or other officers of the house or the caucus. Because representatives are free to pursue an independent course of action, party responsibility is almost entirely lacking.

MACHINES AND BOSSES

The freedom of action which permits parties to serve the cause of democracy also may be turned to the advantage of ambitious and sometimes unscrupulous leaders and their smoothly functioning organizations, enabling them, directly or indirectly, to dominate and to manage the elections and eventually the governments. The organizations in point are called *machines;* the leaders, *bosses.* Unfortunately, national and state party organizations not only tolerate corrupt local bosses and machines but also assist them with patronage and rely on them to deliver large votes for the party candidates for the presidency and governorships.

Party Machines. A party organization may be converted into a political machine which functions with such ruthless precision that it can defeat rival parties and suppress independent movements within its own ranks. The machine may be operated by a small clique or ring, but it is usually under the autocratic control of a boss. Party machines (such as Tammany in New York) may have a continuous existence and control of government from generation to generation.

Party Bosses. In general, party bosses—whether or not they hold public or party offices—have complete control over the party organization; control over the nomination, election, and, virtually, the appointment of executive officers, judges, and members of legislative bodies; and, as a result, almost complete control over the government. A boss may be motivated by a love of politics or power, but many bosses have amassed wealth by methods ranging from "honest graft" to sharing payments made by criminal elements for protection against arrest.

Corrupt Machines and Bosses. The existence of corrupt party organizations and leaders has been explained in many ways. They are usually found in areas which are dominated by one party. Some derive their support from the foreign and illiterate elements of the population and retain it through manipulation of registration, election, and vote-counting. Some ingratiate themselves with the poor by performing services and distributing charitable doles. Some use the ancient demagogic trick of blaming the rich for all the ills of society, at the same time granting accommodation and favors to the rich for a price.

It is a fair question, however, whether bosses and machines are strong or their rivals are weak. The willingness of many businessmen to make deals with a boss lessens the chances for the success of reform movements. Reformers often underestimate the difficulties in setting up an organization which will reach voters; especially they are prone to follow the American habit of organizing for one election campaign only. The unswerving allegiance of many voters to a national party aids bosses in corrupting local politics; the power of local bosses and their machines in turn corrupts national politics and elections. Irresponsible officials handle too many elections and too much public wealth; there is too little insistence upon integrity in government by the electorate.

The problem is by no means confined to the United States. Nor is dishonesty in government attributable to party spirit. The competition of alert parties in a normally functioning party system is one of the best safeguards for an honest administration of public affairs.

13 Public Opinion and Influences Upon It

All forms of government are tuned to public opinion—with the intention of respecting and abiding by it or with the intention of controlling it.

"Government by the people" is usually taken to mean that the electorate may make its opinion known at specific times, on specific issues or general policies. In a modern industrial state, it is almost impossible to obtain the opinion of every individual. However, the opinion of a majority is made public at election time. In a democratic state, this "public opinion" or will of a majority of the electorate should stand on all the important and controversial issues.

Here we are concerned not only with the nature, measurement, and importance of public opinion, but also with the forces which bring pressure to bear upon it under both democratic and totalitarian governments.

ANALYSIS OF PUBLIC OPINION

The idea of government by "public opinion" is based on a number of assumptions: (1) that man is an intelligent being capable, after the completion of elementary schooling, of understanding the problems of government; (2) that man is rational, and that therefore he will be guided by his judgment and not by his emotions or prejudices; and (3) that man is interested in public affairs and will devote time and energy to informing himself concerning the merits and defects of new proposals.

On the popular level it is assumed that all people have equal interest in government, and it is further assumed that the opinions of individuals should not vary greatly. (Presumably, the sum total of individual opinions constitutes public opinion, in accordance with which government should always be conducted.) In our analysis of the nature of public opinion, we shall consider to what extent these assumptions are true.

Meaning of "Public." Desirable as a national public opinion might be, it would be practically impossible to achieve. Communication among people is difficult; most individuals are confined to their limited spheres of activity from which they obtain public information, supplemented by a small measure of knowledge which they absorb from sources such as newspapers (with relatively local coverage), magazines, books, radio, and television. Each individual associates with his fellow workmen, members of his clubs and residents of his own community. He is likely to think that the expressions of opinion that he hears represent the consensus, but a quite different set of opinions may be expressed, during the same period, in another section of the country or even among another occupational group or social class in his own region. Instead of one "public," there are likely to be dozens of "publics" within a democratic state—each convinced that it is expressing the representative opinion or will of the whole.

Meaning of "Opinion." The word "opinion" is used popularly to indicate a belief on almost any topic. Political scientists, however, limit its application to beliefs on questionable or debatable topics.

Few statements concerning controversial public affairs result from the voter's own analysis of the facts, his personal judgment as to what they mean, or his decision as to the course which his government should pursue in relation to them. Consciously or unconsciously, most of his expressions are borrowed from or influenced by others. They are often colored by prejudices, by likes or dislikes, or by considerations of personal interest. Furthermore, they may be mere parrotings of ideas skillfully disseminated by propagandists.

Measurement and Importance of Public Opinion. "Straw votes," which are taken by a newspaper or private organization to test the effectiveness of an election campaign—and often to influence the result—are a well-known but not highly respected device. As random samplings they have some value, but their validity depends on the methods and honesty with which they are conducted. Early in the present century, the popular news weekly *Literary Digest* conducted a poll in presidential election years, sending out millions of return postcards to a mailing list compiled from telephone directories and automobile registrations. Its findings proved fairly accurate so long as the electorate continued to follow middle-class leadership; they proved false during the New Deal landslides of the 1930's. Later there were developed the so-called "scientific sampling" techniques which were based on the proposition that the polling of a very small percentage of the electorate, provided it was a completely representative cross section, would yield practically the same result as the polling of a much larger group. A polling industry grew up and prospered until the presidential election of 1948, when it was discovered that a good many subjective estimates as to what is a "representative" cross section and as to how long a sampling of opinion remains accurate combined to discomfit all the pollsters.

Many observers continue to hope for the perfection of a scientific polling method. Of this group, a considerable number feel that polls are instrumental in (1) interesting voters in pertinent issues and (2) presenting the tenor of opinion on current issues to government officials, politicians, and others. In addition, compilation of the results of individual polls conducted over a period of time may provide useful long-term forecasts of trends in public opinion.

MEANS OF INFLUENCING PUBLIC OPINION

In a totalitarian state, the means of influencing and controlling public opinion are very important. However, democratic nations also make use of devices for forming opinions; and citizens of democracies combine in groups in order to influence agencies of the government. The main forces acting on public opinion are propaganda[1] and pressure groups.[2]

---

[1] "The utilization of words, objects, or persons in an attempt to influence or control the opinion and overt actions of groups and individuals."—E. C. Smith and A. J. Zurcher, *Dictionary of American Politics*, an Everyday Handbook (New York: Barnes & Noble, Inc., 1955).

[2] Organizations "which promote specific economic, moral, or other causes by employing paid agents or lobbyists to influence legislators and public officials, by endorsing candidates nominated by political parties, or by conducting systematic educational or propaganda campaigns among the general public."—*Ibid.*

Propaganda. In the United States, propaganda is greatly in evidence and many individuals unconsciously ignore large portions of it each year. However, it is dangerous to be unaware of it, because not all propaganda is harmless or easily discernible or even easily traceable to its source. Within the past half-century, the once-respectable word *propaganda* has become associated with the one-sided presentation of a point of view, with tricks of appealing to emotions rather than reason, and with downright deceit. Whereas an honestly educational project would present all sides of a question in order that individuals might make balanced judgments, propaganda presents one viewpoint only, often with half-truths and arguments masquerading as facts and with ready-made, logical-appearing conclusions to follow from them. Propaganda, in short, is an effort to manufacture a "public opinion" favorable to a single interest.

PRIVATE PROPAGANDA. A propagandist is a self-styled "public relations counselor or educator" who purports to be engaged in an educational project for the dissemination of information or the removal of misconceptions from the minds of people. Although political parties use the services of the propagandist they cause relatively little harm,[3] because almost everyone realizes the source of the propaganda and the field is open for rebuttal. For many years, private organizations, such as business corporations, have engaged in spreading propaganda. Their purposes vary considerably, however: many simply wish to obtain the good will of the public by presenting relevant facts, but others attempt to influence in unfair ways. Contrary to political parties, many private interests deliberately attempt to conceal their own connection with their propaganda. Often, they prepare news and feature stories and even editorials, which they distribute to newspapers and magazines in the well-founded hope that a number of editors will print them. Sometimes they handsomely subsidize the writing and the publishing of books with the understanding that the author's name and his professional rank, usually in a respectable university, will appear on the title page—and that there will be no reference anywhere to the source of financial support which makes the publication possible.

---

[3] A real menace may arise when the party in power disseminates political propaganda under the guise of government information.

It may be inferred from such practices that concealment of the origin of propaganda is obviously not in the public interest.

OFFICIAL PROPAGANDA. It was not private propaganda which first gave the word "propaganda" its poor reputation, but rather the vast quantities of official statements issued by the governments engaged in World War I. "Our own cause is completely just, our own conduct has been above reproach, but the enemy is worse than savage" was their cry, backed by the sometimes fictional details of sensational atrocity stories.

Later, the Fascist, Nazi, and Communist dictatorships made propaganda, usually handled through a specific government agency, a permanent instrument of public policy. They took advantage of the results of recent psychological research which indicated that man is a somewhat less rational creature than had been supposed. They made use of color, music, hypnotic suggestions, and the contagious enthusiasm of the crowd. They appealed to patriotism, nationalism, and pride in the historical glories of the state, and whipped up feelings of hatred for foreigners and unpopular minorities. Having instituted strict censorship so that nothing might be refuted, official propagandists developed the technique of the "big lie"—that is, a falsehood in itself so atrocious as to be incredible but repeated over and over with infinite variations and additions until the people came to accept most of it as true and to believe the government's "story."

Even in a democratic state, there is a valid use for official propaganda. For the proper functioning of democracy it is essential that government offices should render periodic reports and, furthermore, that these reports should justify their activities and be easily understood. In the United States (and also in Great Britain), most sizable offices now employ qualified public-relations experts. These experts make use of the means of communication (newspapers, magazines, radio, television) for issuing propaganda and information and, in addition, supervise the preparation of pamphlets, films, and exhibits for direct distribution to the public. Democratic governments have not attempted to co-ordinate the publicity efforts of their various departments, for most states regard centralization of government publicity as a political menace.

SEVEN PROPAGANDA TECHNIQUES. Propaganda should be analyzed thoroughly to determine whether words are being used to confuse rather than clarify the facts. The seven most common propaganda techniques are (1) "band wagon" (here the propagandist uses the theme "everyone is doing it," thus playing on the desire of the individual to conform); (2) "name calling" (the propagandist appeals to hatreds, prejudices, and fears by intimating unfavorable qualities in those groups, states, races, issues, and individuals he would have people cite or condemn; (3) "glittering generalities" (the propagandist identifies his plans with respectability by appealing to the common emotions of love, generosity, and brotherhood and by employing words such as *democracy, truth, liberty, the ideals and privileges of the Constitution);* (4) "transfer" (the propagandist invokes the prestige or sanction of an honored and respected force to convince his audience to accept his program); (5) "plain folks" (the propagandist uses this device to win confidence and illustrate that those being publicized or promoted are "just like everyone else"); (6) "testimonial" (here the propagandist quotes a widely-known person as saying that he uses a specific product, such as cigarettes or cosmetics, in the hope that the audience will follow the advice of the individual); and (7) "card stacking" (in this case the propagandist seeks to confuse those searching for facts, which he does not wish to reveal, by employing underemphasis and overemphasis to evade issues, resorting to falsehoods and censorship, omitting and distorting facts, and raising new isues.)[4]

Pressure Groups. Skillful pressure on government by organized groups is one of the distinct phenomena of our time. Some of these groups are altruistic and are sincerely devoted to social reform; others exist frankly for the promotion of the economic well-being of their members. At least a few organizations with high-sounding names represent nothing more than the efforts of one or a few persons to influence the conduct of public affairs; others with large staffs of public-relations experts, legislative counsel, and lobbyists ("legislative agents") represent the attempt of thousands of persons to bring pressure to bear on government officers at national, state, and local levels. Among the most powerful groups with offices at Washington, D.C. are

---

[4] Institute for Propaganda Analysis, "How to Detect Propaganda," *Propaganda Analysis,* I (November, 1937), pp. 1-4.

the American Federation of Labor and Congress of Industrial Organizations representing labor; the National Association of Manufacturers and the Chamber of Commerce of the United States representing business; the American Farm Bureau Federation; and the American Legion and the Veterans of Foreign Wars. In other democratic countries labor, business, farmers', and veterans' organizations are all actively engaged in promoting the interests of their members; in totalitarian states, such pressure groups as exist are generally controlled by agents of the parties in power.

LOBBIES. Lobbying is the process of "addressing or soliciting members of a legislative body, in the lobby or elsewhere, with intent to influence legislation."[5] By and large, lobbying is carried on in the open; nowadays, instances of behind-the-scenes lobbying scandals are actually quite rare.

It is common for interests such as large industries to maintain lobbies at the capital and smaller interests to maintain a lobbyist or "legislative agent." One of the most effective activities of the lobby, lobbyist, or "employed expert" is appearing before legislative committees to argue for or against specific proposals. If lobbyists are unable to influence legislators by analysis and argument, they usually call upon the members of the groups they represent to flood the mails with protests; often this is so successful that bills in question are passed and even the executive may refrain from vetoing them—as a result of the demonstration of "public opinion." In addition, if he happens to be a close friend of a lawmaker, the lobbyist may make use of his friendship, and be instrumental in the introduction of measures favorable to his interest group.

Several states have attempted to curb the influence of lobbies by means of regulation and registration. The Congress of the United States took steps to regulate the public-utility lobby through the Holding Company Act of 1935. In 1946, it passed the Federal Regulation of Lobbying Act which requires the registration of all individuals who provide funds for the support or the defeat of national legislative proposals. This act

---

[5] *Webster's New International Dictionary* (Springfield: G. & C. Merriam Co., 1945). Also see E. C. Smith and A. J. Zurcher, *Dictionary of American Politics*, an Everyday Handbook (New York: Barnes & Noble, Inc., 1955).

has not lessened the practice, but has made known the source of the influence and has enabled officials and legislators to better evaluate pressures.

Stricter regulation of lobbies has been rejected because many groups feel that stronger measures would interfere with the constitutional rights of petition and of association.

GROUP PRESSURES IN THE UNITED STATES. Pressure groups on the American scene are extremely active and effective in the nomination and election of legislators and administrators who are sympathetic to their interests. However, even the defeat of their candidates at the polls does not deter interest groups from bringing pressure to bear on elected officers at all government levels and on political party policies throughout the nation.

The Nature of Pressure Politics. The maintenance of a pressure group's membership depends on its success in influencing officers of the government. The objectives are often not submitted to a vote of the membership but are developed one after another by officers and employes who wish to retain their jobs. Control over the officers is difficult because the groups' elections are usually not conducted in a democratic manner. More often a nominating committee presents a slate, the nominations are closed, and the choice is by acclamation or by one ballot cast by the secretary. In presenting a proposal, the pressure group always rationalizes its own interests to make them appear to be advantageous to the entire population. Thus a protective tariff is pictured as a measure for developing infant industries, for providing public defense, and for maintaining the American standard of wages against the competition of underpaid foreign labor. The general tendency of pressure politics is to insist that officers of the government ought always to obey the "public opinion,"—which has been largely created by the pressure group itself.

Pressures on Political Parties. In the United States, the weakness of the caucus and party authority makes individual members of the legislature and other elective officers targets for pressure-group sniping. An officer's record on policies sponsored by a group is isolated from his whole record and is made the basis for the membership of the group to vote for or against him at the next primary or general election. If they are to be supported, new candidates must be cleared by each important pressure group. After the party nominations are made, a pressure group may endorse the candidate that it considers most favorable to itself. Even if the endorsed candidate is defeated, the group does not accept defeat in good spirit but puts pressure on the successful candidate, or other officers of the government. It has often been pointed out that pressure groups are serious rivals to political parties, and the suggestion has been made for a representation of interests or for a government based on economic groups. Pressure groups themselves are unlikely to accept such a solution, because each desires to concentrate its attention on a narrow field and is completely unwilling to assume the responsibility for meeting all the problems of government.

Pressures on Legislators. The day is past when a lobbyist with a few thousand dollars or shares of stock could corrupt a whole legislature. Today there is the so-called "social lobby" in which the point of view of an organized group and the information it has may be presented informally, but this will be only a small part of the pressure activity. The group drafts bills, finds as many sponsors for them as possible, testifies before committees, and "buttonholes" members of the legislature individually to have the bills reported favorably. Simultaneously, it circulates propaganda to create favorable climates of opinion for the measures and members of the organization contact their senators and representatives. There is an implied threat that if a legislator fails to vote in accordance with the wishes of the organization he will lose the support of its members when he seeks renomination and re-election.

Pressures on Executives and Judges. The manner in which legislation is enforced may be as important as the legislation itself. The pressure group is interested in the kind of office which is set up for enforcement and especially in its personnel. The group will suggest suitable appointees for administrators to the executive, who makes appointments. For example, if a professional association has secured the enactment of a law limiting the admission of persons to practice the profession, it will reason plausibly that none can better administer the law than those who are already members. "Appropriate" interpretations of a law will be suggested, and the ablest counsel will be employed to seek out favorable precedents and show the advantages to the public of strict or lax enforcement. Pressures directed at administrators and judges are even more dangerous than lobbying, because arrangements can be made in secret.

GROUP PRESSURES IN GREAT BRITAIN. On the Continent of Europe, the multiparty system allows each of the larger pressure groups to set up a party of its own, but in Great Britain, organized groups present their proposals to the cabinet, which may adopt them or not as it sees fit. Since individual members of the Parliament vote with their parties, it is not worth while for a group to bring pressure on individuals.

Government officials are elected on the basis of their party's program and in the event of deviation therefrom, may bring about the fall of the party more readily than in many other democratic states. The means for enforcing party responsibility are: (1) a tradition of strong party discipline, (2) the cabinet's power of dissolution, (3) the fact that political careers in Britain usually last a lifetime, thus encouraging reputable and defensible action by politicians at all times, and (4) the general election, held when issues require it rather than at fixed intervals. Moreover, due to the country's small area and homogeneous population, British citizens are more inclined than Americans to pay close attention to national issues.

All these factors increase the importance of a day-to-day evaluation of public opinion on the part of British legislators and administrators and lessen the possibility of pressure on government from groups other than those officially recognized by the cabinet and the electorate.

GROUP PRESSURES IN THE SOVIET UNION. Dictatorships commonly do away with private interest groups, subordinating the interests of the individual and his "gain-seeking" associations to the interests of the state. In the Soviet Union, however, a few associations such as trade unions (which are used by high party officials for maintaining discipline and enthusiasm among the workers and to which membership is almost mandatory) have been retained. But, trade unions and other associations—among which are youth, technical, agricultural, scientific, and cultural organizations—do not exert pressure on the government; rather their officers exert pressure *from* the government on their members in order to promote the causes of the state.

The economic, social, and cultural life of the entire nation is ordered by the Soviet government, but it is extremely difficult for even a totalitarian state to eliminate entirely the interaction between diverse forces. The state trusts, state banks, state organizations, government departments, trading companies, and programming agencies compete for special recognition and treatment, producing a type of subtle "lobbying" to obtain approval or favors from the heads of the communist government.

FREE DISCUSSION AND PUBLIC OPINION

In order to form a genuine public opinion a people must have freedom of thought, speech, assembly, and the means of communication. Through freedom of expression people uncover issues requiring government action, exert control over government, argue correctly and incorrectly, and recognize error and the right. An alert citizenry is desirous of obtaining facts on public affairs, participates in free discussion and, in this way, forms public opinion.

Discussion in Democratic States. Freedom of the means of communication extends the scope of free expression and has to a great degree been responsible for making democracy possible in countries with large territories and populations. Censorship of the instruments of communication is generally considered odious under democratic systems of government, but in time of crisis specific limitation of expression is required usually to protect national security. In peacetime, complete freedom of the press, radio, and television are of vital importance. Even though the forces working to influence public opinion present their viewpoints via the channels of communication, it is hoped that this type of propaganda and pressure will be counteracted by the availability of the facts and by free discussion. It is critically necessary, therefore, that press, radio, and television provide adequate opportunities for factual discussion.

The service of the means of communication covers not only expressing opinion, but also molding it and prescribing government action, if any. The role of communication is to assemble and provide objective and accurate information.

Many problems complicate the efforts of the press, radio, and television to fulfill their responsibilities towards public affairs. Aside from those in small cities and towns, modern newspapers are part of "big business," with huge circulations to be maintained or increased, and often reflecting editorially the opinions of "big business"—especially in dealing with controversial topics. The fight for circulation leads some newspapers and periodicals to cast aside the obligation to mold public opinion; instead, they simply mirror it. In recent years, newspaper chains have increased in number and now they control more than 20 per cent of the dailies in the United States. In Great Britain, this trend has been far more widespread, resulting in near-monopoly.

Despite condemnations of publications in past years, democratic states have generally agreed that government supervision of the press is undesirable and perhaps dangerous. At one time or another, the following measures have been suggested to revitalize the function of the press: (1) the enforcement of the anti-trust laws to prevent further consolidation, (2) the encouragement of self-regulation within the field, and (3) the establishment of uniform journalistic standards.

Although they allow opportunity for one-way discussions and presentations of ideas, radio and television are devoted to entertaining listeners. The problems of radio and television have always been slightly different from those of the press. These media have been semi-monopolistic due to the limited number of licenses available. In the United States, control of broadcasting stations is concentrated in the hands of a few. Licenses are obtained from the Federal Communications Commission, which also has the authority to review and revoke licenses. In Great Britain, radio and television are monopolized by the British Broadcasting Corporation which for the most part was financed until recently by set owners. Traditionally, the B.B.C. has maintained a policy of political neutrality and, therefore, has been cautious in its selection of controversial programs.

Discussion in Totalitarian States. Almost without exception, the government of a totalitarian state monopolizes and operates the communication media. In order to secure his own position and power, a dictator must create (or give the impression that he has created) agreement among the people as to his actions and control: unanimity of public opinion.

Public opinion in the Soviet Union does not result from free discussion nor is it permitted to influence and direct the activities of the government. In theory, the Soviet constitution grants the rights of free speech, press, and assembly and the *means* (mechanical) for using these rights. In practice, none except communist party members are accorded these rights and, of course, communists do not object to a communist government's operation of the *means* (press and radio) provided to make these privileges effective.

Contrary to historical dictatorships, the Soviet Union has not established a central official office for the dissemination of propaganda. But the state and communist party control the means of communication by directing their activities, placing the most loyal members of the party in high positions, and enlisting the censorship agency to enforce its requirements. Further control is maintained by specifying topics to be ignored and topics to be discussed: criticism of communist theory, leaders, party or governmental policy is tabu; usually, economic matters, production records, and political offenses are safe topics for discussion and also permissible are accounts of the success or failure of minor projects and administrations.

In keeping with the tactics of totalitarian states, both the Nazis and the Fascists established central propaganda offices and made similar changes in laws and policies in order to stifle all freedom in channels of communication and to use them as propaganda devices, exclusively: (1) Criticism of government policies became a crime and (2) secret police were planted everywhere—thus making free discussion dangerous or impossible. (3) In order to operate, newspapers, periodicals, and journalists had to obtain government licenses. (4) All publications were forced to file issues with the state—thus, loyalty was constantly investigated and if it was found lacking licenses were revoked. (5) The central agency provided positive government publicity to the press and radio every day—eventually saturating the means of communication and the minds of the people. Like the communists, these states forced their propaganda into the schools and places of work, culture, and recreation.

14 *The Legislature*

The legislative bodies in existence today either are offshoots of the English Parliament or have been established in imitation of it. Parliament itself evolved over a period of many centuries by a slow and often halting process.[1] The origin of representation is even more obscure.[2]

American legislatures, created shortly after the settlement of each colony, have followed a course of development somewhat different from that of Parliament. Some European legislatures have retained the ancient feudal form, but gradually acquired powers like those of the British Parliament; others have copied the British model in form and in powers.

LEGISLATIVE POWERS AND FUNCTIONS

The legislature formulates the will of the state, exercises a degree of supervision and of control over other branches of the government, and is, in general, the chief organ of popular government. The powers of legislatures vary among states; but practically everywhere they include at least a share in the constituent

---

[1] Its roots appear in the Anglo-Saxon *folkmoot* (general assembly of town, city, or shire) and *Witenagemot* (king's advisory council which met several times a year to impose taxes, raise military forces, and, occasionally, elect a king). In the Norman era, members of the "Great Council" were required to attend the king personally. During its early period, attendance at Parliament was not a privilege, but an unwelcome duty imposed by the king. In 1295, when the king needed financial aid, he summoned to the "Model Parliament" not only the great lords but also representatives of the lesser landlords and the merchants—two knights from each shire and two burgesses from each borough. By traditionally petitioning for redress of grievances when it granted new taxes to the king, Parliament established, in the eighteenth century, its supremacy over both the king and the administrative machinery.

[2] It is traced by some to the Teutonic *folkmoot;* by others to the practices of the monastic orders in the Middle Ages, especially of the Dominican Order; and by still others to the medieval legislatures which reflected classes and estates.

and electoral functions as well as in the lawmaking and supervisory powers.

Constituent Functions. The power to amend the constitution is a constituent function. In Great Britain, Parliament may exercise this power completely in the ordinary course of its procedure. In some countries, the legislature has the power to amend the constitution but is under a number of procedural restrictions designed to delay action and protect the rights of minorities. In the United States, constituent action by the national legislature is limited to the proposal of amendments, which may be ratified either by state legislatures or by conventions in the states. (The executive may not veto a proposed amendment.)

Electoral Functions. In France, the two houses of the legislature by joint vote elect the president. In the United States, the members of the House of Representatives, voting by states (each state having one vote), have the power to elect a president should no candidate receive a majority in the electoral college; the senators voting as individuals elect a vice-president under the same circumstances. In countries having a cabinet system of government, the legislature or its more popular branch in effect elects the cabinet; for, although the titular executive asks someone to form a ministry, that body can not function until it has received legislative approval.

Statute-Making Functions. Every legislature has the power to make statutes. Although there are few absolutely new subjects for legislation, technological advances and other changes are so rapid that legislatures are forced to repeal, alter, and add to the provisions of existing law, make it apply to new conditions, provide for better administration, change penalties, and, as far as possible, keep the statute books abreast of the times.

Control of Administration. By far the most important function of the legislature is the supervision which it exercises over the administrative authorities. The legislature has created most existing departments and other administrative agencies, and it may alter or abolish them at will. It may grant them generous appropriations, or it may practically destroy them by granting little or no money. In some states, the legislature or one of its houses must ratify treaties and approve appointments to administrative offices before these become effective. There are several means by which certain legislatures can dispose of an incumbent officer: by impeachment,[3] by address,[4] or by voting lack of confidence. As a necessary adjunct to the exercise of all these powers, the legislature has full power to investigate, to summon witnesses, and to compel the presentation of books, records, and correspondence. The publicity which results from the consideration of appropriations and from investigations keeps the electorate informed of public affairs.

Internal Discipline. In order that the legislative branch may not be interfered with by the executive, a number of constitutional safeguards are provided. Each legislative body is made the sole judge of the election and qualifications of its own members. It may choose its speaker and other officers and adopt its own rules of procedure. Its members may not be arrested while attending sessions or traveling to and from them for any reason except the commission of crimes. They may not be punished for anything they say in debate except by the house to which they belong. But in the United States a member may be called to account by his house and may be subject to punishment ranging from reprimand to expulsion. If a member of Congress takes advantage of his legislative immunity to indulge in the character assassination of private citizens, or if a committee engages in irresponsible "witch-hunting," the house to which the member or committee belongs is squarely responsible and may not shift the responsibility.

LEGISLATIVE STRUCTURE

Under the feudal system the number of assemblies or chambers of a legislature varied from state to state.[5] The bicameral pattern established in England (the nobles were members of the House of Lords and the representatives of small landholders and merchants were members of the House of Commons) was to become the general rule for other modern legislative bodies.

In the current era, legislative bodies have been subject to

---

[3] In most states, the officer is arraigned for misbehavior in office by the lower house and tried for impeachment by the upper house.
[4] The legislature petitions the executive to order the removal of an officer (not subject to impeachment) on grounds of unworthiness to hold office.
[5] Although there was a tendency to recognize three political classes (representing three estates of nobility, clergy, and commons), four or five assemblies might exist in states which separately recognized higher and lower clergy, merchants, and small landholders.

numerous demands. This has served to attract public notice to their manner of functioning, and, in addition, to the advantages and disadvantages of proposals for the reconstruction of legislative systems.

Bicameral and Unicameral Legislatures. Nearly all national legislatures are bicameral in organization. No large federal system has been created without an "upper" legislative chamber, in which the component political units or provinces are represented, and a "lower" chamber, in which the populace is represented. A few of the smaller countries of Europe and Latin America have adopted a structure which consists of a single chamber. Both types of structure have specific advantages for the social and economic organizations which they serve. Unfortunately, in many cases they have disadvantages also.

ADVANTAGES OF BICAMERALISM. Bicameralism is advantageous in six ways. (1) Two houses are less likely than one to be carried away by the excitement of the moment or the influence of a demagogue. Thus, in this system there is greater likelihood of temperate and deliberate discussion, resulting in balanced, equitable, careful legislation. (2) The competition of two houses for prestige should result in more careful scrutiny of legislation by both: the length of time that elapses between introduction in one house and final passage by both reduces haste and carelessness. (3) Again, the existence of two houses may have been the result of a compromise among different interests, in the absence of which national unity could not have been secured: minorities of wealth, class, race, nationality, or region might otherwise be averse to trusting their destinies to a majority which could prove to be self-seeking or tyrannical. (4) The bicameral system is a bulwark of individual freedom against the tyranny of a legislature composed of a single interest. (5) It helps also to protect the independence of the courts and to protect the executive in the exercise of its proper functions. (6) The existence of two houses allows a division of labor through the assignment of certain minor matters to one house or the other.

DISADVANTAGES OF BICAMERALISM. Bicameralism has four major disadvantages. (1) Two houses are often deadlocked, preventing or delaying the transaction of business. (2) There is duplication of effort as both houses seek independently to obtain the same information and as both debate the same questions. (3) Theoretically, the general will of the people is divided when there is more than one chamber. At all events, legislative procedure is more complicated and more difficult for people to follow: voters often suspect that private and selfish interests manipulate the procedure to defeat popular proposals. For this reason, there has been a consistent and fairly steady demand that members of both houses—of the upper as well as the lower house—be chosen by popular vote or else that the powers of the upper house be reduced. Thus in the United States, the Senate was made popularly elective in 1913, and in Great Britain the House of Lords has been shorn of most of its power. (4) The operation of a cabinet system of government may become almost impossible where either house can cause a cabinet to fall just by voting "lack of confidence."

ADVANTAGES OF UNICAMERALISM. National experiments with unicameral legislature have worked well in several small countries with homogeneous social and economic organizations. The structure is simple, and it definitely locates responsibility. Experiments in the state of Nebraska and in most American cities have proved successful, partly because of homogeneity of population and partly because of the protection given by the Fourteenth Amendment and by city charters against the abuse of legislative power.

DISADVANTAGES OF UNICAMERALISM. The factors in favor of unicameralism rest on the supposed defects of bicameralism and, conversely, factors opposed to it are the assumed advantages of bicameralism. Those who oppose unicameralism state the virtues of the principle of checks and balances, and the lessened likelihood that two houses could be subject to radical ideas or subject to a demagogue. In a state with many conflicting interests, it is often impossible to provide a formula for representation in a single house.

Composition of Legislative Chambers. Usually members of the upper house belong to an older age group and are more experienced in public affairs than members of the lower house. The latter more accurately reflect the composition of the population as a whole.

MEMBERSHIP IN UPPER HOUSES. Though there is an increasing tendency toward popular election, membership in upper houses is often the result of historical survivals or of social and economic distinctions. In the British House of Lords membership is largely hereditary;[6] it is appointive in a few national upper houses, consisting of persons who have gained distinction in many fields and whose discussions may wield great influence on the electorate even though the houses may exercise little actual power; in many, membership is determined indirectly by the legislative bodies of the territorial units. The tendency toward popular election of members makes the upper house a duplicate of the lower, except for its smaller size, higher qualifications, representation of different constituencies, and longer terms for members.

MEMBERSHIP IN LOWER HOUSES AND UNICAMERAL ASSEMBLIES. At the present time, direct election on the basis of nearly universal, equal, and secret suffrage is the general rule for choosing members of lower chambers and unicameral legislatures. Former provisions for indirect election, for property qualifications, and for plural suffrage of property holders, have given way to the apparently irresistible advance of democracy. Likewise, qualifications for office based on age or property are disappearing. Today, salaries are paid to members nearly everywhere, thus opening legislative careers to many persons who formerly could not have afforded to attend sessions.

Tenure of Office. The period during which representatives serve may be a fixed term as in the United States, or a maximum term with a possibility of an earlier dissolution as in countries having the cabinet system of government. There is no general agreement as to the ideal term: some political theorists prefer short terms on the ground that a legislature should reflect current opinion; others favor longer terms in order that members may acquire sufficient experience to deal intelligently with problems of public policy. Short terms and frequent elections result in constantly changing legislatures and consequent instability and inconsistency of policy. The present tendency is toward a long term with or without a provision for dissolution. The advantage of this provision is that legislatures may continue for periods of four or five years if they appear to have the confidence of the people, or they may be dissolved if public confidence is lacking.

---

[6] Exceptions are the archbishops and bishops of the Anglican Church, the representative peers of Scotland and Ireland, the lords of appeal, and newly created peers of England.

BASES OF REPRESENTATION

It is assumed that in a democratic state a member of a legislative assembly speaks and acts in behalf of all the people of a constituency, geographical or otherwise, which elected him; this is called "representation." There are wide differences of opinion as to the proper duty of a representative. (1) One theory holds that he is primarily an agent of his constituents committed to follow their instructions and wishes and to look out for their local interests. (2) A contrary theory holds that the representative is an officer of government and should act for the people of the state as a whole, rising above parochial considerations. He has many more opportunities than his constituents to obtain information; therefore, in best serving them and the nation as a whole, he must use independent judgment. (3) A third concept holds that he should consult and act with leaders of his party, subordinating his own personal convictions and the transient interests of his constituents to the general program adopted by the party. In practice, a representative should try to conform to all these theories. He may fail to be re-elected if he ignores his constituents' wishes on matters which a great number consider important; knowing that he can not satisfy everybody as to policies, he seeks to keep his constituents' good will by running errands for them at the nation's capital. He may be supplanted by another if he does not comprehend the ultimate effects of policies and assume a statesmanlike attitude toward national problems. Again, he may go down to defeat with his entire party if he fails to support it. One or another of the three theories is fundamental in existing or in proposed schemes of representation.

Geographical Representation. Geographical representation exists where the state is divided into districts containing, under ideal conditions, an equal number of people who choose one representative. This system has the advantages of being readily understood by the voters and of enabling them to hold the representative accountable for his acts.

If district lines were drawn fairly, there would always be some representation for the minority party. But often the majority party, in a process known as *gerrymandering,* crowds great numbers of its opponents into one or a few districts and arranges the boundaries of others so that it will continue to have a large majority in the legislature. Another abuse of the system is the inattention over a long period of time to the reapportionment of districts, a neglect that continues the dominance of a sectional or economic interest which may have ceased to be a majority.

Geographical representation is the system followed in the United States, Great Britain, and many other states. In Great Britain, where the representative is not required to be a resident of his district, it has resulted in effective national representation.

Proportional Representation. Under a system of proportional representation, the state is divided into large districts each of which elects three or more representatives. Parties or other groups are usually represented roughly in proportion to their numbers. Advocates of proportional representation point out that under geographical representation the minority in a district is practically unrepresented; even though their partisans may be chosen from other districts, their economic and social interests may be entirely different. The two chief methods used to achieve proportionality are the list system used on the Continent and the Hare system (the "single-transferable-vote system") sometimes used in cities of the United States.

THE LIST SYSTEM. Under the list system each party nominates three or more members, according to the number of seats to be filled, and the voters select party lists. When all the votes are counted, each party is accorded a number of representatives roughly in the proportion of its vote to the total. Unless the electorate may also vote for individual candidates, the persons declared elected are those at the heads of the lists. This system is justly criticized because it reposes excessive power in the hands of the party organization and denies to voters the privilege of selecting individuals.

THE HARE SYSTEM. The Hare system seeks to obviate this difficulty by allowing the voter to mark his ballot 1, 2, 3, etc., for candidates in the order of his choice. When the first-choice vote for any candidate equals the quota for election, all surplus votes cast for him are immediately distributed to the candidates named as second choice. Then the candidates who receive the fewest votes are eliminated in turn, and their votes are distributed. Often, third, fourth, and later choices are counted before all the seats are filled. This system is complicated and not readily understood by voters. It may easily be thrown out of alignment by the tactics of one or more parties in practicing "bullet voting"—that is, voting for only one candidate in order to receive aid from other parties while giving none. Also, one may wonder whether a third or later designation by a voter expresses a real choice.

DEFECTS OF BOTH METHODS. In practice, under both the list system and the Hare systems, proportional representation has encouraged the formation of splinter parties, has dissipated energy of the electorate, and has increased the difficulty of insuring majorities to conduct governments.

Functional Representation. The grouping of people for representation according to their occupations has been proposed as being more realistic than either of the major systems because it would tend to bring divergent interests face to face. Under the constitutions of the Third German Reich and the Fourth French Republic occupational chambers were established, but they were given merely advisory functions. Toward the end of its fascist period, Italy had a corporative system in which decrees were issued by the government following the advice of separate assemblies, each of which represented a principal industry. The chief difficulties in establishing functional representation are that many individuals have overlapping interests and that the relative importance of occupations is difficult to fix. If such a system were adopted, it seems clear that the effect would be to emphasize class interests at the expense of national unity.

Other Systems. The *limited vote,* under which each voter is restricted to voting for fewer than the total number of representatives to be chosen, has been occasionally used to secure minority representation. For the same purpose, the state of Illinois has a *cumulative system* under which each voter is given three votes for members of the lower house: he may cast all for one candidate or may distribute them as he pleases.

LEGISLATIVE ORGANIZATION AND PROCEDURE

The problems of the internal organization of a legislative body and of its procedure are so complicated as to be normally left to each legislative house. The Constitution of the United States establishes a majority as a quorum, makes provisions for convening and adjournment, assigns a limited number of special powers to each house, and provides that certain matters must be decided by more than a majority vote. State constitutions and the new constitutions of France and Germany go into greater detail, but it is doubtful whether detailed requirements are of much value.

Legislative Rules. Rules of procedure insure the orderly transaction of business, provide sufficient opportunity for consideration, guard against surprise, and protect the interest of the minority. In the British Parliament there are relatively few written rules (or "standing orders," as they are called): most business is transacted according to precedents, many of which are of long standing. Other legislatures have adapted the British procedure to their own needs by setting down elaborate rules in writing and by allowing precedent also to play a part. Occasionally, rules must be suspended in order to get business done. Also, the House of Representatives of the United States has developed the device of *special order,* which establishes a new rule for the consideration of a particular bill and expires when the bill is passed or rejected. Special orders are proposed by the committee on rules; when the House adopts them, the effect is to interrupt temporarily the regular order of business. In order to insure adequate consideration for a bill, rules may provide for study by a committee and for reading of the bill on separate days. To expedite business, rules may restrict or prohibit debate on procedural motions, limit the time in which members may speak, and provide for the closure of debate on passage of a motion for the previous question. In some legislative bodies (notably the Senate of the United States, where there is inadequate provision for closure), debate may drag on interminably until a measure is filibustered to extinction.

The Speaker. The primary function of the *speaker* or other presiding officer is to enforce the rules. He preserves order and decorum in debate. He recognizes members and may call them to order. When a point of order is made by any member, it is the duty of the Speaker immediately to announce a ruling; and, if not reversed by the House, this ruling may establish a new precedent for the future. He may refer bills and resolutions to appropriate committees and may be vested with power to appoint the members of some or all the committees. The Speaker of the House of Representatives of the United States formerly appointed all committees and was chairman of the *committee on rules.*

Speakers of most state legislatures in the United States still have equivalent powers and thereby become the chief leaders of their parties in legislation. British speakers, who discard partisanship when they take the chair, have greater powers than American speakers in controlling debate and applying closure.

Committees. A *committee* may consist of any number of members from one to the whole body, to which the house details certain functions. It is sometimes said that a committee may be created for any purpose except the final passage of legislation. It may conduct investigations, hear witnesses, introduce or amend bills, recommend their passage or defeat, and debate. A *standing committee* is appointed to serve during the whole life of a legislature and has jurisdiction over all measures that fall within a broad subject of legislation. A *special* or *select committee* is appointed to conduct an investigation or to consider a particular problem, and it ceases to exist when the object has been accomplished. A *sessional committee* may be appointed, usually for administrative purposes, to serve for one session. A *committee of the whole,* consisting of the entire membership of a legislative house, is for debate and amendment, but it works under less rigid rules than those of the house proper. In American legislatures, the standing committees are largely responsible for the determination of policies. They are the "gateways of legislation." In Great Britain, this function is performed by the cabinet, and standing committees are only for debating matters of secondary importance. In France, *commissions,* as they are called, may consider bills in secret session, amend them, and appoint *rapporteurs* to defend a commission's point of view on the floor of the Assembly—even against the introducer of the bill or the minister in whose department its subject matter falls.

Legislative Leadership. A comparison of the British, French, and American committee systems provides food for serious thought on the subject of legislative leadership. In Great Britain, the leadership of the cabinet is so strong as to stifle the initiative of members of Parliament and to nullify some of the advantages of representation. In France, the ministry provides leadership, but the committees are so strong as to become its rivals. In the United States, there is no single authority capable at all times of formulating a uniform program of legislation and of carrying it through to passage. Some presidents or governors have been influential enough to take the lead; at times, however, unity in general policy can be achieved only through agreements among chairmen of individual committees and among party leaders. A meritorious suggestion for improvement advises that major questions of public policy, and only those, should be considered and decided by democratic procedure in the party caucus; and when a decision is thus reached, party members should be morally bound by it.

15 The Executive

In a broad sense, the executive is the branch of government which gives effect to the will of the state. Its discretionary authority is very great, for all the complex and multiform details of administration could not possibly be embodied in statutes. It must not merely execute laws, but must take action on many matters not covered by law. In a very real sense, the executive is the active force in government: this is acknowledged by Americans when they speak of "the administration" and by the British when they refer to the cabinet as "the government." The executive branch is responsible for much of the planning of the modern state. On the basis of its special knowledge and experience, it may suggest projects or methods to the legislature; on the other hand, its exercise of power at a given time may lead the legislature to impose restrictions preventing future performances of the same kind. Both the legislature and the judiciary are essential checks on executive action.

EXECUTIVE POWERS AND FUNCTIONS

It is important to distinguish between "executive powers" as such and the particular powers which may be assigned to an individual president or cabinet head. The general powers of the executive are derived from the constitution and the laws: they include the enforcement of law, the execution of administrative policy, the conduct of foreign affairs, the control of armed forces, and the authority to dispense pardon and amnesty. Where these powers require the approval of a legislative body, that body functions as an executive council.

Enforcement of Law. It is the chief executive's duty to enforce all laws and court decisions. In some instances he may insist upon a rigorous enforcement of the letter of a law; in others he may seek to accomplish equivalent results by enforcing only the spirit.

The power to enforce laws against individuals and groups includes the power to use all appropriate means at the disposal of the executive officer. It is essential that he have authority to appoint subordinates and to direct them in the discharge of their duties; it is also essential that he have authority to remove subordinates who refuse or neglect to perform their duties. (As a result of the manifold services and business activities of the modern state, problems of appointment and removal and of the continuous direction and co-ordination of the activities of a host of public officers and employees have vastly increased; so also have the power and influence of the executive.)

Formulation and Execution of Administrative Policy. Legislatures have come to rely upon the executive branch for working out the programs to be accomplished, the methods to be used, and the necessary organizational details. Legislatures, when making statutes on relatively new subjects, can not possibly foresee the complications and technicalities that may arise. Consequently, they establish only the main outlines of policy and grant to the executive, with suitable safeguards, a sublegislative power. Through this power, the executive issues ordinances that have the force of law when they fill in the details necessary for the application of a statute to specific conditions. Through its "budget-making" authority, the executive tentatively designates an allocation of funds to various public activities and is thus influential in establishing the relative importance of each in the grand scheme of policy.

Control of Military Forces. The executive has the power to determine how and where troops and ships of war may be used in periods of peace and of war. In wartime there is a tremendous concentration of power in the executive. Usually the legislature expressly confers power to control production and transportation, to establish rationing, to institute censorship, and to suspend the operation of certain guarantees of civil liberty; but even when such powers are not so conferred, the executive may take any necessary action to safeguard the state and insure the successful prosecution of the war. Thus, in the exercise of his inherent power as chief executive, President Lincoln established a blockade of Southern ports, emancipated slaves in sections not controlled by federal troops, and suspended the writ of habeas corpus.

Conduct of Foreign Relations. The executive in every state is charged with conducting relations with other states. At his discretion, the chief executive may grant or withhold recognition to the government of a foreign state. He appoints, instructs, and controls the activities of ambassadors, ministers, consuls, and other foreign-service officers. He may dismiss the ambassador of a foreign state. He decides what claims to territory, property, and other rights to advance on behalf of his state or its citizens. He determines foreign policy. By sending representatives to international assemblies and conferences he may co-operate in the solution of world problems; by refusing to send representatives he may commit the state to a policy of isolation. In all countries he has exclusive control of the negotiation of treaties; and, except in the United States and a few other countries, he may promulgate them on his own authority. Even in the United States, by means of executive agreements, the president acting independently may make binding arrangements with foreign states (as when President Franklin D. Roosevelt exchanged fifty overage destroyers in return for 99-year leases of British bases in the Western Hemisphere). The legislative branch may refuse to declare war or to provide appropriations to carry out the terms of treaties, but in practice it may find that the state is committed already to such action.

The Pardoning Power. The chief executive usually has the power to issue pardons for offenses against the state either before or after trial and conviction. Such a pardon either releases a person from the legal consequences of a crime or remits the penalties imposed. The chief executive may reduce a sentence or, by a reprieve, delay its execution (although he may not increase a sentence). Also, he may issue a general proclamation of amnesty whereby a specifically described class of persons is absolved from the legal consequences of rebellion or other actions against the state.

TYPES OF EXECUTIVES

Before the start of the nineteenth century, practically all heads of state were hereditary monarchs; most were absolute monarchs —wielding legislative and adjudicative as well as executive powers.

Since that time, nearly all states have dispensed with hereditary monarchs or else have practically deprived them of power. The governments of many states, such as Great Britain, are still conducted in the names of kings and queens, but the real executive power has been assigned to cabinets or ministries. Some, like France, are conducted in the names of elective presidents, whereas their real power has been assigned to ministries. Some, notably the United States, are conducted in the names of elective presidents whose powers are both ceremonial and real.

Titular and Real Executives. Much confusion will be avoided if this distinction between "titular" and "real" executives be constantly kept in mind.

Titular heads of state, like those of Britain and France, serve as emblems of national unity. By performing ceremonial functions, they are useful in relieving the real executives from numerous public appearances and in enabling them to concentrate upon the solution of governmental problems. Furthermore, insofar as they have the right to be informed and consulted about public issues, they may use their influence to smooth over difficulties or may choose prime ministers when no party has a majority.

The principal forms in which the *real* executive exists today are (1) the presidential system as used in the United States, (2) the cabinet system, sometimes called "parliamentary government," as it functions in Great Britain or in France, (3) the method employed in Switzerland, and (4) the formula practiced in the Soviet Union.

Single and Collegial Executives. The executive, whether single or collegial, is responsible for a great deal of the planning in the modern state. A single executive—a chief to whom all other executives are subordinate—can make decisions and pursue energetically a course of policy at which a collegial executive, such as a cabinet, might fail. The number of persons constituting collegial executives varies from seven in Switzerland to upwards of fifteen or twenty in the cabinet systems of a number of European states.

REPRESENTATIVE EXECUTIVE SYSTEMS

The various executive systems in the modern world tend to function differently in exercising similar powers. The five foremost types of executive are: (1) American presidential system, (2) British cabinet system, (3) French cabinet system, (4) Swiss collegial system, and (5) collegial system of the Soviet Union.

The American Presidential System. Originally derived from the eighteenth-century powers of the British king, the United States' presidential system has developed its own recognizable qualities. In addition, it has become with modifications a pattern for other nations—especially in Latin America—but our discussion deals mainly with it as it functions in the United States.

In a presidential system, all executive powers, subject to a few limitations, are vested in a single chief executive. He is personally responsible for the enforcement of the law, the conduct of the administration, the formulation and execution of foreign policy, the issuance of pardon and amnesty, and the command of the armed forces. The distinguishing characteristic of the presidential system is the basic separation of executive and legislative powers and their independence of each other. In this principle lie the unity and strength as well as the weakness of the system. The principle of the separation of powers requires executive-legislative co-operation whether the president or Congress leads. A strong president may intervene at almost every stage of the legislative process and accomplish many of his objectives; a weak president may allow leadership to fall into congressional hands. A stalemate often occurs when the two branches are controlled by different political parties.

ELECTION AND TENURE OF THE PRESIDENT. The executive is elected by the people either directly (as in a few of the Latin-American countries) or indirectly through the medium of an electoral college. Indirect election in the United States amounts in practice to popular choice within each state: a candidate who receives a majority or plurality in a state obtains all its electoral votes. (Thus a president can claim a mandate from the electorate equal or superior to the mandate given Congress. Some presidents have even professed to be the only officers elected by the whole people inasmuch as members of Congress represent constituent states or congressional districts.) In the United States, the presidential term is fixed at four years, and since 1951 an individual president has been limited to two terms. In some Latin-American states he is ineligible for re-election after serving one or two terms; in others he may be re-elected after an intervening term. Long tenures of office enable the executive to acquire experience, insure his independence, and conduce consistent policies in government. They have the disadvantage of enabling a strong executive to acquire excessive power. Generally, the executive may not be removed before the expiration of his term of office except by the almost unworkable process of impeachment for high crimes and misdemeanors.

PRESIDENTIAL CONTROL OF THE CABINET. The executive, in most cases, appoints officers who are responsible for the administration of their separate departments of government; these officers are referred to collectively as the "cabinet." From the time of Washington, presidents of the United States with few exceptions have held regular cabinet meetings to which, by custom, all heads of departments are summoned; but the president may invite others of his "official family." These discussions are informal and secret. The cabinet may discuss matters affecting a single department or all departments and advise the president on any subject which he submits to them. The president may accept or ignore their votes or advice. In addition, the president may consult informally with other officers, members of Congress, or his own White House staff.

PRESIDENTIAL POWERS OVER LEGISLATION. The Constitution of the United States provides the president with five major legislative powers. (1) Originally a requirement of the Constitution, the "state-of-the-Union" address has been recognized recently as an influential source of legislative action: it enables the president to formulate and present to both Congress and the people a complete legislative program at the beginning of each session. In addition to the annual budget message and the annual economic report, the president may deliver supplementary addresses emphasizing the need for specific legislation. Though Congress is not obliged to follow his recommendations, the burden of proof is placed upon it for refusal. (2) The chief executive may also influence the development of legislative programs through the reports and proposals of cabinet members to Congress and perhaps by intimating to congressional leaders that a proposed bill is satisfactory or unsatisfactory to him, with the result that it is approved, dropped, or modified to suit his views. (3) The Constitution grants the chief executive a suspensive veto over legislation. The president's veto may be overridden by an adverse vote of two-thirds in each house, but it is nevertheless highly effective —not only in preventing encroachments on presidential powers, but also in determining the content of legislation. (4) The president may call Congress into special session, but he can not force it to consider a particular question. In doing this the president fixes the attention of the people on the need for legislation and Congress may be compelled to act on measures which it had previously disapproved or delayed. (5) The chief executive also possesses the power to issue executive decrees and proclamations under powers granted to him by the Constitution or by statute.

THE OFFICE OF GOVERNOR IN THE UNITED STATES. Generally speaking, the office of governor in a state of the United States conforms to the pattern of the presidential system except in two ways: (1) Generally the governor's legislative powers are superior because he may veto separate items in appropriation bills. (2) In name he is the "chief executive," but his constitutional power to control the administration is limited. State officers, whether elective or appointive, are responsible to the law and are not subject to removal at the discretion of the governor, and they may have longer terms than the governor. To exercise effective control over his administration, the governor must often request the legislature to make changes in the laws. It is no accident that many of the presidents who have exercised the most effective leadership, while in office, have had previous experience as state governors.

The British Cabinet System. Although the king is the formal symbol of leadership, the real executive powers are lodged, not in a single person, but in a cabinet which is composed of a prime minister and about twenty other ministers. The members of this collegial body are selected from Parliament; each of these individuals directs one department of government. A distinction is maintained between executive and legislative powers in Great Britain, but in practice they are commingled because of the dual responsibilities of cabinet members.

Contrary to the multiparty cabinet systems, the British system is based primarily on the predominance of one political party, which normally supports the policies of the cabinet. Consequently, this is "party government."

A majority in the House of Commons can force the cabinet out of office, but the cabinet can also dissolve the House and force the members to undergo expensive election campaigns. What is sometimes called the "dictatorship" of the cabinet rests on its ability to carry through successfully a series of delicate adjustments and to interpret constantly the feelings of the party and the electorate.

The chief merit of party government is its responsiveness to public opinion. Its chief defect is an overemphasis on party which keeps many important matters (other than party interests) from receiving an adequate hearing.

APPOINTMENT AND TENURE OF THE CABINET. After a general election, during which 625 representatives to the House of Commons are chosen from mainly single-member constituencies, the titular monarch formally authorizes the leader of the majority party in the House of Commons to be prime minister. The new prime minister chooses his cabinet from among the members of Parliament—the greatest number of seats being given to members of the House of Commons, almost always selected from the majority party. The task of constructing a cabinet is not easy; the prime minister must bring together a body of men who will work harmoniously, defend one another's policies, conciliate various elements within the party, and direct their departments efficiently and defend their operation in Parliament. Members of former cabinets of the party in power are nearly always included, as are the most effective debaters and exponents of party policy in the preceding Parliament. Scotland, Wales, and various sections of England must be represented and so must the principal economic and social interests.

One of the most important differences between the presidential and parliamentary forms of government is that members of the cabinet do not serve for a fixed term; rather they hold office as long as their plans are approved by the majority party in the House of Commons.

ACCOUNTABILITY OF THE CABINET. In this collegial body is concentrated the responsibility for the uninterrupted administration of government affairs. The cabinet must stand or fall as a whole; when the prime minister resigns or a basic policy of his cabinet is defeated in Commons, the cabinet resigns, parliament is dissolved, and a general election follows.

POWERS OF THE PRIME MINISTER. Actually, the prime minister has been the leader in government for two centuries, but his office was not recognized by law or salary[1] until very recently. The prime minister's status has been described as "first among equals." For he appoints ministers, presides over their meetings, and, in the case of serious defection within the cabinet, resigns or forces resignations. In other ways the prime minister is also pre-eminent. He is the leader of his party—a position acknowledged by all voters. As such he is the most successful campaigner of his party and the spokesman whose statements of policy are received with attention throughout the country and, in many instances, throughout the world. Always, unless his vigor is seriously impaired or his party suffers disastrous defeats at the polls, he retains the position of party leader. He is the leader of the House of Commons and, as such, proclaims policy developments and answers questions on important issues. The prime minister is the first person the Crown consults in emergencies. His advice is sought by other ministers on important matters affecting their departments. In situations requiring immediate action, he acts on his own responsibility and expects to be supported by his colleagues.

DUTIES AND POWERS OF THE MINISTERS. The ministers are responsible collectively for the consideration, determination, and co-ordination of the main lines of policy and for the conduct of the departments of government; each minister is also responsible for the management of his individual department.

The principle of collective responsibility has been applied to many of the ordinary activities of individual ministers—such as making speeches in various parts of the country. In the planning and execution of cabinet programs the reason behind collective accountability becomes more obvious. In planning fiscal policy, for example, the needs of various departments are often integrated, bringing the attention of two or more ministers to bear on the plan, rather than just the eye of the minister in whose department the need or suggestion arose.

As for individual responsibility, the minister is the political head of his department but, in modern times, it has been impossible for him to do more than direct the higher permanent officials of the department. In England, administration of a department is carried on by the permanent civil service, subject

---

[1] In days past, the prime minister assumed the office of First Lord of the Treasury.

to the approval of the minister, the cabinet, Parliament, and ultimately the electorate. The minister makes use of the civil service organization and employs the specialized knowledge of its members in developing departmental policies to coincide with the cabinet's program. He is the liaison, so to speak, between his ministry and the cabinet and Parliament.

In order to be valid, every act done in the name of the titular monarch must bear the countersignature of the minister within whose jurisdiction the matter lies. In signing, the minister takes full responsibility for the act even though he may have neither initiated nor supported it.

It is quite common now to assign various ministers to one of the permanent cabinet committees in order to expedite interdepartmental procedures. It has been discovered that in emergencies a body of twenty members is too large to function effectively. Often responsibility for decisions is devolved on an "inner" cabinet composed of the prime minister and a few of his associates.

THE CABINET'S CONTROL OF PARLIAMENT. To a certain extent, Parliament's freedom of action is hampered by the cabinet's power to dissolve the House of Commons. Consequently, the the cabinet controls the legislative procedure at almost every step. As we have said, it does the preliminary planning of the general legislative program, whereas in the United States, this task is performed by the President and the party leaders in Congress. (Some political theorists believe the cabinet does this more effectively.) In developing policies concerning particular subjects, the cabinet does not face the rivalry of standing committees of the Houses. It has a virtual monopoly in drafting and introducing legislation. This monopoly does not necessarily mean that the cabinet is unresponsive to public demands for legislation, but that such demands must be submitted to the cabinet first. There they are scrutinized and adapted to fit into the general policy and the cabinet's view of the specific need for legislation on a particular subject. They may, of course, be rejected altogether. If accepted, they become part of the cabinet's own program. Also, the cabinet controls the "timetable" of the house—that is, the order in which measures are considered and the amount of debate allowed on each one. In the course of debate it is sometimes found that a cabinet measure has serious defects or is unacceptable to party members or to the public. In such a case, the cabinet does not hesitate to propose amendments or even to withdraw the bill.

PARLIAMENT'S CONTROL OF THE CABINET. The efficiency of the cabinet system is enhanced by the control of the cabinet through party caucuses and representation in the House of Commons. The cabinet in power answers to Parliament or, strictly speaking, to the House of Commons. By resolution of censure regarding some administrative performance or by an adverse vote on a bill which the cabinet has declared to be a "matter of confidence" (that is, one on which it has chosen to stand or fall), Commons may force the cabinet to resign. In practice such votes are infrequent because the majority party supports the cabinet, but as a possibility it forces the cabinet to adapt its policies to the wishes of members of its own party in Commons or pay the consequence—appeal to the electorate.

The people may also look to the opposition party for thoroughgoing criticism of the cabinet's measures. The "shadow" cabinet ("opposition bench," composed of leaders of the opposition party) subjects them to pitiless scrutiny and points out defects and inconsistencies. It may obtain their modification or withdrawal; but the grand objective of the opposition is to convince the electorate that the government's policy is wrong, so that in the next general election the opposition may form the government. One of the best opportunities for the opposition is in the daily "question hour" in which grievances against the administration can be aired, and in which it may force a minister to make a damaging statement. The minister defends the actions of civil servants in Parliament but excoriates them for their mistakes when he returns to the department. The knowledge that their errors will become subjects of parliamentary debates makes civil servants more amenable to control.

The French Cabinet System. The French government is one example of the cabinet system as used in a state having a multiparty system. Unfortunately, the people of France have experienced government instability under the Fourth Republic as well as the Third. Similiar instability has existed in Italy, another nation in which the multiparty system exists. In Scandinavia, Belgium, and the Netherlands a reasonable degree of stability, achieved under similar systems, is attributed to a keen sense of responsibility on the part of political leaders who do their utmost to avoid ministerial crises.

In contrast to the system in Great Britain where national election campaigns are held following dissolution of Parliament, elections in France are based mainly on the calendar. Each candidate appeals to his particular constituency on his own record. Once elected, the deputy joins with others of similar political views in the Assembly and, in this way, gains strength for his causes and manages to become a member of a parliamentary group and the commissions on which it is entitled to be represented.

POWERS, ELECTION, AND TENURE OF THE PRESIDENT. In France the President is elected by majority vote of the National Assembly and the Council of the Republic meeting in joint session. He holds office for seven years and may be re-elected once. The President is the titular head of the French state and a national symbol of dignity and stability, in much the same way as the British monarch. He presides over the Council of Ministers, promulgates the laws, and may veto bills temporarily; with the approval of the Premier, he may return bills for further consideration. He signs and ratifies all treaties. At the beginning of a Parliament the President selects a new Premier, subject to majority approval in the National Assembly.

POWERS, ELECTION AND TENURE OF THE PREMIER. When nominating a Premier, the President confers with the presidents of the two chambers of the legislative body in order to assure selection of an individual who will receive the support of the majority. Once named, the prime minister submits his program (which will be the policy of his yet-to-be-appointed cabinet) to the National Assembly. If it is accepted by the majority of that body, he submits his choices for the Council of Ministers to the Assembly, where he hopes both he and his cabinet will receive a vote of confidence from a majority of the deputies on roll call. He and his cabinet are formally appointed by the President of the Republic when this has been accomplished.[2] Actually, the premier is the director of the government; he makes decisions and policy and proposes laws. He is the spokesman for the cabinet rather than a strong executive. Under the constitution

---

[2] This system is called "double investiture.'

of the Fourth Republic, votes of confidence can be taken only on motion of the premier, and, along with motions of censure, they can be voted on by roll call following a delay of a full day. An absolute majority vote of the National Assembly is necessary in order to cause the fall of the ministry.

POWERS, ELECTION, AND TENURE OF THE COUNCIL OF MINISTERS. In selecting ministers, the premier seeks the co-operation of a number of political parties whose combined membership constitutes a majority of the National Assembly. He finds it necessary to bargain and compromise on policies and on men in order to form his cabinet. It always contains many men who were in the preceding cabinet, for the fall of the government is due usually to the defection of one or more political parties whose places need to be filled by others. The ministers are accountable as a body to the National Assembly (not to the Council of the Republic) for cabinet policy and are responsible as individuals for their personal activities. Legislative and executive powers of the French Council of Ministers are similar to those of the British cabinet. Administration is handled in a manner not unlike the British, except that in France the standing consultative commissions are influential in shaping policy and in controlling the timetable of legislation.[3] The secretariat performs routine duties and provides an avenue of contact between the cabinet and the Fourth Republic's four representative assemblies: (1) the National Assembly, the most forceful of the four, (2) the Council of the Republic, which assists in the formulation of legislation, (3) the French Union, which gathers advice from overseas colonies on problems affecting the entire empire, and (4) the Economic Council, an advisory body operated according to the functional organization of the state. Resignation of the entire cabinet results when the National Assembly fails to grant a vote of confidence. The fall of a French cabinet does not necessarily entail a dissolution of the legislature or a general election.

PARLIAMENT'S CONTROL OF THE CABINET. In France the power of the deputy is pre-eminent. This is due mainly to the peculiar functioning of the multiparty system and the cabinet's lack of

---

[3] Under the Third Republic (1870-1940), *interpellation* (an adaptation of the British question hour) was followed by an immediate vote of confidence in which a vote of a majority of those present could cause the fall of the ministry.

power to force dissolution. The National Assembly may vote censure and force the resignation of the cabinet by withholding a vote of confidence. Contrary to the British system, the Conference of Presidents (composed of the vice-presidents and presidents of the chamber plus the presidents of grand committees and the parliamentary groups) controls the agenda. Even the commissions may question the cabinet on legislation. The power of dissolution lies with neither the cabinet nor the Assembly. The President of the Republic (with the advice of the premier and the President of the Assembly) can dissolve the National Assembly during the last 42 months of its life if there have already been two crises in any eighteenth-month period. The crises can be brought on only by the action of the Assembly in voting censure or refusing to pass a vote of confidence. In case of dissolution, the cabinet with the exception of the prime minister and the minister of interior remains in office and the President of the Republic names the President of the National Assembly as the premier. He, in turn, designates a minister of interior, subject to the approval of the secretariat and the assembly. A general election takes place 20 to 30 days after the dissolution.

The Swiss Collegial Executive. The population of Switzerland is composed of four linguistic groups, a fact which might indicate a problem in maintaining stability; but actually there is none. Switzerland is governed under a multiparty political system in which the popular legislative chamber, once elected, serves for four years.

APPOINTMENT AND TENURE OF EXECUTIVE COUNCIL. Each new chamber, jointly with the upper house (composed of representatives of the cantons), elects seven members to an executive council which also serves for four years. Usually, former councilors are re-elected. As a rule, new councilors are chosen from the legislature; in this case, they lose their membership in either house, but may participate in the work of both chambers without voting privileges. Meeting in joint session each year, the houses designate one councilor to be president and another to be vice-president (rotating the offices among the linguistic groups). These officials have little more authority than the other councilors. The Executive Council itself assigns each of its members to head one of the seven departments of the Swiss administration. Each councilor enforces laws and manages his department, subject to the approval of the Council as a whole and subject to the strict orders of the legislature. The councilors may draft bills or modify those referred to them, as detailed bills almost always are; they participate in debate and submit explanatory reports on their activities. The defeat of a policy which a councilor (or council) supports has no effect on his tenure of office.

SUPREMACY OF LEGISLATIVE BODY OVER EXECUTIVE. In spite of their total legal subordination to the legislature, the members of the Council have great legislative influence because of their long experience and knowledge of the practical effects of the application of laws. The highly successful operation of the Swiss collegial system is a challenge to theorists who insist on a single executive head or on the necessity for the real executive to resign when its policies and acts are not approved by the legislature.

The Executive in the Soviet Union. Executive power in the Soviet Union embraces not only the ordinary duties of law enforcement and administration but also the operation of an all-embracing industrial corporation as well as control of the police and education. In any consideration of the Soviet government, the distinction must always be kept in mind between the constitutional powers and the actual exercise and control of power by the hierarchy of the Communist party (the country's only political party). From outward appearances the government and the communist hierarchy appear separate, but in reality their structures, personnel, and functions are almost identical.

APPOINTMENT OF THE COUNCIL OF MINISTERS. According to the constitution, the highest executive organ is the Council of Ministers. This is a large body including ministries for such varied subjects as the rubber industry, cinematography, and food reserves who are designated by both houses of the legislature meeting in joint session. The chairman of this group is referred to as "premier," and is comparable to the prime minister in Britain; the vice-chairmen of the council may number as many as fifteen.

SUPREMACY OF THE COUNCIL. On paper, the Supreme Soviet is the legislature. In actuality it is in session for approximately one month each year during which time it appoints a Presidium, composed of about thirty members, and it vests this group with all its constitutional powers for the rest of the year. The Presidium exercises a great deal of legislative authority. Though supposedly it lacks executive powers, it appoints high officials, grants honors, orders the mobilization of the armed forces, proclaims martial law, and issues pardons. The chairman of the Presidium receives foreign ambassadors. Its judicial powers extend to the interpretation of laws and the annulment of judicial decisions which it finds contrary to law.

Although it is explicitly made responsible to the Supreme Soviet or the Presidium, the Council is in reality responsible to neither. Its basic policies are those of the communist party. Many decisions announced by the nominal legislative and executive organs are first made, proclaimed, and carried into effect by the party. Under its chairman and vice-chairmen, the council controls and directs the whole social, cultural, and economic activity of the Soviet Union. The decrees and ordinances which it issues far outweigh in number and importance the combined legislation of the Supreme Soviet and the Presidium.

16   *The Judiciary*

In a modern state the liberty of individuals depends upon the fairness of courts in protecting them both from other individuals and from tyrannical or overzealous governmental officers. The maintenance of tranquility within the state is as dependent upon the justice with which disputes are settled as upon the use of force.

Separation of the judiciary from the control of legislative and executive powers is considered essential to the preservation of individual liberty. The judiciary, with its studied nonpartisanship and its presumed aloofness from political controversy, usually attracts less public attention than do the other governmental branches; yet, its functions, its organization, and its procedure demand an equally critical understanding.

FUNCTIONS OF THE JUDICIARY

The over-all function of the judiciary is to apply the law with certainty and uniformity to specific cases as they arise.

Ordinarily, judges will not act in the absence of a bona fide case between parties. When a case is presented, the duty of a court is first to find the facts and then to discover the law applicable to the case. Sometimes the law is not clear because the statute-makers did not foresee the circumstances of the case, or because the wording of the statute is ambiguous, or because two or more laws applicable to the case are in conflict. The court must resolve these difficulties. In determining the exact meaning of the law, expanding its details, and applying the general principles of justice, the judge may become the virtual creator of part of the law for the particular case at hand.[1]

---

[1] This raises the purely academic question as to whether judges "make" or "discover" the law. Some theorists hold that they can and do make law. Others hold that they merely reveal pre-existent law.

The weight which courts give to previous decisions varies in different states. In Roman-law countries each decision must be based on the code or on statutes, and judges rarely refer to previous cases. In Anglo-American jurisprudence (based on the common law) each decision is regarded as a precedent for future decisions. This principle is known as *stare decisis* ("to stand by decisions"). It has been attacked because it may perpetuate errors if the original decision was based on a misconception or was otherwise unjust. However, the principle has been defended on the ground that it assures uniformity in the application of the law.

The function in applying the law includes the settlement of disputes, the prevention of wrongful acts, issuance of declaratory judgments, judicial review (in the United States and a few other countries), and a host of miscellaneous activities which are less judicial in character, but which require the knowledge and authority of a judge.

The Settlement of Disputes. Both civil and criminal cases are brought before the courts in the ordinary course of judicial business. A *civil case*[2] is a case between individuals. In deciding it, judges settle claims to property, award damages, or take other appropriate action. A *criminal case* is a case brought in the name of the state against a person accused of a misdemeanor or felony. The court may determine whether a person is innocent or guilty and may invoke the penalties provided by law.

Preventive Justice. By means of writs and restraining orders, courts may act to prevent threatened infractions of the law. In England and in the United States such matters come within the jurisdiction of equity courts, and the principal writ is the injunction which requires a person to refrain from specific acts. Failure to obey an injunction constitutes contempt of court and may be punished by fine or imprisonment. In the United States, some judges formerly abused their authority by issuing temporary "blanket injunctions" directed to members of labor unions who had gone on strike against their employers. A hearing was necessary in order to make the injunction permanent, but often before the hearing was held the strike had been broken. Blanket

---

[2] Civil cases may be either actions *at law* or suits *at equity* in English and American courts.

injunctions have now been forbidden by law. Far worse violations of personal rights have occurred under recent dictatorships which ordered individuals to be punished by the courts merely because their minds were supposed to harbor disloyal thoughts.

Declaratory Judgments. Several countries, including the United States, provide by law that courts may, in actual controversies, render declaratory judgments—that is, judicial determinations of the rights of parties existing under statutes, contracts, wills, or other documents. Such judgments enable the parties to ascertain their respective rights without becoming involved in wasteful litigation and without having to prove that any wrong has been done or is immediately threatened. Although declaratory judgments do not grant relief, they are binding on the parties.

Judicial Review. In Great Britain, an Act of Parliament is supreme, but courts can declare illegal some executive orders and the enactments of minor legislative bodies. The United States Supreme Court will try actual cases that challenge the legality of specific executive acts or legislative statutes. That is, it will examine the acts or statutes to determine whether or not they are prohibited by the Constitution or are in excess of the powers granted by it; if they are, it will declare them void. Judicial review[3] has already been defined and briefly discussed in the section dealing with the enforcement of written constitutions in Chapter 10. Here it is desirable to add some further comment to bring out the relationship between the judiciary and the other governmental branches.

REVIEW OF EXECUTIVE ACTS. The United States Supreme Court has sparingly used its power of judicial review over executive acts even when suits have been brought against presidents as individuals. It has not interfered when a president has proclaimed that certain territories belong to the United States or when a president has intervened with armed forces to suppress disorders within foreign states; rather it has asserted that such matters are "political questions," with which it has no concern.

---

[3] The practice of judicial review is Anglo-American in origin, although it has spread to the high courts of countries elsewhere. It must be distinguished from the mere refusal of a court to apply a law because the provisions are self-contradictory, fail to express the clear intent of the legislature, or lack sanctions for enforcement. Probably every court in the world has faced these latter problems at one time or another.

It has never declared a treaty unconstitutional, although it asserts that it has the power to do so. The United States Supreme Court has refused to order state governors to extradite fugitives from justice in other states. It has usually upheld those acts of cabinet officers which have been committed under presidential direction. On the other hand, it has often declared void the administrative determinations of cabinet officers in cases involving such matters as taxes and patents; it has held minor officials of the executive department to strict legal accountability for their public acts; it has issued *writs of mandamus,* ordering officials to perform duties clearly prescribed by law.

REVIEW OF LEGISLATION. With respect to legislation, the practice of the United States Supreme Court has been more rigid. Though it can not compel Congress to take affirmative action and though it does not interfere in legislative procedure, it has declared about one hundred federal statutes void because of conflict with the terms of the federal Constitution. Moreover, it has voided a thousand or more acts of state legislatures because they encroached on federal powers or because they violated constitutional guarantees of individual liberty, of rights to property, and of equal protection under the laws.

Although judicial review is a valuable check upon headstrong executive or legislative action, its exercise is heavily charged with political implications. Here is a typical instance: a legislature has determined to embark upon a policy that lies beyond the periphery of its recognized powers and has passed an act without precedent; a case is brought through one or two stages to the Supreme Court, and the Court upholds or voids the legislative act. But, critics point out, the Court thereby upholds or voids the political policy; sometimes it does so by a majority of one Supreme Court justice (five-to-four decisions); occasionally, it upholds a policy during a certain political era and voids the same policy during another.[4]

The frequency of five-to-four decisions on highly contentious issues and the reversals of interpretations of the Constitution

---

[4] In some eras, the Supreme Court has insisted upon *strict construction* of the Constitution (that is, upon literal adherence to the wording); in others, it has insisted upon *loose construction* (that is, upon the need for interpreting the intentions of the framers of the Constitution rather than their words). Thus in one era, by strict construction, it voided child-labor legislation; and in another, by loose construction, it upheld such legislation.

have led to various proposals for revising the present procedure of judicial review. In order that the bias of a single justice may not decide the constitutionality of a statute, it has been proposed that each Court decision require the concurrence of six instead of five justices. Furthermore, it has been proposed that Congress be empowered to override Supreme Court decisions. Also it has been suggested that the power of judicial review be abolished altogether by constitutional amendment.

Nonjudicial Functions. Some foreign countries and a few American states impose on the courts the duty of rendering opinions to officers of the government concerning the legal effect of statutes when no case has been brought to the courts. The United States Supreme Court has refused to render such opinions on the ground that they would involve it in nonjudicial activities. Interesting as such opinions might be to executive and legislative officers, they could not properly be regarded as precedents for decisions in later cases.

Among other functions of courts are a variety of important everyday activities, which are conveniently assigned to judges for responsible handling. These include such matters as granting licenses, appointing receivers in bankruptcy, appointing guardians of minors and administrators of estates, and naturalizing aliens.

ORGANIZATION OF THE JUDICIARY

In establishing a judiciary, the goal is to create a court structure that will be convenient for litigants and that will be expert and certain in its application of the law. Convenience is attained in such a large country as the United States by a territorial distribution of courts; in Great Britain, which emphasizes other than geographical considerations, it is attained by centering in London the hearing of all important cases. Expertness is attained in most states through the creation of specialized courts—for example, courts that hear only civil, criminal, children's, domestic-relations, probate, labor, commercial, or equity cases. Certainty is attained through the establishment of appellate courts to review the decisions of lower courts and to correct their errors.

The Structure of Court Systems. Written constitutions contain articles which provide for the structure of the judicial sys-

THE JUDICIARY

tem and the jurisdiction of each court within it and leave to the legislature the power to determine the number of judges in each court.[5] Regardless of differences in systems of law, every state organizes its courts in a hierarchical structure.

COURTS OF SUMMARY JURISDICTION. At the base of the hierarchical structure are a great number of minor courts each in charge of a justice of the peace or of a magistrate whose function is to try and pass sentence upon persons accused of misdemeanors, and to decide petty civil disputes. In large cities, there may be specialized divisions such as civil, criminal, juvenile and domestic-relations courts. At this level procedure is informal, and records are often incomplete.

COURTS OF GENERAL JURISDICTION. Next are courts in counties or districts whose functions are to try persons accused of crimes and to hear important civil cases.[6] There may be specialized criminal, commercial, probate, and other divisions. Courts at this level are courts of record; that is, they keep complete and accurate statements of testimony and proceedings which may be reviewed by higher courts if a case is appealed.

INTERMEDIATE APPELLATE COURTS. In many (though not all) states there are intermediate courts between courts of record and the supreme court which hear appeals and review the proceedings in cases originally tried and decided in courts of record. In some states, their decisions are final when confined to specific subjects. In all appellate courts, each case is heard by a group of several judges.

SUPREME COURTS. At the apex of the judicial structure, the supreme court has final jurisdiction to decide all cases which may be brought before it by appeal or otherwise[7] from the lower courts. Through its appellate jurisdiction, a supreme court maintains uniformity in the application of the law throughout the state.

Hierarchies of Courts in Federal Systems. In states having federal forms of government, the judicial structure is arranged in

---

[5] In the United States, courts not established by the federal or state constitutions are created and may be abolished by legislative act.

[6] In Anglo-Saxon countries each of these courts is in charge of a single judge, but on the Continent they consist of several judges sitting together.

[7] Most of the cases in the Supreme Court of the United States are brought before it by *writ of certiorari* (application for review of the decision of a lower court).

either one or two hierarchies of courts. At the extreme of simplification, Switzerland and the Soviet Union vest the administration of both local and national law in the courts of their respective cantons or republics (their national supreme courts provide final appellate jurisdiction). At the opposite extreme, the Bonn Constitution of West Germany provides individual hierarchies for the component *Laender* (or constituent states) and a completely independent hierarchy for the nation—with a Federal Constitutional Court above both to decide on the interpretation of the constitution, the relative powers and duties of the local and the national governments, and the relations between these governments.

In the United States, fear that state courts would not properly enforce federal law resulted in the creation by Congress (1789) of a complete system of federal courts. These now include district courts, circuit courts of appeals, and the Supreme Court, which is both the highest national court and the supreme tribunal of the federal system. A separate hierarchy of courts exists in each state for the trial of cases which arise under its constitution and laws.

State courts in the United States have jurisdiction except when the nature of the question or the nature of the parties falls under the jurisdiction of the federal courts. The jurisdiction of the federal courts is exclusive as to *subject* in cases arising under the Constitution of the United States, or under federal laws and treaties, or in admiralty and maritime law. It also has exclusive jurisdiction as to parties in cases between two or more states, cases concerning foreign diplomatic agents, cases in which the United States is a party, cases between citizens of the same state claiming lands under grants of different states, and cases between a state or the citizens thereof and foreign states, citizens, or nationals. Only those cases which arise between citizens of different states and in which considerable sums of money are involved may be removed to federal courts at an early stage on application of the defendant. Cases tried in the highest state courts may be appealed to the Supreme Court of the United States if the appellants can show that a federal question, such as the denial of due process under the Fourteenth Amendment or interference with a proper function of the federal government, is involved.

Hierarchies of Administrative Courts. Some countries of Continental Europe, notably France, have a distinct hierarchy of courts to apply *administrative law,* that is, law regulating the conduct of public officials and determining the rights of individuals when they deal with public officials.[8] The judges in administrative courts perform both judicial and executive acts. They hear cases concerning public officers accused of having acted in excess of their authority and may punish them for abuse of their powers. When they find that an individual has suffered a wrong from public action, they award compensation from the public treasury. Although their decisions have no effect on the contents of statutes passed by legislatures, these courts often annul ordinances made by administrative officers.

Until recently, the courts of the United States and of Great Britain have given less protection than have French administrative courts against individual wrongs committed through the negligence or illegal acts of governmental officers. Anglo-American common law has indeed made government officials personally responsible for their acts, but it has provided no recourse when these officials are not financially able to meet the judgments against them. But since 1946 and 1947 respectively, the United States and Great Britain have provided by statute that individuals may bring suit against the state as well as against an officer for wrongful acts committed in the course of carrying out official duties.

Unification of Court System. In European countries, all courts are integrated into single systems under the supervision of a ministry of justice or of high judicial officers.

In the United States, there is an almost complete lack of integration: each court is separate from every other court. Some judges are overburdened at times when others have little to do. It has been proposed that each federal court and each court within an American state be made a branch of the highest federal or state court and be made subject to its control in such matters as rules, staff, and calendar; the highest court or its chief justice or a judicial council might then assign judges or distribute cases

---

[8] In the United States, so-called "administrative" or "legislative" courts—e.g., the Court of Claims, the Court of Customs and Patent Appeals, and the Tax Court—are specialized tribunals whose decisions are subject to review by the regular courts, as are the quasi-judicial decisions of executive departments and commissions.

among various courts of equivalent level and equalize the burden. A central office in charge of all records could secure uniformity and avoid needless duplication. In several states and in the federal government the first step has been taken towards the creation of *judicial councils*—the membership of which usually includes the chief justice, judges of courts of original or appellate jurisdiction, practicing lawyers, and sometimes prominent laymen. Such a judicial council surveys the volume and the condition of business in the several courts, suggests methods for simplifying and expediting it, acquaints judges with the results of experience elsewhere, and acts in an advisory capacity to legislative and executive committees charged with investigating judicial affairs and formulating policy concerning the courts.

PERSONNEL AND TENURE OF THE JUDICIARY

Judicial work requires a thorough knowledge of the law and a thorough knowledge of contemporary social and economic conditions; in addition, it requires developed judgment—the ability to be impartial and nonpartisan—and the highest personal integrity. Judges must be selected by a method which emphasizes these qualities and which minimizes political considerations, and they must be guaranteed conditions of tenure and remuneration that assure their independence of political influence.

Methods of Selection. On the Continent of Europe, where court systems are unified under ministries of justice, the judiciary is a career: after electing it, the young man goes from the university, sometimes as the result of competitive examinations, into the ministry of justice and hopes by hard work to be promoted from court to court until he reaches the highest tribunal. The career system succeeds in securing the services of experienced judges with legal learning; but often it secures men with narrowly legalistic viewpoints or men who have been exposed to a need for pleasing their superiors and perhaps also influential politicians. In the British Empire and in the United States, the judiciary is generally selected from among practicing lawyers (though in the latter country a few come from the faculties of law schools). In Great Britain, judges are appointed by the Lord Chief Justice; in the United States, federal judges are appointed by the president with the approval of the Senate, and state and municipal judges are chosen by executive appointment, popular election, or election of a legislature. Appointment may result in a partisan judiciary. Elective systems frequently secure incompetent judges—because candidates of proper judicial caliber are hesitant to undertake political campaigns, because voters lack the discernment to choose well-qualified judicial candidates, or because political bosses are overly influential. Yet, any of the American methods of choosing judges may be satisfactory provided that executives, legislatures, and party nominating conventions follow the advice of leading bar associations.

Systems of Tenure. Tenure for life or during good behavior with compulsory retirement at a definite age seems to be the most effective way to secure judges of independence and high integrity. Independence is not affected by a judge's knowledge that he will be retired at the age of sixty-five or seventy, nor is integrity hampered by the fact that venal and corrupt judges can be removed through impeachment procedure, judicial trial, or address by the legislature; but both independence and integrity may be affected by the knowledge that an unpopular decision may mean removal from office or failure of re-election. Short tenures, whether by appointment (as in the Soviet Union) or by election (as in most of our own states) tend to place on the bench judges who are under the temptation to please the public rather than to fulfill the law. When they yield to this temptation, their decisions make the law uncertain and inconsistent.

The evil effects of the elective system have been partly overcome in some of our states through the establishment of long terms and the tradition of having incumbent judges jointly renominated by both political parties.

JUDICIAL PROCEDURE

Proper procedure in the decision of cases is as necessary as good judicial organization and personnel. Constitutional guarantees—due process, jury trial, confrontation and cross-examination of witnesses, immunity from compulsory self-incrimination, and the right to have counsel and to have adequate time to prepare a case—all emphasize the importance of judicial procedure. But excessive respect for traditional methods and a desire for absolute perfection in every minute detail often result in excessive delay, undue expense, and the miscarriage of justice. Justice long delayed or made unduly expensive is justice denied. Theoretically, the courts are open to all on equal terms. Practically, they are not accessible to most individuals when going to law means long delays and appeals on trivial grounds, with resulting court costs and attorney's fees.

Rules of Procedure. The purpose of procedural rules is to enable the courts to decide cases with dispatch while giving a fair and impartial hearing to all the parties concerned on all essential points—or, briefly, to get business done justly and promptly. American rules of procedure compare unfavorably with those of Western Europe, where the courts themselves are largely responsible for making the rules and keeping them up to date. Judges, who apply the law, are expert both in recognizing changing needs and in distinguishing among the procedures which are useful in various cases. They readily discern the difference between rules that really protect the parties to litigation and those that only interpose technicalities while appearing to give protection. In the United States, rules of procedure are made by the legislature. They tend to be antiquated, intricate, and cumbersome; to unduly hamper judges in the administration of justice; and to multiply the issues which must be tried. In addition, they allow appeals on merely technical grounds whereas they should restrict appeals to material issues. A noteworthy exception to the general course of legislation on judicial rules is the federal law, drafted and submitted to Congress by judges of the Supreme Court in 1925, which allows the Supreme Court wide discretion in determining what cases may come before it.

The Role of the Judge. In Western Europe, the judge is assigned responsibility for actively directing and controlling the trial of a case. He sees to it that all pertinent facts are discovered and when he believes that the counsel has failed to bring out the essential facts, he asks questions of witnesses. Furthermore, the judge prevents lawyers from posing improper questions and making improper emotional appeals to the jury. In his final summation of a case he not only sets forth the law which governs it, but he also analyzes the testimony presented on both sides in order to aid the jury in reaching a correct decision. In America, such activity on the part of a judge would usually result in a mistrial of a case. Here, the judge's role is largely the passive one of acting as an impartial moderator in a contest of procedural skill between opposing counsel.

The Jury System. In Europe, the jury system is rarely used except for criminal cases; but in the United States, it is often used for civil cases as well. Many proposals for its improvement have been advanced, and some have been adopted by various American states.

In Anglo-Saxon procedure the requirement that a person accused of a crime may be tried only after an *indictment* and convicted only after the unanimous verdict of a *trial jury (petit jury)* of twelve impartial laymen, especially empaneled for the trial of a case, is traditionally regarded as his fundamental right. An *indictment* is a formal written accusation drawn up by the prosecuting officer of a state and endorsed by a *grand jury* of laymen summoned to hear the state's witnesses and to determine whether the evidence justifies holding the accused person for trial.

Because grand juries have tended to become merely mouthpieces of the prosecuting attorneys, more than half of our states have made provisions for dispensing with them by substituting an "information"[9] for an indictment. Trial juries are generally criticized because of the methods used in selecting jurors, the tendency to reach verdicts by compromise, and the frequent mistrials due to the absence of a juror for illness or similar cause; their usefulness in civil cases is especially questioned because of the average juror's lack of familiarity with the complexities of modern economic life. It has been proposed that limitations be placed on the present rights of counsel to challenge prospective jurors. Some states now relax the requirement that verdicts must be unanimous and provide that a vote of three-fourths or five-sixths shall be sufficient for a verdict in civil and minor criminal cases. Some permit alternates to replace absentee jurymen. All permit the accused to waive his right to jury trial in favor of trial by court, and there is a movement towards reserving jury trial for cases that involve felonies or other serious crimes.

Other Procedures. Experience has shown that many issues can be justly and amicably settled through means less drastic than litigation. *Conciliation* and *arbitration* are two such means.

---

[9] An *information* is "a written accusation before a magistrate, made upon oath by a prosecuting officer, which charges one or more persons with having committed a felony or misdemeanor."—E. C. Smith and A. J. Zurcher (ed.), *Dictionary of American Politics,* an Everyday Handbook (New York: Barnes & Noble, Inc., 1955).

CONCILIATION. Conciliation is the attempt of two parties to reach a compromise by submitting the dispute to a third party who is friendly to both; the contending parties are not legally bound to accept the conciliator's advice. Some European states have conciliation courts. In the United States, many labor disputes are settled every year by permanent national and state conciliators; it has even been proposed that all civil cases should be discussed in the presence of impartial conciliators and submitted to courts only if conciliation fails.

ARBITRATION. Arbitration is the voluntary submission of an issue to the hearing, investigation, and determination of a single umpire or a panel by whose decision the contesting parties agree in advance to be bound. The value of arbitration in the settlement of international disputes was fully recognized in 1899 by the establishment of the Permanent Court of Arbitration at the Hague. In the United States, contracts often provide that any disputes arising under them must be submitted to arbitration; in 1925 an act of Congress made arbitration proceedings valid, irrevocable, and enforceable.

17 *Public Administration*

The term *administration* is used in two broad senses: (1) as an abstract noun, it designates the art and science[1] of managing governmental affairs, enforcing law, and fulfilling public policies and (2) as a concrete noun, it designates the entire body of officials (both elective officers and civil service appointees) who carry out these functions.

The functions of administration crosscut the traditional division of governmental powers into "legislative," "executive," and "judicial" branches. Administrative bodies must in the course of their work exercise sublegislative, subexecutive, and quasi-judicial powers and initiate policies that are later incorporated by the governmental branches into statutes, proclamations, or directives. Those political scientists who classify all government under the three traditional headings usually consider administration to be a specialized part of the law-enforcing machinery of the executive branch. Others look upon all governmental activities as being primarily divisible into (1) "political" functions having to do with the formulation of policies and (2) "administrative" functions having to do with the execution of policies. Still others consider administration in the modern state as a "fourth branch of government."

During the past fifty years, the complexity of administrative problems has increased commensurately with the tremendous expansion of governmental activities, and the number of employees in civil service offices has skyrocketed. (It is estimated

---

[1] Administration is an "art" insofar as it concerns practical management of men and materials for the public interest; it is a "science" insofar as it concerns a knowledge of the ways and methods for efficient fulfillment of public policy.

that in the United States one among every nine gainfully employed persons now works for the federal, a state, or a local government; the proportion is far higher in countries which have greater socialization.) The expansion of civil service calls, of course, for frequent—almost continuous—reorganization of administrative structure; but proposals for reorganization invariably meet strong opposition from officeholders and from all who profit by an existing order.

In the United States, administrative organization has often been fundamentally faulty. It has grown haphazardly through temporarily expedient legislative acts and has lacked over-all direction. Theoretically, almost all the administrative agencies of the federal government are responsible to the president, but so many agencies have been created outside regular executive departments that effective presidential supervision is impossible. Although a few American states have made important strides toward carefully planned administrative structures, the agencies of the forty-eight state governments do not always have even a centralized responsibility.

Here we will (1) define the relationship of administrative functions to the legislative, executive, and judicial branches of government; (2) examine the types of administrative organization found in the United States and elsewhere; and (3) compare the administration of the United States' Civil Service with that of other countries. Throughout the chapter, consideration will be given to proposals for improvement.

RELATIONSHIP OF ADMINISTRATION TO THE THREE BRANCHES OF GOVERNMENT

For illustrative purposes, it is helpful to liken the flow of authority in governmental administration to that in private corporations. In such an analogy, the legislature roughly corresponds to a "board of directors" which determines over-all activities and policies. The executive roughly corresponds to a "general manager" who, with the approval of the directors, supplies immediate leadership, directs activities, and assumes responsibility for making important staff appointments. Members of governmental administration correspond to the rank and file of department heads and subordinates who perform specified tasks as responsibly as possible within their limited spheres and give impartial treatment to the public.

At all times, administrators are liable to censure by the legislature, to discipline by the executive, to overrulings by the courts, and to criticisms from the public—which range from general charges of "bureaucracy" to complaints about inefficiency in the performance of particular tasks. Administrators may sometimes initiate policies that are adopted by their superiors, but they usually conduct their work efficiently without expecting more than a small measure of recognition; sometimes no recognition at all has been forthcoming.

Legislative Control of Administration. The legislature determines the activities in which a government will engage, designates the agencies by which these will be carried out, and (in conjunction with the executive) declares the policies and the methods to be followed. Its control rests not merely in its power to create but in its power to abolish administrative offices or to refuse them appropriations. In the United States, its control rests also in its power to withhold confirmation of executive appointments and in its power to investigate administrative acts through congressional committees.

The exercise of these powers should be neither too strict nor too lax. Since legislators can not be experienced in all the intricacies of administrative problems, they should not attempt to enact excessively detailed regulations, which prevent administrators from making adjustments to needs which constantly arise. The opposite policy of granting excessive discretionary powers to administrators opens the way to abuse of power. A sound middle course is for the legislature to formulate a clear statement of policy, to set definite limits to the exercise of discretionary powers, and to require administrators both to keep accurate records and to submit reports at regular intervals or on demand. Moreover, there should be standing committees in each legislative chamber and a staff to check the fidelity and efficiency with which administrative work is being performed.

Executive Control of Administration. The executive has immediate control over administrative activities and methods. It co-ordinates the multitudinous administrative activities of the modern state and instructs officers as to how legislative acts shall be enforced. The executive assigns individuals to the chief offices, directs them in the performance of their tasks, and supplies them with essential information. Furthermore, it maintains discipline and requires co-operation throughout the service. It has a duty to promote good morale, pride in civil government, and job satisfaction among civil servants.

Judicial Control of Administration. The courts enforce the fundamental principle that all public officers and all employees are strictly accountable to the law. They try civil and criminal cases involving official misconduct. Moreover, they can issue *writs of mandamus* to compel the performance of clearly required duties and *injunctions* to prevent wrongful acts by administrative officers.

When judicial control is excessively strict, administrative efficiency is reduced. Public servants, fearful lest their acts may involve them in lawsuits, often take refuge in established procedures and become slavishly devoted to red tape. Because judges do not have an intimate knowledge of administrative problems, and because judicial delays prevent the prompt performance of official duties, most states have found it necessary to grant wide discretionary powers to administrative officers in order to facilitate performance.

Experience has proved, however, the necessity for judicial control over the actions of administrative officers. When the United States was rapidly expanding its administrative services, Congress hastily granted sublegislative and quasi-judicial powers to administrative offices without imposing effective limitations, and too often an administrator became legislator, policeman, prosecutor, judge, and jury. After widespread complaint, Congress passed the Administrative Procedure Act of 1946. Among other requirements, this act required the publication of the orders issued by every agency, a definite procedure in conducting hearings before any quasi-judicial determination might be reached, and a review by the courts upon application of any person who might claim to suffer wrong as a result of the conduct of an agency. Under this law, the courts may compel action if it is withheld or unreasonably delayed; they may set aside administrative determinations that are arbitrary, capricious, unconstitutional, in excess of statutory authority, unwarranted by facts, unsupported by evidence, or arrived at without observance of procedural requirements.

ADMINISTRATIVE ORGANIZATION

Experience has proved that failure to emphasize a sound administrative structure results in conflicts of authority, duplication of work, and other inefficiencies and wastes; hence, every state should reorganize its constantly expanding "officialdom" frequently. The essentials of good administrative organization are two: there should be (1) an over-all administrative structure to provide efficient supervision and (2) an internal unit structure suitable to the kind of work it is to perform.

The Over-all Structure. The ultimate goal of administration is an organization in which all units function harmoniously under effective supervision. The over-all structure should include (1) an adequate number of *staff agencies* to obtain information and to provide technical assistance to executives, (2) an efficient grouping of *operative* or *line agencies* to carry on administration at various levels of authority, and (3) a sufficient number of *auxiliary* or *service agencies* to provide financing, personnel, equipment, and other common needs of operative agencies.

STAFF AGENCIES. Staff agencies perform investigative, advisory, and planning functions. (In the United States, they include the offices of the various economic advisers, which keep the president in touch with current business conditions and prospects, and the Office of the Director of the Budget; in Great Britain, they include services for bill-drafting, for the management of administrative methods and personnel, and for budgeting.) In order for a president or a cabinet to obtain the information needed for the proper direction and supervision of all the activities and the officers of a state, an adequate staff is necessary to study problems and supply facts, to compare methods of operation in different departments and bureaus, and to analyze costs. Generally, the executive handles the reorganizations which are inevitable within the staff.

OPERATIVE (LINE) AGENCIES. Operative or line agencies fulfill executive orders, perform the day-to-day functions of administration, and carry out governmental objectives in a variety of fields, such as in nuclear research or in the daily distribution of mail. These agencies are so very numerous that supervision is necessary at various levels. Units with similar functions may be grouped into homogeneous bureaus, related bureaus may be subordinated to divisions, and divisions may be placed within appropriate departments which are in general directly responsible to the president.

AUXILIARY (SERVICE) AGENCIES. Auxiliary or service agencies may oversee many different types of operations such as personnel administration (e.g., the conduct of civil service examinations), collection of taxes, custody and disbursement of funds, public accounting, procurement of supplies, and miscellaneous hosts of housekeeping tasks. The problems of proper organization of auxiliary agencies are generally similar to those which have been discussed in connection with operative agencies.

The Problem of Continuous Reorganization. The complicated hierarchy of offices in administrative organization could be diagrammed as a triangle with the chief executive and his staff at the apex, the intermediate operative and auxiliary departments, divisions, and bureaus at various central levels, and the primary units at the base. But administrative reorganizers should guard against creating on paper a "too-perfect" triangle by crowding together units with dissimilar functions. True, it is necessary for reorganizers to keep the flow of authority as direct as is practicable and to eliminate all superfluous intermediate offices; but if they begin their studies by considering the services and needs of each basic unit, they will often find that it is wiser to create more—in place of fewer—supervisory divisions and bureaus. They should first discover the best organization for each unit by comprehending its needs, not on the top level but on the operational level.

The Structure of Units. Each unit should be organized to perform its specific task. The functions of most units can be accomplished under the supervision of *single administrators;* however, some require *commissions* and others can best be managed by *government corporations.*

UNITS UNDER SINGLE ADMINISTRATORS. Ordinarily, administrative work requires unity of purpose and promptness in execution. These aims are most often executed efficiently by placing single administrators in charge of offices which are engaged in the enforcement of laws and the performance of day-to-day tasks.

COMMISSIONS. A commission should supervise a unit (1) when the work of the unit requires bipartisan representation, (2) when it involves controversial issues that are unprecedented in public regulation, or (3) when it demands extensive use of sublegislative and quasi-judicial powers.

GOVERNMENT CORPORATIONS. A government corporation is a corporate business enterprise conducted by the state in the interest of general social and economic welfare.[2] Its organization is similar to a private corporation: it has a legal charter, capital stock (wholly owned by the state), a board of directors, and a management responsible to the directors. Like a private corporation, it provides goods and services to the public and in turn receives payment.

Governmental corporations are freer than regular agencies from direct legislative or executive control: from dependence upon specific legislative appropriations of funds, from minute executive supervision, and from civil service specifications on staffing and salaries. (The government corporations of the United States lost some of their autonomy in 1945 when Congress subjected their financial operations to the scrutiny of budgeting and accounting authorities. Those of Great Britain are attached to appropriate ministries which they are obliged to consult on matters of policy. In Russia, on the other hand, there has been a trend towards transferring authority from heads of governmental departments to independent corporation directors and managers.)

THE CIVIL SERVICE

The *civil service* includes all appointed officers or employees of government except members of the armed forces. Although the term excludes legislators and executives, it includes high administrative officers such as the assistant secretaries in the United States and the undersecretaries who manage ministries in European governments; professional experts, such as the economists who furnish data for legislative and executive decisions and the

---

[2] In many countries, the provision of adequate water supplies and the provision of adequate means of communication and transportation are considered matters for governmental rather than for private enterprise. The United States has both regional and federal government corporations. One *regional corporation* is the Port of New York Authority, which is owned by the states of New York and New Jersey and which operates the greatest seaport and three of the most important commercial airports of the world. The many *federal* corporations include the Tennessee Valley Authority (TVA), the Home Owners' Loan Corporation (HOLC), and the Reconstruction Finance Corporation (RFC). For a compact survey of government corporations, see Jack Taylor, *Business and Government: An Introduction*, College Outline Series (New York: Barnes & Noble, Inc., 1952), pp. 209-25.

scientists who conduct research in governmental laboratories; publicly employed accountants and clerical workers; and many skilled and unskilled public employees such as policemen, letter carriers, and manual workers in arsenals and shipyards.

Since public administration can not be more efficient than the men and women who operate it, civil servants should be selected with extreme care and should be guaranteed conditions of tenure, promotion, and discipline that will foster devotion to duty—certainly, any condition should be avoided that would impair a civil servant's obligation to give unqualified loyalty to his government or to grant equal treatment to all persons.

Appointment of Personnel. Personnel may be chosen through the so-called "spoils system," through a merit system (as in most European countries), or through a combination of the two (as in the United States).

THE SPOILS SYSTEM. The expression *spoils system* derives from the slogan that "to the victor belongs the spoils of the enemy." It signifies a wholesale dismissal of civil service incumbents whenever a newly elected party takes power and a wholesale redistribution of appointive offices to applicants who have worked for the success of the winning party or who enjoy the patronage of winning politicians. Under such a practice, every newly appointed officer has a strong temptation to subordinate public interest to the interest of his party or patron and to grant favors accordingly; even if he does not yield to the temptation, his activities still will be open to suspicion. Use of the spoils method degrades the civil service by filling public administrative offices with many who are poorly qualified and by excluding or discharging many who are well qualified; it degrades political parties, too, by injecting sordid motives into campaigns which should revolve upon issues of public interest.

THE MERIT SYSTEM. The *merit system* of selecting personnel is based upon candidates' demonstrations of capacity for public office. Under a merit system, tenure is permanent so long as the government needs a particular type of service and so long as an individual appointee is competent to provide it. Thus the appointee is freed from fear of removal on partisan grounds and in return is required to disregard his own party affiliations and to co-operate impartially with all superiors.

In order that political pressures may be minimized, the merit system is operated by a nonpartisan, or at least a bipartisan, body (e.g., in the United States, the *civil service commission*). Such a body recruits personnel by advertising opportunities for public employment, by giving written examinations, by interviewing applicants, by studying credentials, and by supplying a list of certified candidates to the authorities who make appointments. It (or another agency) classifies civil service positions according to broad types of work and within each class establishes grades and subgrades so that those who do equivalent tasks will receive equal pay.

PRACTICE IN THE UNITED STATES. The United States tends to rely less generally than do European countries upon a merit system of appointment and to insist much less strongly that public administration is a unique career that requires special preparation.

Since the passage of the Pendleton Act of 1883 the federal government has gradually extended its use of the merit system; today nearly all federal offices are filled by competitive examination. Yet important positions are likely to be filled by nomination of the president plus the approval of the Senate; that approval, under the custom of "senatorial courtesy," is often contingent upon the preferences of the senators from a particular state. Many American state and municipal public agencies are staffed by out-and-out spoils methods. Some states did not begin to use merit systems until 1939, when Congress required its use in the selection of personnel for activities financed in whole or in part by federal grants.

Conditions of Appointment and Promotion. Most European merit systems differ from those of the United States in the following ways: (1) They attempt to create a professional civil service, in which governmental workers as a body are distinguished by special training from other civilian workers, and they attempt limit shifting back and forth between public and private employment. (2) Within the civil service they draw definite lines between classes of employees ranging from a high administrative class to various technical, clerical, and manual classes. Critics have charged that European merit systems really stratify the civil service according to the ranks of European society. Furthermore, they place primary emphasis upon the development of the "administrative" class. Persons wishing to enter this class must first complete a specified and rigorous course of study at a university or special training school: diplomas and recommendations will be taken into account together with ratings in competitive examinations. In Great Britain, candidates for this class must undergo written examinations which ordinarily are passable only by honor graduates of the great universities; candidates for technical and clerical positions must undergo tests of intelligence and of aptitude as well as of proficiency; those for manual jobs are usually selected from the lists of regular employment agencies and are excused from written examinations on the fairly substantial ground that no written examination can measure a person's capacity to do physical labor. (3) European systems are designed for the recruitment of young men and women who will make lifetime careers of government service and who will be promoted from position to position within their respective classes. Promotions from class to class, though sometimes possible, are rare; but a young man who enters, say, the administrative class hopes to rise by successive stages until ultimately he may reach the position of bureau head or permanent undersecretary. Such promotion policies have resulted in a relatively low turnover of personnel in the civil service systems of Europe.

The United States, on the other hand, has taken few steps towards creating a specially trained civil service. Maximum age limits for eligibility to the civil service are much higher than in Europe. Where merit systems are used, appointments and promotions to the lower positions commonly depend upon the taking of written examinations separately keyed to each particular job; for more important posts, the applicant is required to submit his credentials and samples of his work. Although experience in civil service work is given preference, qualified newcomers may take examinations and step into good positions which senior civil service employees long to secure. Discontent with promotional methods is cited as a principal cause for the huge personnel turn over in the American civil service.

Conditions of Discipline and Removal. In the civil service, it is easier to avoid disciplinary problems than to solve them. Discipline within the system depends partly upon the preservation of an efficient group morale within each agency, partly upon the supervisor's power to raise or lower the civil service ratings of those under him, and partly upon more positive measures. Where there is a good *esprit de corps,* lazy, careless, or indifferent employees will usually feel the opprobrium of their fellows. Where this is ineffective, loss of privileges, reprimands (entered upon the record of each civil servant), suspension without pay, and removal are successively in order.

Although a civil servant is protected from arbitrary discharge, many reasonable grounds exist for removal—ranging from inefficiency and excessive partisan activity to dishonesty. In the United States, under federal civil service regulations, an employee is entitled to a written statement of the reasons for his discharge and is authorized to make a written reply. Under most state regulations, he is allowed an open hearing on the charges and an opportunity to defend himself. Proof of charges of incompetence or inefficiency, of course, is difficult; supervisory officers often refrain from making charges against an incompetent individual and allow him to remain in the service.

18 Public Finance

One of the knottiest problems of politics is to maintain a balance between popular pressures for new or better governmental services and popular resistance to increased taxation. Sooner or later all public services must be paid for by the people. Consequently, certain questions must be asked: Will the creation of a particular service impose an excessive tax burden? How can waste be prevented in administration? Which tax system will be preferable? What conditions justify going into debt? How can the debt be retired?

The science of *public finance* seeks to provide answers to these questions and to many others that concern expenditures, financial administration, taxation, and public indebtedness. It links the principles of sound economics with the principles of good government. Without it, governmental extravagance and financial mismanagement could lead successively to unjustly burdensome taxes and debt loads; to overissues of paper currency, inflation, and dislocations in the economy; and, finally, to severe internal crises.

GOVERNMENTAL EXPENDITURES

Extraordinary spending is frequently justifiable in times of emergency; yet it may be in times of quiet and prosperity that administrators become most susceptible to slogans about "spending as usual" and most tempted to overlook the legitimate reasons for expenditures and the sound principles which should govern all outlays of public funds.

Reasons for Expenditures. In the United States the majority of legitimate expenditures can be classified as essential for (1) national defense, (2) public services, and (3) public relief during economic emergencies.

NATIONAL DEFENSE. By far the greatest expenditures have to do with defense and warfare. These comprise costs of military preparedness, actual expenses during war, and the payment for past wars (pensions to veterans, interest on war debts, and retirement of debts).

PUBLIC SERVICES. At all times, expenditures are necessary to pay the salaries of governmental employees, to carry on the administration of justice, to support public education, to see that highways are built and repaired, and to provide countless other services which may not be easily measurable as to value but which go far *in toto* towards spelling the differences between good and bad government.

EMERGENCY RELIEF. Heavy expenditures are required to meet crises in peacetime. Stable governments must be prepared to supply large-scale employment on public works and to undertake other relief measures in periods of depression.

Principles of Expenditure. Executive plans for spending and legislative curbs upon it must be in accord with sound principles.

OVER-ALL CONSIDERATIONS. All expenditures must be directed towards public welfare; even though such outlays as those for subsidization of private businesses may benefit special groups, their only justification lies in their immediate or ultimate benefits to the state as a whole. Total public expenditures should not be allowed to exceed indefinitely total national revenue: legislators, executives, and the public itself must sometimes be reminded that maximum limits exist in proportion to the wealth and income of the people beyond which governmental spending can not safely go. Expenditures must be explained to the public: since the public is the party most interested, it has a right to understand the reasons for important governmental outlays and to compare the intended benefits with the costs.

CONSIDERATIONS RELATING TO NEW SERVICES. It follows that a government should undertake to provide new services only when available and anticipated revenues are adequate to cover the cost, that preference should be given to the services that will prove most beneficial to the public, and that future administrative and operative expenses should be carefully estimated before a new service is created.

CONSIDERATIONS RELATING TO PUBLIC WORKS. Administrators should plan the construction of public buildings and public works far ahead of actual needs so that they may take advantage of low prices for materials in times of depression and may give gainful employment to laborers who have been laid off by private business.

CONSIDERATIONS RELATING TO GOVERNMENT BUSINESS ENTERPRISES. Administrators must weigh the impending sacrifices of tax revenues against the estimated benefits of proposed government business enterprises. Whether such enterprises are operated at a profit or at a loss, the public must ultimately pay for the services.[1]

CONSIDERATIONS OF ECONOMY. Administrators should take advantage of the great savings that are possible through centralized purchasing and through the buying of goods of standard specifications in bulk.

GOVERNMENTAL FINANCIAL ORGANIZATION

Efficient financial organization requires (1) a budget system for the planning of balanced expenditures and revenues and (2) a system of control and audit for proper custody of funds—this means a controller's office (frequently under executive jurisdiction) to check disbursements, and an auditor's office (frequently under legislative jurisdiction) to examine the accounts of administrative agencies.

The Budget System. A *budget* is a detailed financial program (prepared in advance of the fiscal year to which it applies) in which anticipated expenditures and anticipated revenues are itemized and exactly balanced. The word "balance" demands stress; for a so-called *unbalanced budget* (a program in which expenditures exceed ordinary revenues) is really a contradiction of terms. Good budget practice even underestimates anticipated tax receipts in order to safeguard against any possible decline in revenues during the year, and it plans its expenditures to conform to that underestimation. It is considered wise, particularly during peacetime, for administrators to refrain from making ex-

---

[1] Some European states monopolize the tobacco and match industries and use the profits for revenue, whereas other states leave these industries to private enterprise and impose an excise tax upon production. In the first case, the public pays the revenues when it buys the goods from the government; in the second, it pays the revenues when it buys the goods from manufacturers.

penditures that exceed the national income rather than continuing to increase the public debt.

Of course, there are emergency occasions when governments have to resort to heavy borrowing. Moreover, small governmental units, such as American states and cities, sometimes find an advantage in keeping not merely a balanced *current budget* that provides for routine expenditures on a "pay-as-you-go" plan, but also a *capital outlays budget* that requires borrowing for extraordinary necessities, like new school buildings, which are to be of long-time public benefit and which can be afforded only through spreading costs over several years.

Experience shows that budgets are best prepared under the personal responsibility of the chief executive and then submitted to the legislature for emendation, approval, and the voting of necessary taxes. On the one hand, the executive is in a position to know administrative needs and their costs. On the other, the legislature is in a position to give closer and more disinterested scrutiny to a proposed program if it has had no share in the preparation.[2]

EXECUTIVE PREPARATION OF THE BUDGET. Where budget-preparation is assigned to the executive, as in the federal government of the United States and the government of Great Britain, the following steps are customary: (1) Long before a budget is due to be presented to the legislature, the budget officer (in the United States, the Director of the Budget; in Great Britain, the Chancellor of the Exchequer) calls upon heads of departments and independent administrative units to submit estimates of the funds they shall need during the forthcoming year. (2) After he receives the estimates he makes a detailed investigation to determine to what extent they are reasonable. (3) He then drafts an itemized statement which combines the needs of all the spending agencies and balances it against a statement of anticipated income; if there is a discrepancy, he makes suggestions for increases in current tax rates or for new taxes. (4) The budget officer tenders his balanced draft to the executive (whether president or cabinet) for revision and approval. (5) The executive assumes complete responsibility for the budget and presents it to

---

[2] Nevertheless, some of our forty-eight states do vest preparation of the budget in legislative committees or in commissions representing legislature and governor.

the legislature with recommendations of needed taxes and possible increases in the public debt.[3]

LEGISLATIVE ACTION ON THE BUDGET. The legislature now critically studies the balanced program of the executive, approves or revises its details, makes appropriations, and provides for raising the necessary revenues.

The House of Commons of Great Britain has a long-standing rule against either increasing estimated expenditures or adding new items. It may reduce proposed expenditures and it may eliminate items from the budget. Furthermore, through the work of its Committee on Accounts, the House approaches the task of raising funds expertly with full information about the successes and failures of past governmental operations.

In the United States, on the other hand, either house of Congress may increase outlays or add new items at any point. Hence, Congress reopens the entire question of expenditures;[4] it completely vitiates the principle that the president's budget should be studied as a balanced whole, for both houses begin by separating the study of expenditures from the study of revenues. The problem of expenditures is assigned to the Senate and House committees on appropriations, that of revenues respectively to the Finance Committee and the Committee on Ways and Means.

Control and Audit. After the budget has been modified and accepted by the legislature, careful watch must be kept over the handling of public funds. This means that there must be (1) a *controller's office* to examine vouchers and see that they are in proper form, that they are signed by responsible officers, and that they are restricted to items for which appropriations have been made, and (2) an *auditor's office* to analyze all accounts and see that those who receive and disburse public funds can answer for all the money which passes through their hands. Auditing presents a most complex and difficult problem, for few governments actually know where they stand at any given time or how well their undertakings are conforming to the budgetary program.

Although control is essentially an executive function and audit

---

[3] In the United States, this is the occasion of the president's "annual budget message."

[4] Individual congressmen and congressional committees may be willing to reconsider the requests which department heads make for funds, even though these have been overruled by the executive and even though department heads are forbidden to go directly to Congress.

essentially a legislative one, the office of Comptroller General of the United States[5] was set up by Congress in 1921 in such a way as to make it practically independent of the executive; and, unfortunately, this office has emphasized the control function to the neglect of the auditing function. Administrative experts now recommend that control should be placed under the Treasury Department and that an "Auditor General's" office should be created to supply Congress with information about the fidelity and efficiency with which administrators handle public funds.

TAXATION

A *tax* is a compulsory payment exacted by legislative authority for the support of the government and the maintenance of public services. It may be levied against persons (either individuals or "legal persons" such as corporations) or against property. Its purpose may be *fiscal* (designed primarily to bring money into the public treasury), *regulative* (calculated to achieve other governmental ends, such as the betterment of domestic industry), or both. In effect, it may be *direct* (so imposed that the immediate taxpayer must bear its whole burden—as he must with poll taxes, sales taxes, personal income taxes, inheritance taxes, and some forms of property tax) or *indirect* (so imposed that the immediate taxpayer may shift the burden to others—as he may with customs duties and excises).

Over-all Considerations. Taxes supply practically all revenues of a modern government.[6] No matter how they are levied, they must be paid from the income or the accumulated savings of the public; hence, tax policies will affect the trends of industry, investment, and consumption within the state. It is the problem of a legislature to adopt tax policies which will insure adequate revenue and which will distribute tax burdens equitably.

THE SHIFTING OF TAXES. The individual who pays the tax

---

[5] For details concerning the appointment and duties of the Comptroller General, see E. C. Smith and A. J. Zurcher, *Dictionary of American Politics,* an Everyday Handbook (New York: Barnes & Noble, Inc., 1955).

[6] Governments do receive important, but scarcely major, amounts of revenue from fees (imposed for the issuance of licenses and for other services), fines, forfeitures of property, and special assessments (such as those placed upon property owners who are to benefit from street improvements). They also receive whatever profits may accrue from state-owned corporations or other business enterprises.

collector is not necessarily identical with the person on whom the burden of any tax falls. All *indirect* taxes are shiftable. In our world of trade, businessmen compensate for indirect taxes by raising prices, their customers compensate by raising prices in turn, and, finally, the ultimate consumer pays the amount of the tax. Furthermore, many so-called "direct" taxes are partly or wholly shiftable; thus, renting an office or a house means paying a percentage of the landlord's real-estate tax and buying a factory-made article means helping to pay the manufacturer's taxes on buildings, machinery, and materials.

EXEMPTIONS FROM TAXATION. If public welfare is a main reason for taxation, it would be inconsistent for governments to tax organizations that are themselves devoted to promotion of public welfare. Therefore, most states exempt property of recognized organizations which is used for exclusively educational, philanthropic, or religious purposes. Under the Constitution of the United States the forty-eight state legislatures may not tax federal bonds, and the federal government may not tax state and local bonds.

Some constitutions permit legislatures and local government bodies to grant other exemptions. But questions of serious concern arise. Is a local government justified when it induces business firms to settle in its community by guaranteeing them low taxes? Or is it justified when during a housing shortage it promises remission of taxes for a period of years to corporations that agree to construct needed buildings? In either example, immediate public welfare must be weighed against the injustice of unequal taxation. National legislators face the same dilemma.

Constitutional Provisions. Most constitutions place basic checks upon the use of tax money and upon the taxing powers of legislators. Thus the Constitution of the United States restricts use of the proceeds of federal taxation to promotion of general welfare, provision for common defense, and payment of public debts; it forbids the taxing of exports; it requires that Congress levy taxes uniformly (i.e., that it show no favoritism to particular states or to particular economic groups). Yet it places no maximum limit upon tax rates (legally these could be set so high as to amount almost to confiscation of property), and makes no distinction between taxpayers on the basis of either their ability to pay or the benefit they derive from membership in the state. Hence, the Constitution leaves wide latitude to the discretion of Congress.

Kinds of Taxes. Many different taxes are levied by governments and their subdivisions. Some have the merit of producing large revenues. Others contribute little to the public treasury, but accomplish desirable social purposes. Some taxes impose greater proportionate burdens than others on different groups in the population. Taxes vary greatly in the relative ease or difficulty of assessment and collection.

INCOME TAXES. In the United States, an *income tax* is "a tax levied upon corporate and individual incomes in excess of specified amounts and less certain deductions permitted by law."[7] A small specified exemption is permitted for subsistence, but net incomes exceeding this amount are taxed with proportionately increasing rates according to the "financial bracket" of each taxpayer—the theory being that a person's ability to pay taxes increases more rapidly as his income becomes higher and higher.[8]

Income taxes have been the chief source of federal revenue in the United States since the ratification of the Sixteenth Amendment in 1913, and they are important sources of revenue in many of the forty-eight states. Income taxes are direct; they allow little if any opportunity for a corporate or individual taxpayer to shift his burden. Income tax laws are difficult to administer because they pose serious problems for both taxpayer and collector in the determination of taxable net income, and they often leave the way open to tax avoidance.

ESTATE, INHERITANCE, AND GIFT TAXES. An *estate tax* is one levied upon the total net value of the property of a deceased person. An *inheritance tax* is one levied upon that part of an estate which each heir receives. A *gift tax* is one levied upon the value of goods or the amount of money which may be bestowed by one living person upon another (such a tax is intended to prevent avoidance of estate and inheritance taxes by those who give away property and money in anticipation of death). Laws concerning estate and inheritance taxes may allow exemptions or deduc-

---

[7] H. S. Sloan and A. J. Zurcher, *A Dictionary of Economics,* an Everyday Handbook (New York: Barnes & Noble, Inc., 1953).

[8] Corporation income taxes constitute a real exception because each stockholder's share of the profits is taxed at the same rate, regardless of the size of his own income.

tions for gifts to educational, philanthropic, and religious institutions. As with income taxes, they exempt small estates and small bequests but apply sharply progressive rates to larger ones. The laws usually provide varying rates of inheritance taxes according to the relationship of an heir to the deceased, making them lower for widows and children than for distant relatives.

All such taxes provide important (though somewhat unstable) sources of revenue for federal and state governments. Many authorities think that rates should be made generally higher in order to help equalize disparities of wealth among taxpayers.

PROPERTY TAXES. Property taxes include the *general property tax* levied upon all kinds of property in proportion to their value, the *land tax* levied usually upon unimproved land, the *real-estate tax* levied often upon both unimproved and improved land, and the *personal property tax* levied variously upon stocks and bonds or such items as home furnishings.

Until the present century, general property taxes were the chief source of revenue in the forty-eight states of our country; today, real-estate taxes (and sometimes personal property taxes which are assessed at lower rates) may still be main sources for states and smaller units such as counties, townships, and municipal corporations. Property taxes may be hard to administer: in an agricultural economy where nearly all property is "tangible" (i.e., consists of land, buildings, and livestock), general property taxes are fair and equitable; in a more advanced economy where much property is "intangible" (i.e., consists of stocks and bonds), such taxes are difficult to assess fairly.

CUSTOMS DUTIES (EXTERNAL REVENUE[9]). A *customs duty* is a tax levied on important freight at the place of entry. This duty may be *ad valorem* (assessed according to the value of the goods) or *specific* (assessed according to the physical characteristics of the goods, such as their weight or bulk). The rate of duty is called a *tariff*.

Customs duties may be either fiscal or regulative. If fiscal, such duties are frequently levied upon goods which can not be produced sufficiently within a country, and legislators try to make tariffs high enough to yield satisfactory returns yet not so high as to impede consumption; these customs duties were for a long

---

[9] Taxation of imports is called *external revenue;* other forms of taxation are collectively called *internal revenue.*

time the chief reliance of our own federal government for revenue and they are still a mainstay. If regulative, such duties are confined largely to goods which compete with domestic produce, and legislators try to make tariffs so high as to discourage consumption of imported articles. Sometimes tariffs are *discriminatory* (set unequally upon the imports received from different countries) and *retaliatory* (used as a bargaining device to compel specific foreign countries to reduce their artificial trade barriers); often they are *protective* (designed to safeguard the welfare of domestic industry as a whole against foreign competition,[10] or to safeguard certain selected domestic industries against the dumping[11] of foreign products).

Customs duties are indirect and relatively easy for governments to administer. They are indirect because the importer immediately pays the duties and adds their amount to the prices for the goods. They are easy to collect because they are levied upon goods at the port of entry.

EXCISE TAXES. An *excise tax* is a tax placed upon some phase of the production or the distribution of goods within a country. Although the term is often loosely applied to all internal revenue taxes except those on income, it means essentially a tax collected from manufacturers rather than from retailers. Such a tax is rarely placed upon foods and other necessities of life, but if it is to yield worthwhile revenue it must be levied upon articles that are widely consumed. Excise taxes are indirect; often they are unfair to different groups of consumers because they usually place a heavier proportion of the burden upon the poor than upon the rich. (Theoretically, the poor could ameliorate their burden by purchasing fewer goods, but actually other groups can more easily adjust their habits of consumption.)

---

[10] Slogans about insuring "a balanced economy," combatting "cheap foreign labor," and saving "the American standard of living" are repeatedly employed by beneficiaries of protective tariffs; but economists point out that the whole structure of international trade depends upon equivalence of importation and exportation. For a brief record of the ups and downs of protective-tariff policies in our national history, see E. C. Smith and A. J. Zurcher, *Dictionary of American Politics,* an Everyday Handbook (New York: Barnes & Noble, Inc., 1955), pp. 365–6.

[11] Broadly the term means "selling a product in a foreign market below the price for which the same product is sold in the domestic market." A concise explanation of *dumping* will be found in H. S. Sloan and A. J. Zurcher, *A Dictionary of Economics,* an Everyday Handbook (New York: Barnes & Noble, Inc., 1953).

SALES TAXES. A general *sales tax* differs from an excise in two important respects: (1) it is usually collected not from the producer but through the retailer and (2) it is placed upon practically every article of goods sold (though it may exempt goods that are considered necessities of life).

Sales taxes are fiscal in intent: in the United States they were first widely used by state and local governments during the Depression of 1929, and they have continued to be used for state and local revenue. Sales taxes are felt most by the poorer classes of society. Sales taxes are not everywhere easily administered: since local tax rates differ, some buyers can evade local rates or even avoid paying taxes by making purchases in neighboring areas where taxes are lower or nonexistent.[12]

The Essentials of a Good Tax System. Obviously there is no perfect tax. A taxing system should include several taxes in order that the good and bad points of each may be balanced. Although the fundamental objective in levying taxes is to provide adequate revenue for governmental operation, the best taxes, as has been implied, are those which show the greatest consideration for taxpayers and those which are the most efficient and economical to administer. Certainly a good system should have nothing to do with *nuisance taxes*—taxes which cause hardship or inconvenience that is out of proportion to the amount of revenue they yield.

To provide adequate revenue (1) total collections must be sufficient to cover governmental expenses (though the rates should never be so high as to dry up the sources of revenue); (2) the system should be sufficiently flexible to insure adequate public income throughout cycles of prosperity, depression, and recovery; and (3) the system must be readily adaptable to extraordinary emergencies, such as war.

In fairness to taxpayers (1) exactions should be uniform among groups of similar economic status, (2) rates should be adjusted to the ability of individuals to pay, and (3) payments should be required at the seasons most propitious to taxpayers' systems of accounting and receipts of income.

For efficient administration (1) the tax system must bring the government net returns that are commensurate with the money

---

[12] Some state and local governments have endeavored to preclude evasion by levying a *use tax* upon articles purchased outside their bounds, but such a tax is hard to collect.

exacted from the public (no tax is justifiable if it requires so many assessors, collectors, inspectors, and reviewers that the money collected amounts to little more than their combined salaries); (2) tax laws must be so definite that collectors and taxpayers understand what is really demanded; and (3) laws regulating payments must be so simple and clear that collectors may reasonably demand co-operation from taxpayers and may prevent evasions.

PUBLIC DEBTS

Practically all states and their subdivisions are deeply in debt; practically all have serious budgetary problems of paying interest upon debts and of amortizing them. The time has long since passed when rulers could solve such problems simply by compelling wealthy subjects to make "loans" that might never be repaid. Governments today, if they are economically and politically stable, must devise valid programs for repayment.[13]

Reasons for Governmental Borrowing. If tax revenues could be quickly expanded to meet the costs of emergencies and to provide funds for imperatively needed improvements, there would be little reason for governmental borrowing. Most debts are incurred during times of war or other real emergency. Some of the remainder are incurred to construct toll bridges, buildings for government business enterprises, or public works that should prove self-liquidating.[14] Some debts are incurred (especially by local governments) to provide roads, schools, and other benefits which should prove useful for a long period of time and the cost of which, it is felt, can justly be shared with future taxpayers. Some are incurred because legislators dodge the responsibility of imposing taxes sufficient to cover current expenditures.

Methods of Borrowing. Compared with private borrowers, most governments are in an enviable position: their credit is good and their interest rates are low. (Investors know that a

---

[13] Desperate governments do sometimes resort to the printing press and issue paper currency that amounts to a forced loan. Almost always (unless it has sufficient backing and the issuance is adequately controlled), the currency is looked upon with suspicion. "Bad money drives out good"; serious inflation and successive devaluations of the paper money follow, and economic and political stability vanishes.

[14] Governments of course are obligated to pay their creditors whether or not the investments prove financially successful.

government, through its taxing powers, does have means to repay debts; consequently, they are willing to accept smaller interest on governmental than on other types of securities.) Governmental securities normally consist of (1) short-term *treasury warrants* issued to sustain a small floating debt in anticipation of tax receipts, (2) *treasury notes* issued for relatively brief periods and carrying a larger amount of public debt, and (3) *government bonds* sold preferably to individals rather than banks and issued for longer periods—the latter carry by far the greatest part of the public debt.

Methods of Payment. Public debts are paid off from the proceeds of taxes. Governments should follow these sound practices: (1) make provision for repayment at the time they borrow; (2) pay off their debts as rapidly as possible; (3) issue bonds which mature at definite dates within twenty years or less; and (4) set aside annually from tax receipts sums sufficient to pay off the bonds.

The primary merit of borrowing through bonds that mature in five, ten, or twenty years is that governments are under continuous pressure to pay them off. Both Great Britain and France have had unfortunate experiences with perpetual loans, which lulled their governments into a sense of false security. Subsidiary or local governments frequently find it advisable to issue *serial bonds,* a certain number of which mature each year over the period of a loan: this device is economical and provides for the systematic retirement of bonds.

Another device to facilitate repayment is the *sinking fund,* into which a certain amount of tax revenue is required to be paid each year. Such a fund is invested and, if the investment is well managed, permits the retirement of government bonds when they mature—or better yet permits its trustees to buy in the open market and retire the bonds before the date of maturity.

However, governments often resort to refunding—to the issuance of new bonds in exchange for old ones which have come due. This means the postponement of debt retirement. Refunding is disadvantageous, unless alert treasury officials can take advantage of temporarily low interest rates for the conversion of the debt into bonds with lower interest rates than the old.

19   *Local Government*

A *local government* (the term includes French *departements*, British counties, American cities, and a wide variety of other organizations) is a subordinate territorial unit that owes its creation and existence to a state and that derives its powers from general laws or from charters or other specific grants made by that state. Usually it has a more or less complete governmental framework, all or some of whose officers are elected by resident voters; in most cases it has been given limited taxing powers.[1] In France and in other Continental countries, local governments are rigidly supervised by the central system and possess little freedom of action; contrariwise, local governments in the United States usually are autonomous except insofar as they are subordinate to the state.

STATE POWER OVER LOCAL GOVERNMENT

Local governments are established on the principles of both decentralization and deconcentration of state power, and they are created for the following reasons: (1) They are of administrative convenience to the state because it would be unwise for a state legislature to spend time trying to obtain information about the varying needs for governmental services among the many territorial groups within its populace. (2) They satisfy the practical demands of the populace for self-government in matters that are not of state-wide concern. (Certainly the local populace knows

---

[1] Legally, local governments bear close resemblance to those units of administration (Chapter 17) that have been endowed with sublegislative powers and with discretionary powers to enforce laws or to carry on business enterprises. They must, however, be sharply distinguished from administrative districts (like internal revenue collection districts), which are controlled by a central national office.

177

TERRITORIAL SUBDIVISIONS OF FRANCE, GREAT BRITAIN, AND THE UNITED STATES

LOCAL GOV'T.	FRANCE	GREAT BRITAIN	UNITED STATES
			States (48)
FIRST TERRITORIAL SUBDIVISION FOR LOCAL GOVERNMENT	Department (90) Most important political and administrative subdivision.	Historic County (52) Important for political and judicial purposes.	
SECOND TERRITORIAL SUBDIVISION FOR LOCAL GOVERNMENT	Arrondissement (279) Of little administrative significance. Chiefly for electoral purposes.	Administrative County (62) 19th - century creation; of growing importance for administrative purposes.	County (called a "parish" in Louisiana) (over 3,000) With definite administrative importance everywhere except in New England.
THIRD TERRITORIAL SUBDIVISION FOR LOCAL GOVERNMENT	Canton (About 3,000) For judicial and electoral purposes only. Of no importance as a unit of local self-government. Commune (About 44,000) Both rural and urban. The most important basic unit of local self-government.	Rural district which in turn is divided into 643 Rural parishes. Urban (about 13,000) County Borough, boroughs large enough to be separate counties. Borough, urban units with corporate status. Urban district, 778 urban areas not yet elevated to borough status.	RURAL OR SEMI-RURAL Town Township Magisterial District Precinct The above are variously known depending on the part of the country where found. URBAN City County City Town; i.e., the incorporated town. Village Borough

Special Districts—These are found in all three countries. Their boundaries may coincide with those of other units, or may include two or more other units or parts of units.

Common types of special districts are:

1. Drainage
2. Sanitation
3. Port Development
4. Irrigation
5. Highways
6. Schools
7. Public Utility
8. Parks
9. Public Welfare
10. Planning
11. Police
12. Public Works

better than a distant legislature what should be done about such things as the local building ordinances and local traffic problems; also, it can more satisfactorily designate how local revenues should be spent.) (3) They are good for civic morale because they help to foster an interest in and responsibility for public affairs which may be carried into the larger realms of democratic government.

The Creation of Local Governments. In establishing local units and in assigning powers to them, states should observe the following norms: (1) They should attempt to set up units that have homogeneous populations whose affairs need common local management. (2) They should retain the right to rearrange the units without constitutional amendment when local conditions change. (3) They should guard against designating an excessive number of units—so many that there would be overlapping of powers, duplications of functions, and consequent wastage of public funds. (4) They should center the responsibility clearly within each unit, so that separately appointed officers will not find it easy to dodge duties. (5) They should reserve an executive power, if not to appoint, certainly to remove officers entrusted with the administration of state laws. (6) They should properly supervise the exercise of power within local governments—that is, they should work towards the prevention of dishonesty, waste, and inefficiency.

The Supervision of Local Governments. Supervision over local governments may be exercised by the courts in declaring void any acts which are contrary to law or in excess of the powers granted; by the legislature in changing general laws or special acts which apply to localities; and by administrative officers. Of the three, administrative control is regarded as the most effective under modern conditions. State agents from appropriate departments may inspect local units. The state may require uniform systems of accounting and of reporting activities from local units and officers. It may send auditors to audit their accounts. It may set uniform standards in police, educational, and other matters which are important to the state as a whole and may limit taxing and borrowing powers. One of the most effective means of obtaining a local government's co-operation in carrying out state policy is the *grant-in-aid,* by which the state contributes toward the financial support of a local activity on condition that minimum standards set by the state are maintained.

SYSTEMS OF LOCAL GOVERNMENT IN EUROPE AND IN GREAT BRITAIN

The accompanying chart shows the contrast between the French system, which was deliberately created, and the Anglo-American systems of local government, which are the products of a long historical evolution. Patterned after the French model, most Continental systems are distinguishable from each other mainly in the amount of deconcentration of authority which each state permits. There is not a long tradition of local autonomy among them.[2]

Local Government in France. French local governments are rigidly supervised by the Ministry of Interior. The Ministry controls local government services as completely as the postal service is controlled in the United States; it also appoints and instructs local police chiefs. The *departement,* the highest local government unit, makes regulations concerning a limited number of functions through its elective council. Its chief administrative officer is its president; the administration of the *departement* and of its *communes* are constantly supervised by a "prefect" (appointed by the Minister of the Interior). Each *commune* (which may be a tiny village or a large city) has a wide ordinance power which is entrusted to a mayor elected by the council. The prefect of the *departement* may suspend the council and remove the mayor. There is local government in France, but not "local autonomy."

Local Government in Great Britain. In Great Britain the administrative counties and urban units are small democracies with extensive powers delegated by Parliament. The central authorities may set minimum standards but may not suspend or remove local officers. In each local government unit an elective council possesses the power to make appropriations, levy taxes, and adopt local regulations. The actual work of administration

---

[2] In the Soviet Union (which is not shown on the chart), there is a closely knit hierarchical structure for territorial administration reaching down to local town and village soviets. These supervise local production, retail stores, motion-picture theaters, and, in short, a far wider variety of functions than local governments in the West. They are designated officially not as "local governments," but as "local units of state power." The germ of local government exists, however, in the fact that the local soviets are popularly elected, receive detailed "instructions" from their constituents, and are subject to popular recall by majority vote.

LOCAL GOVERNMENT

is done by civil servants under the general supervision of committees of the council. The mayor presides over the council and has ceremonial duties but no greater power than any other councilor. Such an organization appears to be inefficient, and it would be so if the council and its committees did not strictly refrain from dabbling with the details of administration.

PROBLEMS OF RURAL LOCAL GOVERNMENT IN THE UNITED STATES

Though wide variations exist among the local governmental systems of the states of the United States, a definite pattern is discernible. In New England, the town, an area of some thirty or forty square miles around a church, early became the principal unit for local administration. (This did not include judicial administration.) In the South, the county became almost the only local administrative area. In the Middle States, the county and its subdivisions, the towns or townships, were about equally important. As settlement proceeded westward, the Southern and Middle States systems expanded on practically parallel lines. Special districts were also created for particular functions. Though rural local government units usually have no charters of incorporation, they may hold property, make contracts, and sue or be sued in the courts. It is generally characteristic of American local government that each small unit has legal powers distinct from those of larger units.

Counties. Except in New England, where it is chiefly a unit of judicial administration, the county has a great number of functions. Generally these include the construction and upkeep of roads and bridges, the keeping of local records, poor relief, health and welfare administration, the conduct of elections, the assessment and collection of taxes, and the enforcement of state laws. Most counties were created during an era of slow transportation when small counties were considered necessary. Under modern conditions many are too small for economical administration; yet desirable county consolidations have been made in only a few states. Most officers, including the clerks of courts, are popularly elected and are individually responsible to the law for their acts, rather than to a central county authority. For local affairs, the principal governing body is a board or commission which levies taxes, allocates funds, appoints employees, and directs administrative work. Usually it performs its own duties badly and lacks power to control other officers.

All local functions should be centralized in a single responsible commission which should, as in British local government, merely supervise the work of administrators appointed under civil service regulations. In the larger counties which should be created, a county manager should direct the actual work of administration under the general supervision of the county commission.

Deconcentration of state powers to county officers has been excessive. Local prosecuting officers, for instance, may refrain from obtaining indictments and may prosecute some cases half-heartedly or not at all, thus practically nullifying state law. It is highly desirable that those who exercise state functions should be under the supervision and control of appropriate state authorities.

Towns and Townships. The New England town, which performs nearly all the functions that are delegated to counties elsewhere, is sometimes a highly expensive and inefficient local government unit. In other states the towns or townships have diminished in importance as the state has taken over the maintenance of roads or concentrated it in counties.

Special Districts. A special district is a unit created by law for the administration of a single function. It has power to borrow money, to levy taxes, and to apply the proceeds from its operations to the amortization of its debts. The most common special districts are for the administration of education; they were created originally to take the school system out of politics. Other special districts have been created to build and operate public works, such as levees, irrigation systems, and interstate bridges. The activities of most special districts should properly be transferred to reorganized county governments.

SYSTEMS OF MUNICIPAL GOVERNMENT IN THE UNITED STATES

When a small area within a county becomes densely populated, its inhabitants feel the need for additional police and fire protection and for a sewerage system, waterworks, and other facilities which often the county can not legally provide. The individuals of such a community petition the legislature for a charter creating it as a municipal corporation.

This charter is a strictly limited grant of powers. It can not be construed liberally by the courts. It imposes obligations as well as privileges. The municipal corporation may be held liable for damages inflicted on private persons as a result of negligence in the operation of any of its business enterprises. A taxpayer's suit may prevent levying taxes for a project not fully authorized by the charter. Unless county functions are specifically transferred, county officers continue to exercise them within the boundaries of municipal corporations. The state may supervise the city and may amend or take away its charter.

Methods of Granting Charters. In the United States state legislatures have granted city charters in three major ways: (1) by special legislative act, (2) by the classification system, and (3) by the optional charter system.

SPECIAL ACT OF THE LEGISLATURE. At first, every city charter was granted by a special act of the legislature and was amended in the same way. The great expenditure of the legislature's time on such matters and its lack of knowledge of local conditions led to the constitutional prohibition of special acts and to provision for a general charter enacted by law and applicable to every municipality. However, this provision proved to be inflexible. Large cities had insufficient powers to carry on all the functions which their situations required; small cities were overburdened with an unwieldy administrative structure for which they had no use.

THE CLASSIFICATION SYSTEM. Under the classification system, the state legislature enacted a series of three or more charters, each of which was supposed to fit every city within a certain population range. The neglect of factors other than population in setting up this system soon became obvious.

THE OPTIONAL CHARTER SYSTEM. Popular demand then led to the adoption of an optional charter system. Under it the state legislature enacted a greater number of standard charters providing for diversified forms and powers of government. The inhabitants of a city were allowed to choose the charter which suited them best. The optional charter system protects both the state and the locality.

Municipal Home Rule. A large number of state constitutions have from time to time provided for a "home rule" charter system. The charter is drawn up by a charter commission elected by the voters of a city, but the voters must also approve the final draft in a referendum. They may thus provide for any form of government they desire. They may also include within the powers of the municipal corporation anything that is of local concern and that is not prohibited by the federal and state constitutions and laws. Home rule has the manifest merits of (1) enabling the people to make their own charter rather than forcing them to accept one that is handed down to them; (2) stimulating popular interest in local government; (3) placing the responsibility squarely on a locality if things go wrong; and, in such a case, (4) enabling the people to redress their own error. The principal disadvantage of the system is that the legislature frequently feels obliged to alter the provisions of general laws relating to cities in order to prevent local encroachments on state functions or local maladministration. The home rule system does not mean all that the phrase implies.

The Forms of Municipal Government. The earliest American cities had governments copied from the council-and-committee system which was then, and still is, used in Great Britain. It seemed to Americans to violate the principle of separation of powers. Besides, it worked badly in America due to the strong interconnections which prevailed among federal, state, and local party politics. After a time, it was supplanted by the mayor-council form in which there is a single executive. This form is still in effect in about half the cities; but within the present century, the commission form and the council-manager form have become widely used.

THE MAYOR-COUNCIL FORM. Generally speaking, the mayor-council form of government divides and confuses responsibility. The mayor, who is the head of the city administration, is popularly elected. If he lacks the powers of veto and of sole appointment and removal, he is termed a "weak" mayor; if he possesses these powers, he is called "strong." In most examples of this form of government he prepares the budget. The members of the council are elected by the voters—by wards, or from the city at large, or occasionally by proportional representation. The council votes the taxes, makes appropriations, grants franchises to corporations, and passes ordinances making minor regulations on many matters.

THE COMMISSION FORM. The commission form of government

usually consists of three to seven members, one of whom is sometimes elected mayor. In the better-governed cities the mayor's functions are similar to those of the commissioners. Each commissioner is directly elected or assigned to head one of the departments into which the city government is divided. The commission form centralizes total legislative and executive power in a group which appears small enough to be co-operative. However, the concentration of each commissioner on the affairs of his department tends to make them rivals rather than a team which is collectively responsible to the city. In addition, (1) the group is too small to be adequately representative of a large city, (2) the highly technical work of administering departments is usually in the hands of amateurs, and (3) the commission must supervise the work done by each of its own members. The last can scarcely be done without either recrimination or toleration of lax methods.

THE COUNCIL-MANAGER FORM. The council-manager plan provides a remedy for the most serious defects of the commission form. Legislative and executive powers are concentrated in a small elected council, which usually makes ordinances, votes taxes and appropriations, grants franchises, and exercises general supervision over the administration. Contrary to the commission form, the members of the council do not administer the departments; the council appoints a manager for this purpose as well as for appointing subordinates (with due attention to civil service regulations), enforcing state laws and municipal ordinances, and drawing up the budget for council approval. He is responsible to the council in all these things. The plan works well where the manager is the best-qualified man to be found, regardless of whether he was a resident of the city when appointed. In some cases, the council elects a mayor to preside over the council and over ceremonial functions. In this form of government the line of power is drawn, not between the executive and the legislative, but between policy-making and policy enforcement. The council is expected not to interfere in details of administration, but only to set general policies and standards. The council-manager plan is rapidly supplanting the commission and mayor-council forms. It usually provides efficient administration under the control of popularly elected representatives.

Metropolitan Areas. Wherever there is a large city, a group of satellite cities and villages grow up around it. The whole area has a close social and economic interdependence, resulting in the need for governmental co-operation. The problems of metropolitan areas are sometimes acute, especially when the areas cross county or state lines. Methods for solving the problems include (1) the annexation of the satellites to the city; (2) federation of the cities in the area into a "greater" city with subordinate boroughs; (3) sale of services, such as water supply, by the city to the suburban units; (4) creation of special districts for bridge and tunnel connections, port development, sanitation, parks, and water supply; and (5) voluntary co-operation among the cities and towns through long-range planning and exchange of data. When the metropolitan area includes parts of two or more states each state must be consulted and the consent of Congress is required for any agreement among them.

20 *International Relations and Associations*

Political theorists have long been concerned with the relationships among states. Dreams of peaceful co-operation among peoples through universally accepted regulations and of interstate unity are not new. In the early seventeenth century, Henry IV of France (or his minister the Duc de Sully) devised a scheme for a European federation; at a later date, William Penn envisioned a federation that would include not merely the states of Europe but those of all the world. Ideas for promoting international peace formed a part of the political thinking of Immanuel Kant, of Jean Jacques Rousseau, and of Jeremy Bentham. But such proposals were considered "impractical"; at least they came to nothing in an era of rising nationalism and of increasing belief in the doctrine of state sovereignty. Yet dreams have persisted and have had some tangible influence.

Factors such as economic and human geography affect the power of a state in international affairs; other factors to be considered are its political history, national psychology, and economic, military, and foreign policies.

FACTORS UNDERLYING THE POWER OF STATES

Under the conditions of modern warfare, any state which is fully armed and capable of launching an attack at a moment's notice has a tremendous short-term advantage. Military preparedness strengthens its diplomatic position. However, unless it is rich in resources, the maintenance of excessive armaments over a long period will drain its strength and may provoke the rest of the world to combine against it. As a result of many factors, some of which can not be fully controlled, the power of states in relation to one another is constantly changing.

Geographical Factors. The permanence of geography makes it a fundamental factor influencing the power of states. Climate, rainfall, topography, and the fertility of the soil affect the ability of a state to produce food and other products. Location on a seacoast turns the attention of the people to commerce with overseas countries and emphasizes the need for naval power. An interior location, especially if a state is large and populous, may enable it to control lesser states through its ground and air forces. Until at least the twentieth century, a state was in a strong position if its territory was compact rather than dispersed over a wide area. Mountainous terrain is one of the types of easily defended natural boundaries which states, as part of their military policies, have wanted to secure.

Availability of Raw Materials. Completely self-sufficient states are rare; almost every state lacks one or more valuable raw materials. Adequate food supplies, coal, iron ore, and oil are extremely desirable and, for purposes of war, highly essential. Modern steel manufacturing requires a great variety of metals in order to provide the qualities required for all uses. The list of critical materials is long and the need for them can not always be met by devising substitutes or by stockpiling materials in times of peace.

Technological Development. A state may be rich in raw materials and yet be poor, if its resources are undeveloped. In measuring the power of a state, one must take into account its advancement in *technology*—which includes its capacity to produce, the efficiency of its industrial plants, its industrial research, and its development of synthetic materials. Worn-out or obsolete machinery is a handicap because it requires an excessive diversion of manpower to manufacturing and to the maintenance of machinery.

Economic Considerations. When a nation lacks essential materials, it may be able to obtain them from other countries. For Great Britain, which produces only about one-fourth of its own foodstuffs, the maintenance of an effective seagoing commerce is of vital importance. (It is readily understandable why Great Britain emphasized the importance of a navy strong in surface ships, and why her enemies concentrate on submarines.) Trade balances and foreign exchange are often matters of great concern to governments. So, too, is a financial reputation which may enable a state to borrow in the international money market.

Demographic Factors. A state with a large population is not necessarily strong: much depends on the educational advancement and adaptability of the people. A state which is overpopulated sometimes directs its governmental policies toward expanding its territory; but it might better solve its economic problems by directing its policies towards development of manufacturing or, in a lesser degree, towards providing means for emigration.

A state which is underpopulated in relation to its resources is in a happier position because it can add to its numbers by a controlled system of immigration and by encouraging the internal migration of its people. Potentially the best prospects for large population increases are in countries like the Soviet Union, Canada, Australia, and South Africa, where there is still unoccupied land and incomplete development of manufacturing industries. It is estimated that the populations of the Western European states, which have been in the forefront of industrial production, will hereafter remain static or will beyond that start to decline.

Political Considerations. Of course, political factors exert a great influence on the power of states. Democracy and totalitarianism seem to be about equally balanced in their ability to use force in the international field. For swift preparation against a vaguely foreseen danger, totalitarian rulers have the advantage because their plans can be executed without discussion. On the other hand, the energy and adaptability of a democracy under the capitalist system can often make up for the disadvantage of a later start.

Psychological Considerations. National history and ideologies evince strong and unified emotional responses from peoples. Sometimes a traditional enmity prevents a nation from following its own best interests. Suppositions as to the intentions of foreign governments are influenced by national likes and dislikes. The attachment of a people to its own form of government and its own institutions—in other words, its "popular morale"—is an important factor in its strength or weakness.

LEAGUE OF NATIONS

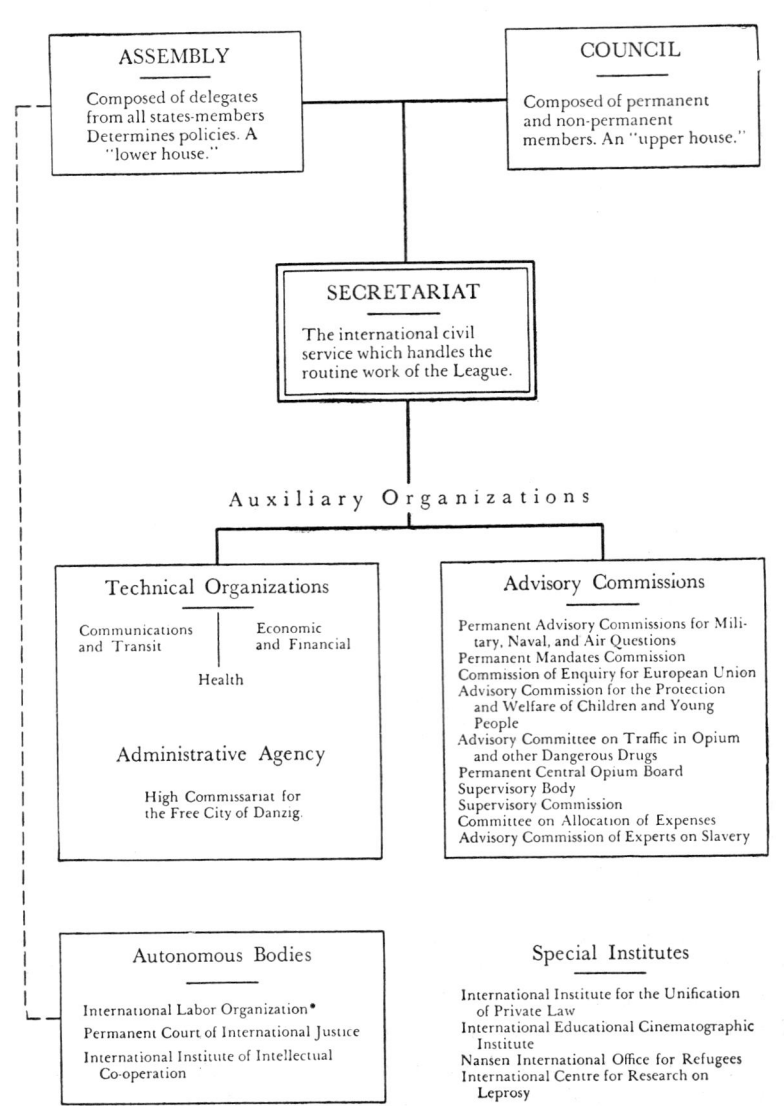

ASSEMBLY
Composed of delegates from all states-members. Determines policies. A "lower house."

COUNCIL
Composed of permanent and non-permanent members. An "upper house."

SECRETARIAT
The international civil service which handles the routine work of the League.

Auxiliary Organizations

Technical Organizations
Communications and Transit | Economic and Financial
Health

Administrative Agency
High Commissariat for the Free City of Danzig.

Advisory Commissions
Permanent Advisory Commissions for Military, Naval, and Air Questions
Permanent Mandates Commission
Commission of Enquiry for European Union
Advisory Commission for the Protection and Welfare of Children and Young People
Advisory Committee on Traffic in Opium and other Dangerous Drugs
Permanent Central Opium Board
Supervisory Body
Supervisory Commission
Committee on Allocation of Expenses
Advisory Commission of Experts on Slavery

Autonomous Bodies
International Labor Organization*
Permanent Court of International Justice
International Institute of Intellectual Co-operation

Special Institutes
International Institute for the Unification of Private Law
International Educational Cinematographic Institute
Nansen International Office for Refugees
International Centre for Research on Leprosy

*See Organization of the United Nations

POLICIES FOR MAINTAINING THE MATERIAL INTERESTS OF STATES

National policies for the utilization of a state's economic resources and opportunities follow patterns of self-interest and aggrandizement. Generally, the emphasis is upon immediate national advantage rather than upon long-run national advantages that might inure from the establishment of an orderly international economic system. Policies such as economic nationalism, colonialism, imperialism, and regionalism lead constantly to international tensions which are often the causes of war.

Economic Nationalism. Since 1776, most economists have held that the surest path to national wealth is for a state to produce those articles for which it is best fitted and to buy others in the cheapest markets. Despite this fact, few states have followed free-trade policies. The present almost universal trend is to reserve the domestic market for domestic products and to exclude foreign goods by means of high tariffs, artificially high exchange rates, inspection fees, and other measures (such as excessive delays in granting clearances to ships). Under present world conditions, this policy is justifiable only for articles that are of critical importance in time of war; furthermore, it is sometimes justifiable as a temporary expedient when a state is beginning its industrialization and its producers need help in establishing a market. The trouble with such a policy is that the individuals who benefit look to their own selfish interests and not to the national interest. They argue that any relaxation of trade restrictions would cause dislocations in the national economy, create unemployment, and reduce the standard of wages (because of competition from cheap foreign labor). The domestic consumer (through higher prices) pays directly for the policy. All who are engaged in producing staples suitable for export pay indirectly, because foreign states retaliate by closing off their own markets. The ultimate effects on all countries which practice economic nationalism are (1) a turning of the basic economy of the state from profitable export production to a less profitable and more static type that depends on local consumption; (2) a creation of monopolies; (3) a tendency to continue the use of obsolete machinery because there is no effective foreign competition; (4) a tendency to produce inferior products for the domestic market; and (5) a threat of economic and perhaps military pressures from strong states which are impatient to break out of the "strait jacket" imposed by the system.

Colonialism. *Colonialism* consists of a state's resettlement of people in sparsely inhabited areas which are owned by it but are outside its domestic territory. Under the mercantilist theory, the economic function of a colony was to produce raw materials for export to the homeland and to provide a market for manufactured goods; the military function was to support garrisons at strategic locations. It is interesting to note that the possession of colonies has enabled small states to become world powers. During the seventeenth and eighteenth centuries, rivalries among states which sought colonies frequently caused wars. England's experience shows (1) that colonies, after developing a stable economy, demand both political and economic independence from the mother country; but (2) that ties of language and sentiment are important in maintaining the peoples as friendly, cooperative members of the economic and political atmosphere of the land of origin.

Imperialism. *Imperialism* consists in the extension of a state's territory or effective control to areas which are already fully populated and which (because of climate, etc.) are unsuitable for colonization by inhabitants of the homeland. The motives for imperialism are many—to obtain exclusive possession of markets, secure strategic locations, exclude a rival power, and insure adequate supplies of raw materials. The usual methods of imperialism have been wars of conquest, military or naval occupation to restore order after the murder of missionaries and traders or the destruction of the property of a national, and the establishment of spheres of influence (which leads to protectorates over native governments and finally to annexation of the territories). Soviet imperialism, however, has developed a technique of "ideological penetration" through support of a world-wide communist movement. The results of imperialism are wasteful exploitation of economic and human resources, forced labor, and sometimes debauchery of native inhabitants. The effects upon the imperial power itself are the same as those of economic nationalism. With the spread of nationalism throughout the world, native peoples are demanding independence and are often willing to court the favor of an outside power in order to expel current imperial masters. International tensions in the disintegration of imperialism are likely to be as great as in its establishment.

Regionalism. We describe the policy as *regionalism,* whenever states in a specific area of the world unite their efforts for economic or political promotion and protection of their common natural or cultural resources. Other factors, such as political history and cultural geography, tend to influence and limit this type of relationship.

THE AMERICAN "REGION." The Monroe Doctrine, under which the United States prevented the reconquest of independent Latin American countries and the establishment of new colonies and outposts in the Western Hemisphere, is the oldest existing regional system. As a "corollary" to the doctrine, the United States early in the twentieth century sent armed forces into several Caribbean countries to compel them to meet their international obligations and, thus, to forestall European intervention. Through a policy of "dollar diplomacy," the United States aroused the anger of Latin American peoples against economic exploitation from the north. Since 1933, through the "good-neighbor" policy, the United States has sought the co-operation of other American states in hemispheric defense.

OTHER REGIONAL SYSTEMS. There are six other areas of the world in which regional policies have functioned: (1) For many years, the "open-door" policy kept the markets of China open on fairly equal terms to all foreign countries. (2) The "Benelux" grouping—Belgium, The Netherlands, and Luxembourg—has been one of the most promising regional arrangements because it has broken down artificial barriers (such as quotas) to production and to trade. (3) Prior to World War II, the Japanese envisaged a "Greater East Asia Co-Prosperity Sphere," which was designed to insure Japanese economic and military supremacy in the Far East. (4) The satellite states east of the "Iron Curtain" form another regional group which to all purposes and results is part of the new Russian empire. (5) The North Atlantic Treaty Organization is a regional alliance for defense against the threat of aggression from the huge ground and air forces of the Soviet Union. (6) The Southeast Asia Treaty Organization is a similar buffer against aggression by Communist China.

THE STATE SYSTEM

The international community is composed of about seventy independent states and a few others of subordinate status existing together in a condition of common distrust. In contrast to the situation in domestic politics, there is no unifying ideal or general public opinion in international politics. Each state regards the preservation of its own independence as the highest law and seeks all available means to maintain it. This condition in which states, in the absence of genuine world government, look out for themselves by diplomacy, balancing alliances, and wars is called a *state system*.

In the ancient world several state systems successively developed in the Near East, in Greece, and in the central Mediterranean; but in each of these regions one state finally swallowed up all the others by conquest. For a thousand years after the fall of the Roman Empire, political power was dispersed among petty feudal lords. The modern state system began in Europe with the rise of strong monarchies in France, Spain, and England at the end of the fifteenth century; and it was formally recognized at the Treaty of Westphalia in 1648. The United States, from the beginning of its existence as a nation, resolutely strove to avoid entanglement with the European state system. American participation in World War I was intended to "make the world safe for democracy" and not to redress the balance of power in Europe. In the ensuing two decades this nation reverted to its policy of isolation, but by the end of World War II it had become fully involved in the state system and was one of the two greatest powers. By that time the state system had extended to all parts of the world.

Theoretical Premises. It is now appropriate to examine in some detail the principal characteristics of the state system as it has existed during the past three hundred years.

NATIONAL SOVEREIGNTY. Most states consider themselves to be sovereign and independent, but their international situations are such that these concepts, in pure theory, do not always apply. The doctrine of "sovereignty" was first developed in order to provide justification for a king to compel obedience from all his subjects. In international relations, it has been applied in a distorted form to mean the complete freedom of a state from all external control. Though every state has in fact signed multilateral treaties which impair its freedom of action, the fiction persists that its sovereignty remains unimpaired. Adherence to a distorted doctrine of sovereignty in external affairs prevents a state from relinquishing its power to judge disputes in which it is a party, to use armed forces at its discretion, and to impose artificial barriers to the free flow of world commerce.

THE EQUALITY OF STATES. In diplomatic intercourse, the fiction that all states are equal is scrupulously observed. The fact is that gross inequalities exist by almost any standard. Difficulty in obtaining unanimity long proved a stumbling block to general international agreements. But, in the documents creating the United Nations, practical recognition was given finally to the inequalities that exist between the great powers and the lesser powers.

THE SUBJECTION OF INDIVIDUALS. In international affairs little attention is paid to people except as members of a state. Until fairly recently in human history, the lands of the prince and the people who lived on them were considered as his to dispose of as he wished; the inhabitants owed personal allegiance to the prince alone. With the beginning of nationalism, allegiance shifted to the state. The effects of this shift on international politics were (1) demands by separate linguistic and other national groups for statehood, which resulted in the formation of various new states; (2) severe tensions arising from *Irredentism* (desire of states to regain lost territory, e.g., Italy in 1878); and (3) intensification of national loyalties. Educational and other policies of the typical state were directed toward proving the superiority of its own culture and the consequent inferiority of foreign cultures. Thus, peoples were driven farther apart, and the hope of developing an international public opinion grew more and more remote. In addition, new instruments of warfare multiplied the horrors of war.

The Balance of Power. With the growth of the modern state system there developed the idea of "balance-of-power." Its main tenet is to prevent any single power from achieving a position of strength sufficient to threaten the existence of other states. On it, nations relied for the maintenance of peace in the international scene. Almost everywhere men have sought equilibrium in dealings among states and have developed systems for administering

ORGANIZATION OF

THE GENERAL ASSEMBLY
PRESIDENT
7 Vice Presidents

Members:

Afghanistan, Albania, Argentina, Australia, Austria, Belgium, Bolivia, Brazil, Bulgaria, Burma, Byelorussian S.S.R., Cambodia, Cameroun, Canada, Central African Republic, Ceylon, Chad, Chile, China, Colombia, Congo (Brazzaville), Congo (Leopoldville), Costa Rica, Cuba, Cyprus, Czechoslovakia, Dahomey, Denmark, Dominican Republic, Ecuador, El Salvador, Ethiopia, Federation of Malaya, Finland, France, Gabon, Ghana, Greece, Guatemala, Guinea, Haiti, Honduras, Hungary, Iceland, India, Indonesia, Iran, Iraq, Ireland, Israel, Italy, Ivory Coast, Japan, Jordan, Laos, Lebanon, Liberia, Libya, Luxembourg, Malagasy Republic, Mali, Mexico, Morocco, Nepal, Netherlands, New Zealand, Nicaragua, Niger, Nigeria, Norway, Pakistan, Panama, Paraguay, Peru, Philippines, Poland, Portugal, Romania, Saudi Arabia, Senegal, Somalia, Spain, Sudan, Sweden, Thailand, Togo, Tunisia, Turkey, Ukrainian S.S.R., Union of South Africa, U.S.S.R., United Arab Republic, United Kingdom, United States, Upper Volta, Uruguay, Venezuela, Yemen, Yugoslavia.

Committees:

GENERAL: Steering committee composed of the President of the General Assembly, the seven vice presidents, and the following committee chairmen:

Political and Security
  Ad Hoc Political (Special)
Economic and Financial

Social, Humanitarian, Cultural
Trusteeship
Administrative, Budgetary

Legal

Representatives of all the member nations are members of these committees.

THE SECURITY COUNCIL

Permanent Members:
China
France
U.S.S.R.
Great Britain
United States

Other Members:
Ceylon (Expires 1961)
Chile (Expires 1962)
Ecuador (Expires 1961)
Liberia (Expires 1961)
Turkey (Expires 1961)
United Arab Republic (Expires 1962)

DISARMAMENT COMMISSION

(Composed of members of the Security Council plus Canada.)

MILITARY STAFF COMMITTEE

(Composed of the Chiefs of Staff, or their representatives, of the five permanent members of the Security Council.)

THE UNITED NATIONS

THE ECONOMIC AND SOCIAL COUNCIL
PRESIDENT

Members:

Terms Expire 1961	*Terms Expire 1962*	*Terms Expire 1963*
Afghanistan	Brazil	El Salvador
Bulgaria	Denmark	Ethiopia
New Zealand	Japan	France
Spain	Poland	Italy
United States	U.S.S.R.	Jordan
Venezuela	United Kingdom	Uruguay

THE TRUSTEESHIP COUNCIL
PRESIDENT

Members:

Australia	France	U.S.S.R.
Belgium	India (Exp. 1963)	United Arab Republic
Bolivia (Exp. 1963)	Italy	(Exp. 1962)
Burma (Exp. 1962)	New Zealand	United Kingdom
China	Paraguay (Exp. 1962)	United States

THE INTERNATIONAL COURT OF JUSTICE
PRESIDENT

Members:

Argentina (Expires 1964)
Australia (Expires 1967)
China (Expires 1967)
El Salvador (Expires 1964)
France (Expires 1964)
Greece (Expires 1967)
Italy (Expires 1970)
Japan (Expires 1970)
Mexico (Expires 1964)
Panama (Expires 1964)
Peru (Expires 1970)
Poland (Expires 1967)
United Arab Republic (Expires 1967)
United Kingdom (Expires 1964)
United States (Expires 1970)

THE SECRETARIAT
SECRETARY-GENERAL

SPECIALIZED AGENCIES

International Labor Organization
Educational, Scientific, and Cultural Organization
International Bank for Reconstruction and Development
International Telecommunication Union
Food and Agriculture Organization
International Civil Aviation Organization
International Monetary Fund
World Health Organization
Universal Postal Union
World Meteorological Organization
Inter-Governmental Maritime Consultative Organization

relations between nations, in order to keep a constant balance of power among the strongest states.

MAINTENANCE OF THE BALANCE OF POWER. The outstanding characteristic of the balance of power is the idea that no nation will dare attack if opposing forces are kept in equilibrium. When a strong state is suspected of having aggressive intentions an alliance is soon made against it; this leads to a counteralliance. An unstable peace results until one group in possession of improved armaments decides to risk the consequences of war. However, the balance of power may be maintained over a long period if one strong state refrains from any permanent alliance and lends its support only temporarily, now to one side and now to the other on conditions that tend to maintain peace. Such was the role of Great Britain during the nineteenth century; the maintenance of the *pax Britannica* benefited not only Great Britain but the countries of Europe as well. Even in the hands of a skillful balancer, the principle of the balance of power does not ensure permanent peace; rather it tends to ensure the independence of the states within the system.

WAR. Although the state system has provided for an elaborate organization of diplomacy to settle disputes, nationalistic passions—usually aroused by an ambitious ruler's dreams of conquest—have often resulted in war. In fear of aggression, some states arm themselves for defense; their action begets fear of aggression in other states. An armaments race results. Among the great powers agreements have sometimes been reached for reducing the size of armed forces to a certain ratio; but such agreements have proved to be temporary. All but a few states renounced war as an instrument of national policy through the Kellogg-Briand Pact (1928); however, no effective means was found to implement it. (This defect appears in most of the agreements made between states under the state system.)

Current Status of the State System. At a time when goods used in everyday living are produced in distant countries, and when rivers, mountains, and even oceans are no longer sure defenses against invasion, the world still lives under the state system, which has undergone little fundamental change since the seventeenth century. Advancements in communication, transportation, and technology have far outstripped progress in international social adjustment.

INTERNATIONAL ASSOCIATIONS

During the past century many international associations have been established—first, in the form of international administrative unions and world tribunals and, later, in the more ambitious forms of the League of Nations and the United Nations.

International associations are difficult to classify juristically. Some are scarcely distinguishable from loose confederations. Some are created to accomplish only a single purpose or several specified purposes. Some are only effective regionally. All are based upon stipulations of treaties among states which have no intention of surrendering individual sovereignty by establishing an over-all state. Yet the associations have this much in common: all are expressions of a universal longing for peace and orderliness in world affairs.

International Administrative Unions. International administrative unions are organized associations created by multilateral treaties for the regulation of common nonpolitical activities. Most of them have permanent staffs which collect and disseminate information, keep records, make recommendations on which member states are invited to act and sometimes to formulate codes of rules in the hope that the states will accept them as binding. Conferences of the member states are held from time to time. Voting is by states, though by agreement expenses are usually apportioned according to the wealth of each state. Though most of the unions are limited to single objectives and have small staffs, their continued operation over long periods has demonstrated the value of international co-operation; in a specialized way, each is a part of international government. Most of the unions that were established before World War II have been absorbed into the United Nations. Although dozens of international unions were created in the nineteenth and twentieth centuries, here three will be described to show their great diversity of organization, powers, and functions and also to indicate their measures of success.

THE UNIVERSAL POSTAL UNION. Established in 1874, the Universal Postal Union expedites and regularizes the handling of mail between states.

THE INTERNATIONAL LABOR ORGANIZATION. One of the largest and most successful of the administrative unions is the International Labor Organization which was created by the Treaty of Versailles (1919) and has since been, respectively, an autonomous part of the League of Nations and an affiliated agency of the United Nations. Its purpose is to improve the conditions of the working classes throughout the world. The governing body of the ILO consists of an executive and a policy-making council. Annually it holds conferences to which each state sends four delegates, who represent both employers and employees, who (since they vote individually) sometimes oppose one another on given issues; the results of its conferences are framed into recommendations and referred to the member states for action. A subsidiary, the International Labor Office, headed by a director, carries on research and maintains contact with the states. It establishes various permanent and temporary committees which consider such problems as health of laborers, migration, and conditions among refugees.

THE PAN AMERICAN UNION. The Pan American Union (which traces its origin to 1890) is the administrative organ of an association among the independent republics of the Western Hemisphere. Its staff collects and disseminates information, keeps records, makes recommendations on which member states are invited to act, and sometimes decides upon rules in the hope that the states will accept them as binding. It holds international conferences from time to time in order to determine basic policies for the future.

The League of Nations. The League of Nations was formed as a result of the efforts of a number of idealists, especially in Great Britain and the United States, during World War I. Through the efforts of President Woodrow Wilson, the Covenant of the League became the first twenty-six articles of the Treaty of Versailles (1919). The Annex to the Covenant named thirty-two original members and contained the names of thirteen other states that were subsequently invited to join. Fully autonomous dominions and colonies were enabled to become members in their own right. Germany was not permitted to join until 1926, Turkey was accepted in 1932, and the U.S.S.R. was finally admitted in 1934; the United States never became a member, chiefly because of isolationist sentiments, constitutional difficulties, and political disagreements. At one time, fifty-four states were members. The withdrawal of Germany and Japan in 1935, after a required two-years' notice, greatly weakened the influence of the League. It was finally dissolved in 1946, when its assets were transferred to the United Nations.

PURPOSES AND AIMS. The League was an association of states for the purpose of international co-operation, the settlement of disputes, and the prevention of future wars. Its Covenant provided for a number of agencies for the promotion of health, education, and economic development, as well as for the suppression of illicit traffic in women, children, and drugs. Under the auspices of the League, the Permanent Court of International Justice (popularly known as the "World Court" and open to member and non-member states alike) sat at The Hague for the purpose of settling controversies and offering advisory opinions on matters having to do with international law.[1] The League itself had specific powers to enforce provisions of the peace treaties relating to the protection of minorities in the new countries carved out of the former Austro-Hungarian, Russian, and Turkish empires. It had immediate supervision over the Saar region and Danzig, and it had general supervision over the former colonies of Germany and the possessions of Turkey which were assigned as mandates to be administered by various members of the League. An evident motive of the great powers that entered the League was to maintain the *status quo* as determined by the peace treaties.

ORGANIZATION. The principal organs of the League were the Assembly, the Council, and the Secretariat. The Assembly, which met annually, was composed of delegations from the member states, with each state having one vote. It adopted a budget, approved the work of the Council, Secretariat, and other organs, and adopted draft conventions to be referred to the member states for ratification. The Council was composed of representatives of each of the great powers and of nonpermanent members elected by the Assembly from the smaller states. Its principal function was to act as a commission of inquiry and conciliation in any disputes referred to it and to recommend action to enforce the obligations of the Covenant. The Secretariat was the permanent staff of the League.

---

[1] This court has been replaced by the International Court of Justice (*see* p. 205).

OBLIGATIONS UPON MEMBER STATES. Each state agreed (1) to submit every dispute to arbitration, judicial settlement, or inquiry by the Council if that dispute was likely to lead to war; (2) to abide loyally by the award, decision, or report; and (3) to refrain from resort to war until three months afterwards. If a state went to war in violation of its pledges, the other members were to break off diplomatic and other intercourse with it. Thus the Covenant provided for a "cooling-off period" and for economic sanctions. It contained only a vague provision for military sanctions.

ACCOMPLISHMENTS AND FAILURES. During its quarter-century of existence, the League gave economic assistance to Austria, Estonia, Greece, and Hungary; it helped Poland fight typhus; it aided China in flood relief; it settled disputes between Sweden and Finland, Germany and Poland, and Poland and Czechoslovakia; it stopped wars between Turkey and Iraq and between Greece and Bulgaria; and it performed many other humanitarian services. Its conspicuous failures were in dealing with the aggressive actions of strong powers in the 1930's—the Japanese invasion of China and the Italian war against Ethiopia.

REASONS FOR COLLAPSE. The downfall of the League has been ascribed to many causes among which the following are outstanding: The refusal of the United States to join deprived the League of objective leadership. The assembly fell under the domination of the Council and the Council fell under the control of France and Great Britain: France used the League in furtherance of her policy to encircle Germany; Great Britain pursued her historic policy of balancing the forces on the Continent. The principle of unanimity in both the Assembly and the Council prevented the reaching of decisions. There was no effective means of enforcing the determinations of the League. (Note the reappearance of one of the defects of the state system here.)

The United Nations. Profiting from lessons learned from the League, the nations which engaged against the Axis powers in World War II determined to establish a new and stronger international organization. Three or four years before the close of the war, conferences were held among leaders of these nations or their representatives to set up organizations for relief and to plan a new world order. In 1945, a general conference among various powers met in San Francisco, and, after long deliberation, the Charter of the United Nations was signed on June 26. The Charter was thus dissociated from the peace settlements which remained to be made later. Presumably, the United Nations was to have a hand in making necessary later adjustments and was not to be bound, as the League had been, to maintenance of the *status quo*. The Charter recognized the realities of the world situation in providing for the use of force to stop aggression. At the same time, in providing for the Economic and Social Council and other agencies, it recognized the necessity for developing friendly international relations, harmonizing the actions of states, and thus eliminating many of the causes of war. The powers of the United Nations are much greater than those of the League, and its organization is better adapted to achieve its ends.

THE GENERAL ASSEMBLY. Today the General Assembly is composed of five delegates from each state. Annually in September, the Assembly meets in regular session and also it may be called into special sessions. It is authorized to discuss any matter within the scope of the Charter. It elects the members of the Economic and Social Council and six members of the Security Council. On the nomination of the Security Council, the General Assembly appoints the Secretary-General. Each state delegation has one vote. A two-thirds majority is required for questions relating to peace and security, to the admission or suspension or expulsion of members, to the adoption of the budget, to the operation of the trusteeship system, and to any proposals for amending the charter. A simple majority is sufficient for the decision of other questions. The voting procedure is significant because it means that the smaller member states may be bound against their wills. The General Assembly lacks the full powers of a legislature; rather, it is to be regarded as an international forum to discuss, investigate, and recommend questions for the consideration of the states and the peoples of the world.

THE SECURITY COUNCIL. The real controlling body in the United Nations is the Security Council. This is composed of representatives of the five great powers—the United States, the U.S.S.R., Great Britain, France, and China which are permanent members—and of six other members elected for two-year terms by the General Assembly. Its eleven members are in continuous session.

Powers. The Charter of the United Nations expressly confers on the Security Council the primary responsibility for the maintenance of peace and security. Members agree to submit disputes to mediation, arbitration, or judicial decision; but the Security Council may intervene at any stage by recommending procedures or terms for settling a dispute. It may determine what sanctions of an economic or military nature are necessary to enforce its decisions. Although it has no international force at its disposal, it may call upon member states to supply contingents. Furthermore, the Security Council has a Military Staff Committee to give advice and make plans for forcible action. There is also an Atomic Energy Commission and a Commission for Conventional Armaments, both of which are designed for the purpose of regulating and reducing the armaments of the various states. Russian objections have thus far prevented the commissions from functioning.

Voting Procedure. Each member has one vote. Seven votes are necessary for a decision on procedural matters. When, however, a question concerns the peaceful settlement of disputes, the majority must include the votes of the five great powers. If one of the powers is a party to a dispute, it must abstain from voting. If the question is to apply sanctions, either economic or military, all of the five great powers must be included in the majority of seven, even though one of them is involved; in other words, any of the five has a veto over such action. This veto means that sanctions can not be applied against a great power.

THE SECRETARIAT. The Secretariat is the permanent civil service of the United Nations recruited from nationals of every state. It is headed by the Secretary-General, who is the chief administrative officer of the United Nations. He is authorized to bring any question threatening the peace to the attention of the Security Council. He controls the property of the United Nations, arranges the agenda for its meetings and those of other international associations, and prepares reports on its activities. Assistant secretaries-general are in charge of each of the eight departments into which the Secretariat is divided.

THE ECONOMIC AND SOCIAL COUNCIL. The Economic and Social Council is the agency which is engaged in positive action for the improvement of conditions throughout the world. It is composed of eighteen members elected by the General Assembly for terms of three years. Six members are elected each year.

Determinations are by a simple majority vote. Its functions are to investigate, recommend, and promote voluntary co-operation among states in such matters as improvements in living standards, health, welfare, education, and individual freedom. One of its commissions has drafted a Declaration of Human Rights; others are engaged in studies relating to transportation, communications, the status of women, and traffic in narcotics. The Council may propose agreements on economic problems and refer them to the respective member states for adoption, call conferences on matters within its jurisdiction, and provide technical advice and assistance to the member states and the United Nations.

THE TRUSTEESHIP COUNCIL. The Trusteeship Council has jurisdiction over the former mandates of the League of Nations, over territories taken from Japan and Italy at the end of World War II, and over any other territory which a state may voluntarily confide to its care. The Council is composed of one member from each state administering trust territories, one member from each of the five great powers which are not trust territory administrators, plus others elected by the General Assembly. It receives reports from the administrators of trust territories, makes annual inspections of their conditions, and receives complaints and petitions from the native inhabitants.

THE INTERNATIONAL COURT OF JUSTICE. The judicial tribunal of the United Nations is the International Court of Justice consisting of fifteen judges elected for nine-year terms by the General Assembly and the Security Council. This is the successor to the Permanent Court of International Justice, which was an organ of the League of Nations; like its predecessor it sits at The Hague in the Netherlands. It has jurisdiction over cases involving the interpretation of treaties, breaches of international obligations, reparation for wrongs suffered by a state, and questions of international law; but it can not take jurisdiction unless the parties to a dispute voluntarily submit a case to it. Several nations have signed the so-called "Optional Clause" by which they have agreed that the court may try all cases, or cases relating to specified subjects, which may arise in the future; but most have hedged or at best specified a limited number of subjects on which they will accept jurisdiction. Once a case has been brought before the Court, the parties to the dispute must abide by its decision. The Security Council may enforce compliance from a recalcitrant state. Advisory opinions may be requested from the Court by the General Assembly, the Security Council, and certain other organs of the United Nations.

SPECIALIZED AGENCIES. A number of specialized and affiliated agencies have been set up which together cover a wide field of international activities. (1) The International Monetary Fund exists for the purposes of stabilizing currencies and stimulating world trade. (2) The International Bank for Reconstruction and Development provides capital to restore devastated areas and develop resources. (3) The Food and Agriculture Organization (FAO) is devoted to raising standards of nutrition and living, promoting more efficient farming methods, developing fisheries, and providing improved marketing conditions. (4) The World Health Organization (WHO) provides technical assistance to governments to promote research, prevent epidemics, improve sanitation, and control malaria, yellow fever, and venereal and other diseases. (5) The United Nations Educational, Scientific, and Cultural Organization (UNESCO) seeks to promote international understanding. (6) The International Refugee Organization (IRO) is engaged in the repatriation of refugees and displaced persons, and in finding means of resettling people who are unable to return to their homelands. (7) The International Trade Organization (ITO) is devoted to efforts to remove tariffs and trade discriminations, encourage new industries, and settle trade disputes. (8) The International Civil Aeronautics Organization seeks to provide equal opportunities for states to engage in international operation of air transport consistent with safety and economy. (9) The International Telecommunications Union assigns radio frequencies, attempts to secure speedy and economical delivery of telegrams and cables, and deals with problems arising in connection with these activities. (10) The World Meteorological Organization provides for the exchange of weather data. (11) The International Labor Organization (*see* p. 199f.) attempts to improve the condition of the working peoples of the world.

Progress Toward World Government. Undoubtedly much progress has been made by the United Nations, but in many quarters there are complaints of its insufficiencies. Events seem to indicate that the nations which co-operated during World War II in resistance to a common danger have lost the will to co-operate after the enemy has been defeated. The excessive use of the veto power (chiefly by the U.S.S.R.) has been a stumbling block to the operation of the United Nations. The continuance of "power politics," as evidenced by an armaments race and by a military and economic penetration in Asia, has resulted in some disillusionment among sincere advocates of a world order.

There continues to be agitation for a genuine federal union on the analogy of the United States. One group wants a federation which would include the whole world; another seeks a federation of Western Europe. The difficulties in the way of either proposal are tremendous. Racial, linguistic, cultural, and political barriers would have to be broken down in a new federation.[2] Not the least difficulty would be to determine the basis of representation, such as population, wealth, resources, or present power. Trade barriers would have to be broken down. The jealousies and rivalries of centuries would have to be forgotten. Genuine federation waits upon the submergence of nationality and the development of a popular loyalty to the ideal of world unity. It would be well to keep in mind these facts: (1) The United Nations is an organization already in being. (2) In spite of great obstacles, it has substantial accomplishments to its credit. In the North Korean police action, its military forces, composed of contingents from several states, maintained the independence of the Republic of South Korea. It has won recognition as a legal entity capable of maintaining suits against states. It has also produced much international legislation. Above all, it has actively and consistently kept the ideal of international co-operation before the public opinion of the world.

---

[2] At the time of its creation, the United States was composed of people who spoke the same language, had similar cultural and political ideals, and had previously lived under the control of one power, Great Britain.

21 International Law

International law is composed of principles which the community of nations considers as obligatory in their relations one with another. Like national or municipal law it deals with persons; but the "persons" here are states or other international persons, not individual human beings as such. *International administrative law* applies to rules made by international bodies (for example, the Universal Postal Union) which have been created for the regulation of the universal rational and physical affairs of states. *International private law,* sometimes called "conflict of laws," deals with conflicting national systems of law affecting private rights, that is, the rights (and obligations) of individuals when these are acquired in one state and enforced by another; familiar cases in international private law include questions of the authenticity of foreign marriages, wills, and contracts involving different systems of law.

THE NATURE OF INTERNATIONAL LAW

At the time the European state system was being established, international law was being developed as a means of alleviating the horrors of war. For the first time jurisprudence was separated from theology and ethics in *De Juri Belli* (*The Law of War,* 1598) by Alberico Gentili, professor of civil law at Oxford. Credit for founding international law is usually accorded to Hugo Grotius whose *De Juri Belli ac Pacis* (*On the Law of War and Peace*) was first published in Paris in 1625. Grotius combined natural law concepts of reason and justice with the actual practice of states throughout the period of human history. Later writers of great ability, such as Samuel von Pufendorf (1632-1694), Christian von Wolff (1679-1754), and Emmerich von Vattel (1714-1767), furthered the work of Grotius by codifying the customs of nations and pointing out the differences between good and bad practice.

Today, international law covers most of the problems of peacetime and defines the rights and duties of belligerents and neutrals during wartime.

Sources. International law is customary law: it contains little of a statutory nature. Its principal sources are (1) established practices of nations; (2) writings of jurists; (3) declarations of international congresses; (4) multilateral treaties regulating certain phases of international conduct; (5) bilateral treaties which sometimes contain provisions declaring existing law; (6) proclamations of the heads of state, opinions of their foreign offices, and orders to their military commanders—all of which are frequently cited; (7) decisions of arbitration tribunals, of commissions of inquiry, and of courts dealing with international questions or with prize cases—all of which may constitute precedents for later decisions; and (8) failure of a state to protest against principles to which other states have expressly consented, for such a failure may be taken as evidence of tacit consent.

Means of Enforcement. The *sanctions,* or provisions for enforcement, of international law are extremely weak. If each state is regarded as sovereign, there obviously can not be a higher power to which it owes obedience. Several states have entered into treaties which require them to submit to arbitration all controversies except those involving their vital interests, independence, and national honor. The excepted questions—defined by each state for itself—are the ones that most often cause wars. A third state, acting as mediator or conciliator, frequently is useful in preventing conflicts. *International public opinion*—that is, the opinion of the majority of governments—frowns upon aggressive action; yet, when a state believes that it has international law on its side, there is no means by which it can compel the enforcement of its right.

Validity. Is international law true law? Jurists of the positive school define law as the command of a definitive human superior and answer "No"; they regard international law as a set of moral standards which states ordinarily follow. Jurists of the historical school recognize as law the powerful influence of custom stamped by official approval and answer with a qualified "Yes"; these jurists consider international law to be true law because it is enforced or actively approved by the courts of states. The courts of some states (including Great Britain and the United States) have declared international law to be the "law of the land." Furthermore, the legislatures of some states have passed statutes to enforce international law in many types of cases involving individuals or merchant ships and other property.

Degree of Effectiveness. The provisions of international law which are most faithfully enforced are the ones that provide convenience in regulating interstate relations and not the ones in which the states are vitally concerned. Within the limited field of normal peacetime relations, the enforcement of international law has been surprisingly good. Sometimes it has preserved peace when wars threatened, and often it has circumscribed the scope of wars and mitigated their horror.

RIGHTS AND OBLIGATIONS UNDER INTERNATIONAL LAW

All members of the international community are subjects of international law and may become parties to disputes. The international community is composed of the seventy-odd organized societies that are generally recognized as states and other societies that lack full sovereignty and independence (such as protectorates and trusteeships). It includes (1) states that have had a long continuous existence, (2) new states that have arisen in formerly uncivilized regions, (3) new states that were once parts of older states from which they have declared independence, and (4) new states that have been formed through mergers of previously independent states. New states do not receive general recognition[1] until they are considered capable of performing their international obligations.

Rights. Every state has fundamental rights (1) to existence, (2) to independence, (3) to ownership and to exclusive control over its territory, and (4) to free use of the high seas. Also, it has certain rights that are not regarded as fundamental—for example, the right for its ships to pass through the coastal waters

---

[1] The principle of "general recognition" is, of course, indefinite and hard to apply. Turkey and other Asiatic countries, for instance, were not recognized by all other states until toward the end of the nineteenth century. The recognition of new governments in older states is a different matter: after World War I, some states recognized the Soviet Union and others did not. Similarly after World War II there was disagreement about the recognition of Communist China.

of other states and the right to regulate the conduct of any foreign vessels or crews that are within its ports.

Obligations. For every right there is a corresponding duty. Each state is responsible for any injuries that its officers or agents may inflict upon other states.[2] Each state is required to use reasonable diligence and all means at its disposal to protect foreigners residing within its borders from mistreatment by its officers and its citizens. (This is to say merely that foreigners must be given the same protection and the same means of redress in the courts and elsewhere that are accorded to the state's citizens, not that foreigners are entitled to a greater degree of protection.) The state is fully responsible and must compensate for injuries inflicted in riots which are directed primarily against foreigners. However, it is usually absolved from responsibility for injuries imposed during periods of civil war or insurrection if, in fact, it has been unable to exercise effective control.

REPRESENTATIVE PROVISIONS OF INTERNATIONAL LAW

The following discussions indicate that international law contains satisfactory provisions for settling many controversies which may arise among states during peacetime. The provisions selected pertain to (1) the financial obligations of new states, (2) the interstate boundaries, (3) the acquisition or loss of territory, (4) the marginal sea, (5) the open sea, and (6) the relations of states with foreign individuals or corporations.

Provisions concerning the Financial Obligations of New States. States are assumed to have continuous existence despite changes in forms of government. When a state is divided into two or more independent states, international law decrees that the debts shall be apportioned according to the value of taxable property within each new state.

Provisions concerning Interstate Boundaries. The boundaries of states are almost always fixed by treaties. When treaty stipulations are lacking or when they are not completely clear, the rules of international law in respect to the determination of boundaries are as follows: (1) If the boundary is a river, the dividing line is

---

[2] The Nuremberg Trials (1945-1946) held officers of states to be personally responsible for violations of international law.

the main navigable channel; where there is no navigable channel, the line is simply the middle of the stream. (2) If the boundary is a range of hills or mountains, the line follows the water divide. (3) If the boundary consists of seas or lakes, the line is drawn equidistant from the headlands on either side. (4) If the boundary is a narrow strait, the line is drawn either in the middle or in midchannel.

Provisions concerning Acquisition or Loss of Territory. Territory may be acquired in five ways: (1) by *discovery* followed by effective occupation, (2) by *accretion* (through the gradual accumulation of soil resulting from the natural action of tides or of river currents), (3) by *prescription* (through undisturbed occupation and control over a long period of time), (4) by *conquest* (through accession by a victorious state of all or part of the territory of a vanquished state without a treaty of cession), or (5) by *cession* (through treaties for the purchase or the exchange of territory or, after a war, for the transference of territory from one state to another). Territory may be lost by the reverse of most of these means—including loss by natural causes and loss through defeat in war. When a defeated state cedes a part of its territory to a victor by treaty, the action is assumed to be voluntary.

Provisions concerning the Marginal Sea. In 1702 the Dutch publicist Cornelius van Bynkershoek proposed that a state's boundaries should be extended outward to a distance of three miles from its shoreline. In his period this was the effective range of a cannon shot and hence the distance to which a state could reasonably be expected to exercise control. The "three-mile limit" has since been recognized as the extent of a state's jurisdiction in policing its coastal waters, despite the increased range of coast artillery. A general exception has been made under the principle of international law called *hot pursuit*. This doctrine justifies the pursuit and arrest of vessels that have infringed upon the laws of a state; but the principle also requires that the pursuit begin within the three-mile limit, continue without interruption, and cease when it reaches the territorial waters of another state. Special exceptions have been made by agreements among states that are willing to exchange privileges. Bays and gulfs (such as the Chesapeake and Delaware bays and the Long Island Sound), which are almost wholly surrounded by the land of one state, are regarded as within the territory of that state even if their mouths are more than six miles wide. The state usually claims minerals that lie in the subsurface of the continental shelf; in recent times, exclusive possession of petroleum deposits has been claimed as far out from the shore as the state can extract them.

Provisions concerning the Open Sea. All states enjoy equal rights to navigate and to fish on the open sea outside the three-mile limit. Each vessel, whether public or private, is under the jurisdiction of the state whose flag it flies; crimes committed on board are prosecuted in the courts of the state to which the vessel belongs. The goods, crew, and passengers of a ship are subject to the control of the captain. If two vessels collide on the high seas, the courts of any state may take jurisdiction in a suit for damages and may make an award under the rules of international law. Inasmuch as pirates are enemies of all mankind, any state may seize and punish them. Slave trade also is outlawed under international law. Merchant vessels suspected of piracy or slave trade may be visited and searched, but warships are not subject to such interference. Vessels in a foreign port are exempt from local jurisdiction except when crimes committed on board a merchant vessel affect the peace of the port.

Provisions Concerning Individuals. A state may legally exclude aliens of any or all nationalities and may expel them for any reason. In cases of expulsion, international law requires that they be given sufficient time to terminate their business affairs. Every alien domiciled in a country tacitly agrees to obey the laws, pay taxes, and perform duties (aside from military service) which are required of the state's citizens though he may not be granted the rights of citizens. His own state, however, has the right to protect him abroad and to insist upon fair treatment. When laws conflict, the naturalization of aliens presents thorny problems, which are usually resolved by agreements among states. Naturalization does not absolve a person from obligations previously incurred in his former state. The extradition of criminals, who have fled from one state to another, is ordinarily covered by treaties, but it may also be granted by comity. No state has the right to demand the extradition of persons charged with political offenses, such as rebellion or conspiracy to overthrow a government.

THE LAW OF WAR

War is an abnormal relationship between states. The decision to resort to war is a political rather than a legal act, for the condition of war is essentially a denial of law. Methods of conducting wars are not susceptible to control by law; the international law of war is largely concerned with procedures for conducting hostilities. Before 1914 an elaborate code of rules forbade the use of poisonous gas, explosive bullets, unanchored mines, and the bombardment of undefended cities, towns, and villages. In the recent World Wars, most of these regulations were not recognized. The development of military aircraft and guided missiles to a great extent erased distinctions which the previous code has made between combatants and noncombatants. Extensive use of submarines nullified rules which required the rescue of crews and passengers from disabled ships. However, the rules of international law for ground warfare—provisions for the care and treatment of enemy wounded and prisoners of war, the inviolability of the Red Cross emblem, the government of occupied territory, and the proper care of public and private property by the occupying forces—were fairly well observed.

An entire section of international law deals with the protection of the territory, citizens, and property of neutral states from unnecessary interference by belligerents and with the reciprocal obligations of neutrals to avoid giving aid to a belligerent. Under the conditions of modern warfare, neutrality is practically impossible unless neither group of belligerents finds it advantageous to invade neutral territory.

METHODS OF ADJUSTING INTERNATIONAL DISPUTES

Members of the international family of nations have developed permanent diplomatic services, the agents of which employ traditional means for expediting the discussion, the negotiation, and the adjustment of affairs among states.

Agents of International Intercourse. The conduct of a state's foreign relations involves the handling of a large amount of business both for the government and for private citizens. Every state requires a large staff for its diplomatic and consular services both at home and abroad. The foreign office of each state instructs

INTERNATIONAL LAW

and controls those members of the foreign service who are sent abroad.

THE DIPLOMATIC SERVICE. There are many ranks in the diplomatic service, the chief in importance being an "ambassador extraordinary and minister plenipotentiary" and a "minister resident." Ordinarily there is an embassy at the capital of every important state and there are diplomatic officers of lower rank at the capitals of smaller countries. It is a recognized principle of international comity that a diplomatic agent must be acceptable to the government to which he is accredited. He may be recalled at any time by his own government at the request of the foreign government. Offended states also may dismiss a diplomatic representative from another country. The diplomatic agent serves as the main channel of communication in the conduct of negotiations between his own government and the government to which he is accredited. By international law and courtesy, privileges and immunities are accorded to diplomats and their families and staffs. These include freedom from arrest, inviolability of persons and papers, and the exemption of the embassy from control by the state in which it is located—a fact which in times of violence sometimes makes the embassy a refuge for foreign nationals.

THE CONSULAR SERVICES. The consular service consists of officers of various grades beginning at the top with a "consul general." These officers are stationed at important commercial centers; generally, they negotiate the business and personal problems of individuals. Consular officers are not accorded the same immunity as diplomatic officers. Recently, in order to secure greater efficiency, many states have taken steps to merge their diplomatic and consular services.

Negotiation of Treaties. Most of the relations between states are regulated under treaties: formal written agreements concerning one or a number of subjects. Treaties which may be enforced without further legislation are called *self-executing* treaties. Others (e. g., those providing for payments of money or changes in tariffs) require legislative action before they become fully effective. Political scientists generally agree that treaty-making is a function of the executive branch of government.

There are three distinct steps in treaty-making—negotiation, approval, and exchange of ratifications. The diplomatic agent should usually be specially accredited and carefully instructed before he may begin the negotiation of a particular treaty. After the treaty has been signed by the negotiators, it must be examined and approved by the foreign offices of the governments concerned. (In the United States, all treaties must be ratified by a two-thirds vote of the Senate before the exchange of ratifications can take place.) Failure to enforce a ratified treaty (through a legislative act or through neglect of the executive) constitutes a breach of international good faith. Treaties are usually terminated by expiration of the time limit for which they are made or by mutual agreement of the contracting parties. The outbreak of war automatically suspends the operation of all treaties between belligerents.

Mediation and Arbitration. When disputes can not be settled by diplomacy, an impartial third state may act as an intermediary, offering its advice and urging negotiation. *Mediation* is the friendly examination of the nature of a dispute by a third party which discusses it with the parties and suggests a solution. Through mediation wars have been prevented and overlapping claims between nations have been adjusted. *Arbitration* is the submission of a problem to a third state or a panel whose decisions the disputants agree in advance to accept. This method is used a great deal in the settlement of controversies concerning boundaries and similar questions. Sometimes international commissions of inquiry provide a "cooling-off period" and contribute unbiased conclusions which may become a basis for settlement.

Judicial Decisions. In Chapter 20, the history, organization, and functions of the International Court of Justice were discussed. Here, we will briefly summarize its jurisdiction: it decides international disputes related to boundaries, questions involving international law, the interpretation of treaties, and alleged violations of international rights and obligations. All parties are required to abide by court decisions, which are enforceable by the Security Council of the United Nations.

Selected References

1—The Study of Political Science

Berle, Adolph A., Jr. *Natural Selection of Political Forces* (Lawrence: University of Kansas Press, 1950).

Easton, David. *The Political System: An Inquiry into the State of Political Science* (New York: Alfred A. Knopf, 1953).

Griffith, Ernest S., ed. *Research in Political Science* (Chapel Hill: University of North Carolina Press, 1949).

Roche, J. P. and Stedman, Murray S., Jr. *The Dynamics of Democratic Government* (New York: McGraw-Hill Book Co., 1954).

Soltau, Roger H. *An Introduction to Politics* (New York: Longmans, Green and Co., 1951).

Smith, E. C. and Zurcher, A. J., eds. *Dictionary of American Politics, an Everyday Handbook* (New York: Barnes & Noble, Inc., 1955).

U.N.E.S.C.O. *Contemporary Political Science* (New York, 1950).

Ward, Barbara. *Policy for the West* (New York: W. W. Norton and Co., Inc., 1951).

2—The Historical Background

Bosanquet, Bernard. *The Philosophical Theory of the State* (New York: The Macmillan Co., 1930).

Carlyle, R. W. and Carlyle, A. J. *A History of Mediaeval Political Theory in the West* (New York: Barnes & Noble, Inc., 6 vols., 1909-1936).

Hayes, Carlton J. H. *The Historical Evolution of Modern Nationalism* (New York: The Macmillan Co., 1948).

Hearnshaw, F. J. C., ed. *Mediaeval Contributions to Modern Civilization*, 9 vols. (New York: Barnes & Noble, Inc., 1949-1950).

Lasswell, Harold D., et al. *Study of Power* (Glencoe: The Free Press, 1950).

Lloyd, R. *The Glorious Liberty* (New York: Longmans, Green and Co., 1946).

Mannheim, Karl. *Freedom, Power, and Democratic Planning* (New York: Oxford University Press, 1952).

3—The Purposes and Functions of the State

Amery, Leopold. *Thoughts on the Constitution* (London: Oxford University Press, 1953).

Arnold, W. T. *Studies of Roman Imperialism* (New York: Barnes & Noble, Inc., 1906).
Dahl, R. A. and Lindblom, C. E. *Politics, Economics, and Welfare* (New York: Harper & Brothers, 1953).
Dallin, David J. *The Real Soviet Russia* (New Haven: Yale University Press, 1947).
Earle, Edward Mead. *Modern France; Problems of the Third and Fourth Republics* (Princeton: Princeton University Press, 1951).
Elliott, William Y. and McDonald, Neil A. *Western Political Heritage* (New York: Prentice-Hall, Inc., 1949).
Harper, Samuel N. and Thompson, E. *Government of the Soviet Union* (New York: Van Nostrand Co., Inc., 1949).
Hovell, M., ed. by T. F. Tout. *The Chartist Movement* (New York: Barnes & Noble, Inc., 1950).
Jennings, Sir Ivor. *The British Constitution* (New York: Cambridge University Press, 1950).
Kirchner, Walther. *History of Russia,* College Outline Series (New York: Barnes & Noble, Inc., 1955).
Murray, J. M. *The Free Society* (London: Andrew Dakers, 1948).
Stapleton, Laurence. *The Design of Democracy* (New York: Oxford University Press, 1949).
Wilkinson, B. *Studies in the Constitutional History of the Thirteenth and Fourteen Centuries* (New York: Barnes & Noble, Inc., 1952).

4—Theories of State Functions

Earle, Edward Mead. *Modern France: Problems of the Third and Fourth Republics* (Princeton: Princeton University Press, 1951).
Elliott, William Y. and McDonald, Neil A. *Western Political Heritage* (New York: Prentice-Hall, Inc., 1949).
Grimes, A. P. *American Political Thought* (New York: Holt, 1955).
Holcombe, Arthur. *Our More Perfect Union: From Eighteenth Century Principles to Twentieth Century Practice* (Cambridge: Harvard University Press, 1950).
Hovell, M., ed. by T. F. Tout. *The Chartist Movement* (New York: Barnes & Noble, Inc., 1950).
Jennings, Sir Ivor. *The British Constitution* (New York: Cambridge University Press, 1950).
Kirchner, Walther. *History of Russia,* College Outline Series (New York: Barnes & Noble, Inc., 1955).
Laidler, H. W. *History of Socialist Thought* (New York: Thomas Y. Crowell Co., 1944).
Murray, J. M. *The Free Society* (London: Andrew Dakers, 1948).

SELECTED REFERENCES

Roche, J. P. and Stedman, M. S., Jr. *The Dynamics of Democratic Government* (New York: McGraw-Hill Book Co., 1954).

Schumpeter, J. A. *Capitalism, Socialism, and Democracy* (New York: Harper & Brothers, 1950).

Wright, Gordon. *The Reshaping of French Democracy* (New York: Reynal & Hitchcock, 1948).

5—The Concept of Statehood

Agar, Herbert. *The Price of Union* (Boston: Houghton Mifflin Co., 1950).

Dahl, R. A. and Lindblom, C. E. *Politics, Economics, and Welfare* (New York: Harper & Brothers, 1953).

Davenport, Russell W., et al. *U.S.A.: The Permanent Revolution* (New York: Prentice-Hall, Inc., 1951).

Grimes, A. P. *American Political Thought* (New York: Holt, 1955).

Jennings, Sir Ivor. *Cabinet Government* (New York: Cambridge University Press, 1951).

Knight, F. H. *Freedom and Reform* (New York: Harper & Brothers, 1947).

Towster, Julian. *Political Power in the U.S.S.R., 1917-1947* (New York: Oxford University Press, 1948).

6—Sovereignty

Grimes, A. P. *American Political Thought* (New York: Holt, 1955).

Hawtrey, R. G. *Economic Aspects of Sovereignty* (Toronto: Longmans, Green and Co., 1952).

Marshall, James. *Swords and Symbols, The Technique of Sovereignty* (New York: Oxford University Press, 1939).

Mosse, G. L. *Struggle for Sovereignty in England* (East Lansing: Michigan State College Press, 1951).

Portus, G. U. *Concept of Sovereignty* (Melbourne: Melbourne University Press, 1948).

Shepard, P. *Sovereignty and State-owned Commercial Entities* (New York: Aberdeen Press, Inc.).

7—Concepts of Law

Allen, C. K. *Law in the Making* (Oxford: The Clarendon Press, 1951).

Cardozo, B. N. *The Growth of Law* (New Haven: Yale University Press, 1924).

Jennings, Sir Ivor. *The Law and the Constitution* (London: University of London Press, 1943).

Kelsen, Hans. *General Theory of Law and State* (Cambridge: Harvard University Press, 1945).

Pound, Roscoe. *The Spirit of the Common Law* (Boston: Marshall Jones Co., 1921).

———. *Introduction to the Philosophy of Law* (New Haven: Yale University Press, 1954).

Seagle, William. *The Quest for Law* (New York: Alfred A. Knopf, 1941).

8—Current Governmental Systems

Dahl, R. A. and Lindblom, C. E. *Politics, Economics, and Welfare* (New York: Harper & Brothers, 1953).

Dallin, David J. *The Real Soviet Russia* (New Haven: Yale University Press, 1947).

Davenport, Russell W., et al. *U.S.A.: The Permanent Revolution* (New York: Prentice-Hall, Inc., 1951).

Earle, Edward Mead. *Modern France: Problems of the Third and Fourth Republics* (Princeton: Princeton University Press, 1951).

Elliott, William Y. and McDonald, Neil A. *Western Political Heritage* (New York: Prentice-Hall, Inc., 1949).

Grimes, A. P. *American Political Thought* (New York: Holt, 1955).

Hearnshaw, F. J. C., ed. *The Social and Political Ideas of Some Representative Thinkers of the Victorian Age* (New York: Barnes & Noble, Inc., 1950).

Laidler, H. W. *History of Socialist Thought* (New York: Thomas Y. Crowell Co., 1944).

Landman, J. H. and Wender, H. *World Since 1914*, College Outline Series (New York: Barnes & Noble, Inc., 1955).

Roche, J. P. and Stedman, M. S., Jr. *The Dynamics of Democratic Government* (New York: McGraw-Hill Book Co., 1954).

Sayre, Wallace S. *American Government*, College Outline Series (New York: Barnes & Noble, Inc., 1955).

Schumpeter, J. S. *Capitalism, Socialism, and Democracy* (New York: Harper & Brothers, 1950).

Towster, Julian. *Political Powers in the U.S.S.R., 1917-1947* (New York: Oxford University Press, 1948).

9—The State and the Individual

Avey, Albert E. *Handbook in the History of Philosophy*, College Outline Series (New York: Barnes & Noble, Inc., 1954).

Carr, R. K. *Federal Protection of Civil Rights* (Ithaca: Cornell University Press, 1947).

Chafee, Z. *Free Speech in the United States* (Cambridge: Harvard University Press, 1941).

Corwin, E. S. *Liberty Against Government* (Baton Rouge: Louisiana State University Press, 1948).

Dahl, R. A. and Lindblom, C. E. *Politics, Economics, and Welfare* (New York: Harper & Brothers, 1953).

Hertz, J. H. *Political Realism and Political Idealism; A Study in Theories and Realities* (Chicago: Chicago University Press, 1951).

Holcombe, A. N. *Human Rights in the Modern World* (New York: New York University Press, 1948).

Hunt, R. N. C. *The Theory and Practice of Communism; An Introduction* (New York: The Macmillan Co., 1950).

Mill, J. S. *On Liberty* (New York: The Macmillan Co.).

Myrdal, G. *An American Dilemma*, 2 vols. (New York: Harper & Brothers, 1944).

Simon, Y. R. *Philosophy of Democratic Government* (Chicago: University of Chicago Press, 1951).

Steiner, G. A. *Government's Role in Economic Life* (New York: McGraw-Hill Book Co., 1953).

10—Constitutions

Bagehot, Walter. *The English Constitution* (New York: Oxford University Press).

Barnes, William R., ed. *The Constitution of the United States and the Declaration of Independence* (New York: Barnes & Noble, Inc., 1956).

Corwin, E. S. *The Constitution and What it Means Today* (Princeton: Princeton University Press, 1954).

Earle, Edward Mead. *Modern France: Problems of the Third and Fourth Republics* (Princeton: Princeton University Press, 1951).

Fenn, P. T. *The Development of the Constitution* (New York: Appleton-Century, 1948).

Grimes, A. P. *American Political Thought* (New York: Holt, 1955).

Jennings, Sir Ivor. *The British Constitution* (Cambridge: Cambridge University Press, 1947).

McIlwain, C. H. *Constitutionalism, Ancient and Modern* (Ithaca: Cornell University Press, 1940).

Marx, Fritz Morstein, ed. *Foreign Governments* (New York: Prentice-Hall, Inc., 1952).

Mathews, J. M. *The American Constitutional System* (New York: McGraw-Hill Book Co., 1940).

Sayre, Wallace S. *American Government,* College Outline Series (New York: Barnes & Noble, Inc., 1955).

11—Suffrage and Elections

Blumberg, N. B. *One Party Press?* (Lincoln: University of Nebraska Press, 1954).

Gosnell, H. F. *Why Europe Votes* (Chicago: University of Chicago Press, 1930).

Hartmann, E. G. *The Movement to Americanize the Immigrant* (New York: Columbia University Press, 1948).

Howe, Q. and Schlesinger, A. M., eds. *Guide to Politics* (New York: Dial Press, 1954).

Konvitz, M. R. *The Alien and Asiatic in American Law* (Ithaca: Cornell University Press, 1946).

McCormick, R. *History of Voting in New Jersey* (New Brunswick: Rutgers University Press, 1953).

Schofield, A. N. *Local Government Elections* (London: Shaw & Sons, 1954).

Weintraub, R. G. *How to Secure These Rights* (New York: Doubleday & Co., Inc., 1949).

12—Political Parties

Bulmer, T. I. *The Party System in Great Britain* (London: Phoenix House, Ltd., Macmillan Co., 1953).

Butler, D. E. *The Electoral System in Britain, 1918-1951* (London: Oxford University Press, 1953).

Coker, F. W. *Recent Political Thought* (New York: Appleton-Century, 1934).

Committee on Political Parties, American Political Science Association. "Toward a More Responsible Two-Party System." (*American Political Science Review,* Supplement, September, 1950).

Dahl, R. A. and Lindblom, C. E. *Politics, Economics, and Welfare* (New York: Harper & Brothers, 1953).

Key, V. D., Jr. *Politics, Parties, and Pressure Groups* (New York: Thomas Y. Crowell Co., 1952).

Lubell, S. *The Future of American Politics* (New York: Harper & Brothers, 1952).

Merriam, C. E. and Overacker, L. *Primary Elections* (Chicago: University of Chicago Press, 1928).

Penniman, H. R. *Sait's American Parties and Elections* (New York: Appleton-Century-Crofts, 1952).

Sayre, Wallace S. *American Government,* College Outline Series (New York: Barnes & Noble, Inc., 1955).

Schattschneider, E. E. *Party Government* (New York: Farrar and Rinehart, Inc., 1942).

Turner, H. A., ed. *Politics in the U. S.; Readings in Political Parties and Pressure Groups.* (New York: McGraw-Hill Book Co., 1955).

13—Public Opinion and Influences Upon It

Albig, W. *Public Opinion* (New York: McGraw-Hill Book Co., 1939).

Binkley, W. E. and Moos, M. C. *A Grammar of American Politics* (New York: Alfred A. Knopf, 1952).

Chase, Stuart. *Democracy Under Pressure* (New York: Twentieth Century Fund, 1945).

Childs, H. L. *Introduction to Public Opinion* (New York: John Wiley & Sons, Inc., 1940).

Coase, R. H. *British Broadcasting* (London: Longmans, Green and Co., 1950).

Doob, L. W. *Public Opinion and Propaganda* (New York: Henry Holt and Co., Inc., 1948).

Hocking, W. E. *Freedom of the Press: A Framework of Principle* (Chicago: University of Chicago Press, 1947).

Irion, D. C. *Public Opinion and Propaganda* (New York: Thomas Y. Crowell Co., 1950).

Key, V. O., Jr. *Politics, Parties, and Pressure Groups* (New York: Thomas Y. Crowell Co., 1952).

———. *Southern Politics* (New York: Alfred A. Knopf, 1949).

McCamy, J. L. *Government Publicity* (Chicago: University of Chicago Press, 1939).

McKean, Dayton D. *Party Pressure Politics* (Boston: Houghton-Mifflin Co., 1949).

Moscow, Warren. *Politics in the Empire State* (New York: Alfred A. Knopf, 1949).

Mott, G. F. *Journalism,* College Outline Series (New York: Barnes & Noble, Inc., 1956).

Odegard, P. *Pressure Politics; The Story of the Anti-Saloon League* (New York: Columbia University Press, 1928).

Potter, Allen M. "British Party Organization," *(Political Science Quarterly,* Mar., 1951).

Siepmann, C. A. *Radio, Televivsion, and Society* (New York: Oxford University Press, 1950).

Smith, C. W. *Public Opinion in a Democracy* (New York: Prentice-Hall, Inc., 1942).

The Commission on Freedom of the Press. *A Free and Responsible Press* (Chicago: University of Chicago Press, 1947).

Turner, H. A., ed. *Politics in the U. S.; Readings in Political Parties and Pressure Groups* (New York: McGraw-Hill Book Co., 1955).

14—The Legislature

Bailey, S. K. and Samuel, H. *Congress at Work* (New York: Henry Holt & Co., 1952).

Burns, J. M. and Peltason, J. W. *Government by the People: The Dynamics of American National Government* (New York: Prentice-Hall, Inc., 1954).

Chamberlain, J. P. *Legislative Processes, National and State* (New York: Appleton-Century Co., 1936).

Galloway, G. B. *The Legislative Process in Congress* (New York: Thomas Y. Crowell Co., 1953).

Griffith, E. S. *Congress; Its Contemporary Role* (New York: New York University Press, 1951).

Gross, B. M. *The Legislative Struggle: A Study in Social Combat* (New York: McGraw-Hill Book Co., 1953).

Jennings, Sir Ivor. *Parliament* (Cambridge: Cambridge University Press, 1939).

Luce, R. *Legislative Procedure* (Boston: Houghton-Mifflin Co., 1927).

———. *Legislative Problems* (Boston: Houghton-Mifflin Co., 1935).

Mill, J. S. *Representative Government* (New York: Oxford University Press).

Ranney, John C. and Carter, Gwendolen M. *The Major Foreign Powers* (New York: Harcourt, Brace & Co., 1952).

Sayre, Wallace S. *American Government,* College Outline Series (New York: Barnes & Noble, Inc., 1955).

Walker, H. *The Legislative Process* (New York: The Ronald Press Co., 1948).

15—The Executive

Campion, Sir Gilbert, *et al. British Government Since 1918* (London: Allen & Unwin, 1950).

Corwin, E. S. *The President, Office and Powers* (New York: New York University Press, 1948).

Earle, E. M., ed. *Modern France: Problems of the Third and Fourth Republics* (Princeton: Princeton University Press, 1951).

Harper, S. N. and Thompson, R. *The Government of the Soviet Union* (New York: Van Nostrand Co., 1949).

Hyman, S. *The American President* (New York: Harper & Brothers, 1954).

Jennings, Sir Ivor. *Cabinet Government* (Cambridge: Cambridge University Press, 1951).

Marx, F. M., ed. *Foreign Governments: The Dynamics of Politics Abroad* (New York: Prentice-Hall, Inc., 1952).

Neumann, R. G. *European and Comparative Government* (New York: McGraw-Hill Book Co., 1951).

SELECTED REFERENCES

Towster, J. *Political Power in the U.S.S.R., 1917-1947* (New York: Oxford University Press, 1948).

16—The Judiciary

Amos, Sir Maurice S. *British Justice: An Outline of the Administration of Criminal Justice in England and Wales* (London: Longmans, Green and Co., 1940).
Berman, Harold J. *Justice in Russia: An Interpretation of Soviet Law* (Cambridge: Harvard University Press, 1950).
Binkley, W. E. and Moos, Malcolm, C. *A Grammar of American Politics* (New York: Alfred A. Knopf, 1952).
Ferguson, J. H. and McHenry, D. E. *The American System of Government* (New York: McGraw-Hill Book Co., 1953).
Harper, S. N. and Thompson, Ronald. *The Government of the Soviet Union* (New York: Van Nostrand Co., Inc., 1949).
Jennings, Sir Ivor. *The Law and the Constitution* (London: London University Press, 1943).
Pound, Roscoe. *The Spirit of the Common Law* (Boston: Marshall Jones Co., 1921).
———. *Organization of Courts* (Boston: Little, Brown & Co., 1940).
Sunderland, Edson R. *Judicial Administration* (Chicago: Callaghan, 1948).

17—Public Administration

Carpenter, W. S. *Unfinished Business of Civil Service Reform* (Princeton: Princeton University Press, 1952).
Charlesworth, J. C. *Governmental Administration* (New York: Harper & Brothers, 1951).
Dale, H. E. *The Higher Civil Service of Great Britain* (Oxford: The Clarendon Press, 1941).
Dimock, M. E. and Dimock, G. O. *Public Administration* (New York: Rinehart & Co., 1953).
Hyneman, C. S. *Bureaucracy in a Democracy* (New York: Harper & Brothers, 1950).
Macmahon, A. W. and Millett, J. D. *Federal Administrators* (New York: Columbia University Press, 1939).
Pfiffner, J. M. and Presthus, R. V. *Public Administration* (New York: Ronald Press, 1953).
Sayre, Wallace S. *American Government,* College Outline Series (New York: Barnes & Noble, Inc., 1955).
Report on the Commission on Organization of the Executive Branch of Government (Washington: Government Printing Office, 1949).
Simon, H. A., Smithburg, D. W., and Thompson, V. A. *Public Administration* (New York: Alfred A. Knopf, 1950).

White, L. D. *Introduction to the Study of Public Administration* (New York: The Macmillan Co., 1955).

18—Public Finance

Babb, H. and Martin, C. *Business Law,* College Outline Series (New York: Barnes & Noble, Inc., 1955).

Blough, R. *The Federal Taxing Process* (New York: Prentice-Hall, Inc., 1952).

Hicks, Ursula K. W. *Public Finance* (London: Cambridge University Press, 1947).

Sayre, Wallace S. *American Government,* College Outline Series (New York: Barnes & Noble, Inc., 1955).

Schwartz, Harry. *Russia's Soviet Economy* (New York: Prentice-Hall, Inc., 1954).

19—Local Government

Anderson, W. *The Units of Government in the United States* (Chicago: Public Administration Service, 1949).

Chester, D. N. *Central and Local Government; Financial and Administrative Relations* (New York: The Macmillan Co., 1951).

Council of State Governments. *The Book of States* (The Council, 1951).

Finer, H. *English Local Government* (London: Methuen & Co., Ltd., 1950).

Lancaster, L. W. *Government in Rural America* (New York: Van Nostrand Co., Inc., 1952).

Morlan, R. L. *Capitol, Courthouse, and City Hall: Readings in American State and Local Government* (Boston: Houghton-Mifflin Co., 1954).

Phillips, J. C. *State and Local Government in America* (New York: American Book Co., 1954).

Sayre, Wallace S. *American Government,* College Outline Series (New York: Barnes & Noble, Inc., 1955).

Tait, J. *The Mediaeval English Borough: Studies on Its Origins and Constitutional History* (New York: Barnes & Noble, Inc., 1936).

Wendell, M. *Relations between Federal and State Courts* (New York: Columbia University Press, 1949).

20—International Relations and Associations

Brinton, C. *From Many, One* (Cambridge: Harvard University Press, 1948).

Chase, E. P. *The United Nations in Action* (New York: McGraw-Hill Book Co., 1950).

De Huszar, G. B. and De Grazia, A., Jr. *International Relations,* College Outline Series (New York: Barnes & Noble, Inc., 1953).

SELECTED REFERENCES

Dulles, J. F. *War or Peace* (New York: The Macmillan Company, 1950).
Eagleton, C. *International Government* (New York: The Ronald Press, 1948).
Ewing, A. C. *The Individual, the State, and World Government* (New York: The Macmillan Co., 1947).
Haines, C. G. *The Threat of Soviet Imperialism* (Baltimore: Johns Hopkins Press, 1954).
Hill, N. *International Relations* (New York: Oxford University Press, 1950).
Kelsen, H. *The Law of the United Nations; A Critical Analysis of Its Fundamental Problems* (New York: Frederick A. Praeger, Inc., 1950).
Landman, J. H. and Wender, H. *World Since 1914,* College Outline Series (New York: Barnes & Noble, Inc., 1955).
Levi, Werner. *Fundamentals of World Organization* (Minneapolis: The University of Minnesota Press, 1950).
Mangone, G. J. *The Idea and Practice of World Government* (New York: Columbia University Press, 1951).
Morgenthau, H. J. *Politics Among Nations* (New York: Alfred A. Knopf, 1954).
Perkins, D. *The American Approach to Foreign Policy* (Cambridge: Harvard University Press, 1952).
Schuman, F. L. *International Politics* (New York: McGraw-Hill Book Co., 1953).
Schwarzenberger, G. *Power Politics; A Study of International Society* (New York: Frederick A. Praeger, Inc., 1951).
Strausz-Hupé, R. and Possony, S. T. *International Relations in the Age of Conflict between Democracy and Dictatorship* (New York: McGraw-Hill Book Co., 1954).
Taylor, A. J. P. *The Italian Problem in European Diplomacy, 1847-1849* (New York: Barnes & Noble, Inc., 1934).

21—International Law

Brierly, J. L. *The Law of Nations* (Oxford: The Clarendon Press, 1949).
Canham, Erwin D., et al. *Awakening: The World at Mid-Century* (New York: Longmans, Green and Co., 1951).
Hyde, C. C. *International Law, Chiefly as Interpreted and Applied by the United States* (Boston: Little, Brown & Co., 1945).
Keenan, J. B. and Brown, B. F. *Crimes Against International Law* (Washington: Public Affairs Press, 1950).
Lauterpacht, H. *International Law and Human Rights* (New York: Frederick A. Praeger, Inc., 1950).

Examination Questions

This examination covers most of the major topics discussed in the outline and, therefore, may be used by the student as a trial final examination.

The examination is divided into four parts and makes use of four different types of questions: essay, identification, completion, and association. Answers are supplied for the completion and the association tests (p. 237).

Essay Questions

1. Explain on what grounds political science may be regarded as a true science.
2. Explain the relationship between political science and history.
3. What is the relationship between political science and economics?
4. Explain how the political scientist uses the inductive method.
5. Discuss the five essential characteristics of the state.
6. Explain what is included within the territory of a state besides land area.
7. Explain why component members of federal unions can not be regarded as states.
8. Distinguish between a state and a nation. What are the principal elements of nationality?
9. Explain the probable effects of kinship and religion in the creation of primitive states.
10. Contrast the political organizations (states and empires) of Greece and Western Asia in ancient times.
11. State the contributions of the Roman Empire to modern politics.
12. Discuss the several factors which contributed to the establishment of strong national states at the end of the Middle Ages.
13. Discuss the conditions which made possible the development of the modern democratic state.
14. Explain the difference between the social contract and the governmental contract.
15. Explain which theory as to the origin of the state best conforms to realities and in what respects other theories are lacking.
16. Distinguish between the state and government.
17. Explain why there can be no legal limit to the exercise of power by the sovereign.
18. List, with brief explanations, the principal characteristics of sovereignty.
19. Discuss the problem of sovereignty in a federal system of government.
20. Distinguish between legal sovereignty and political sovereignty.
21. Discuss the attitude of political pluralists toward the doctrine of legal sovereignty.
22. Discuss criticisms of the doctrine of sovereignty by internationalists.

EXAMINATION QUESTIONS

23. Explain the advantages to a state and its people of uniformity of law.
24. Explain the points of disagreement between analytical and sociological jurists.
25. Compare and contrast the systems of Roman law and Teutonic law.
26. Discuss the origin and characteristics of the common law.
27. Explain how equity developed and discuss its characteristics.
28. Discuss the importance of the individual in considering the ends for which the state exists.
29. Discuss various reasons why states engage in business functions.
30. Explain how it is possible for people to be in substantial agreement concerning the ends of the state and yet disagree violently concerning the propriety of the state's undertaking particular functions.
31. Write a brief essay on the reconciliation of liberty with the powers of the state.
32. Explain points of likeness and difference between socialism and communism.
33. Explain the relationship between individual freedom and communism.
34. Explain the reasons for the growth of empirical collectivism and state typical proposals.
35. Distinguish between an absolute monarchy and a limited monarchy.
36. Define the republican form of government and state its essential characteristics.
37. Suggest reasons why some contemporary states have retained the limited monarchy.
38. Compare and contrast an absolute monarch with a contemporary dictator.
39. Describe the political position of subdivisions of a state which has a unitary government.
40. Explain the advantages and disadvantages of unitary government.
41. How do various federal systems differ in the division of powers between the central government and its component units?
42. Briefly trace the principal steps in the development of the constitution of Great Britain.
43. Discuss conflicting views and practices as to the nature of a constitutional convention.
44. What subjects should be included in a written constitution? What subjects should not be included?
45. Distinguish between flexible constitutions and rigid constitutions.
46. Discuss the principle of separation of powers in theory and in practice.
47. Compare the processes of amending the constitutions of the United States and of the Fourth French Republic.
48. Where and how are the initiative and referendum used for the amendment of written constitutions?
49. Contrast American and European views as to the nature of a written constitution.
50. How does judicial review affect the executive and legislative branches?
51. Explain the privileges, obligations, and duties of the citizen.
52. Name and distinguish between the two principles of determining citizenship by birth.

53. Explain the process by which an alien may become a citizen of the United States.

54. What is the importance of natural-law concepts of individual freedom?

55. Show by several examples that constitutional guarantees of civil rights are not absolute, but are subject to limitations.

56. State the duties which an individual may be called on to perform through the exercise of the suffrage.

57. State the principal theories as to the nature of the suffrage.

58. What were the principal arguments for and against the extension of the suffrage?

59. Explain the relative importance of the concepts of equality and liberty in the exercise of the suffrage.

60. List, with brief comment, the disqualifications for the suffrage which exist at present.

61. What are the essential characteristics of the Australian ballot?

62. Explain whether or not you would be in favor of a law imposing penalties for failure to vote.

63. Explain the usefulness of the initiative and referendum in statute-making.

64. For what reasons would you be in favor of, or opposed to, the adoption of the recall of public officers?

65. Compare the administration of elections in the United States and in Europe.

66. What services are performed by political parties in a democratic state?

67. Explain the functions of an opposition party.

68. What are the relative strengths and weaknesses of the biparty system and the multiparty system?

69. State the principal functions of the official party in a totalitarian state.

70. Compare the organization of the Socialist party with that of one of the major parties in the United States.

71. Describe the organization of political parties in Great Britain.

72. What are the principal defects of national party conventions in the United States?

73. Describe the process of nominating candidates by primary elections.

74. What are the merits and defects of the primary election system?

75. Discuss the power and influence exerted by machines and bosses.

76. Comment on the basic assumptions underlying the theory of government by public opinion.

77. What criticisms may be made of the sources of information available to the average voter?

78. Describe methods of propaganda in totalitarian dictatorships.

79. Contrast the effects of group pressures in the United States and in Great Britain.

80. Discuss the methods used by private groups to influence legislative and executive action.

81. What are the chief problems in the making of statutes under modern conditions?

82. Explain the means by which a legislative body may control the administration.

EXAMINATION QUESTIONS

83. What constitutional safeguards exist to protect the legislature from executive interference?
84. Discuss the advantages and disadvantages of bicameral legislatures.
85. Should members of a legislative body serve out their terms or be subject to dissolution?
86. Discuss various theories concerning the duty of a representative.
87. What are the advantages and disadvantages of geographical representation?
88. Explain the underlying theory of proportional representation.
89. Define functional representation and comment on its use in several European states.
90. Compare the list system and the Hare system of proportional representation.
91. What procedural requirements are imposed upon Congress by the Constitution of the United States?
92. Compare the powers of the speakers of the House of Representatives, of the House of Commons, and of the lower house of a state legislature.
93. Compare the functions of legislative committees in the United States, Great Britain, and France.
94. List, with brief comment, the functions of the executive branch.
95. Explain why the power of removal is essential to the executive's duty to enforce the law.
96. Discuss the powers of the executive in time of war.
97. Discuss the executive's powers with respect to relations with other states.
98. Contrast the cabinet system with the presidential system.
99. Describe the composition of the President's cabinet and estimate its influence in the determination of policies.
100. Discuss the powers and influence of the President in legislation.
101. Compare the position of the President with that of the governor of one of the states of the United States.
102. Discuss the relations between the Prime Minister and other members of the cabinet in Great Britain.
103. Describe the position of a British minister in relation to his ministry.
104. Explain whether Parliament controls the cabinet or the cabinet controls Parliament.
105. How does the cabinet system in France differ from the British cabinet system?
106. Describe the composition and powers of the Swiss collegial executive.
107. Discuss the exercise of executive powers by various organs of the Soviet Union.
108. Summarize the principal functions of the judicial branch of government.
109. What considerations should govern in the organization of a system of courts?
110. Discuss judicial organization in a federal system of government.
111. Define the respective jurisdictions of state and federal courts in the United States.
112. Discuss the composition and powers of administrative courts in France.

113. Compare methods of selecting judges in France, Great Britain, and the United States.
114. What reforms might be accomplished by the establishment of a unified court system?
115. Criticize existing rules of procedure in most of the courts in the United States.
116. What modifications of the jury system have been made or proposed?
117. Discuss judicial control over the administration.
118. Criticize the administrative organization of national and state governments in the United States.
119. Describe the functions of each of the essential divisions of a good administrative structure.
120. Explain the relative advantages of single heads and of commissions.
121. Compare the civil services of the United States and Great Britain.
122. What are the advantages of the merit system over the spoils system?
123. Compare methods of examining applicants for the civil service in various countries.
124. Discuss the problems of discipline and tenure in the civil service.
125. What principles should govern in making public expenditures?
126. What are the essential elements of a good financial organization?
127. Define budget. Explain the process of preparing a budget.
128. Compare British and American procedure in legislative consideration of the budget.
129. List the principal taxes in general use and explain whether or not the burden of each can be shifted from the original payer.
130. List, with brief explanations, the essential qualities of a good tax system.
131. Explain points of similarity and difference between excise and sales taxes.
132. Explain the reasons for the creation of local governments.
133. Compare the local government systems of Great Britain, France, and the U.S.S.R.
134. Describe the organization of county governments in the United States.
135. Criticize the methods which state legislatures have used in granting charters to municipal corporations.
136. Describe each of the principal forms of municipal government in the United States.
137. Discuss intergovernmental problems of metropolitan areas.
138. What are the essential characteristics of the European state system?
139. Explain how the doctrine of sovereignty has affected efforts to establish a world order.
140. Explain the influence of nationalism on efforts to establish a world order.
141. Discuss the effectiveness of the balance of power as a means of preserving peace.
142. Classify the underlying factors of state power in the order of their importance.
143. Discuss the advantages and disadvantages which result from pursuing a policy of economic nationalism.

EXAMINATION QUESTIONS

144. Compare the League of Nations and the United Nations as to the sanctions available for the punishment of aggression.

145. State the powers and duties of the Secretariat of the United Nations.

146. Explain the difficulties in the way of world federation.

147. Explain from what sources international law has been derived.

148. Discuss the arguments as to whether or not international law is true law.

149. What are the rights and obligations of states under international law?

150. Discuss the effectiveness of the international rules relating to war and neutrality.

Identification Exercise

Identify each of the following words and phrases:

Public law	Interpellation	Fee
Deductive method	Declaratory judgment	Special district
State of nature	Arbitration	Strong mayor
Thomas Hobbes	Line organization	Dollar diplomacy
Pluralist	Unbalanced budget	Hot pursuit
Natural law	Degressive tax	Optional clause
Machiavelli	Grant-in-aid	Service function
Idealistic theory	Municipal home rule	Politburo
John Austin	Open-Door Policy	Personal union
De facto sovereignty	Embassy	Mandate
Philosophical jurist	Prescription	Montesquieu
Statute	Trusteeship Council	Enfranchisement
Geopolitics	Codification	Indirect election
Juristic theory	Tyranny	Repeating
John Locke	Lord Bryce	Central office
External sovereignty	League	Legislative caucus
Code Napoléon	Satellite state	Gerrymander
Substantive law	Model State Constitution	Cumulative voting
Syndicalism	Nationals	Previous question
Direct democracy	Oath of allegiance	Executive agreement
Rule of law	Preferential vote	Pardon
Protectorate	Third party	Presidium
Petition of Right	Open primary	*Stare decisis*
Preamble	Unicameralism	Conciliation
Procedural right	Limited vote	Loose construction
Long ballot	Sublegislative power	Senatorial courtesy
Personation	Amnesty	General property tax
Optional primary law	Motion of censure	Special assessment
Farm Bloc	Inner cabinet	Kellogg-Briand Pact
Bullet voting	Advisory opinion	Benelux group
Closure	Political question	Accretion
Standing committee	Government corporation	Open sea
Question hour	Comptroller General	UNESCO

Completion Test

Complete the following sentences by writing the appropriate words or phrases in the blank spaces. When you have completed this exercise, compare your answers with those which appear in the key on p. 237.

1. The field of public law includes _____ law, _____ law, and _____ law.
2. The existence of the state is condemned under _____ and _____ theories.
3. _____ sovereignty is based on temporary possession of physical force, whereas _____ sovereignty is based on law and right.
4. In the United States, constitutional law is enforced by the _____ _____ exercising the power of _____.
5. In the Anglo-American legal system, preventive justice may be obtained through _____, but redress for damages already inflicted may be obtained under _____.
6. The theory of individualism regards the state as _____ and holds that state power should be confined to _____.
7. The _____ is the nearest American equivalent to pure democracy.
8. Federalism combines the advantages of _____ with those of _____.
9. In states of the United States wholly new constitutions are drafted by _____ and ratified by _____.
10. Provisions of the Bonn (West German) constitution relating to _____ and _____ are not subject to amendment.
11. The fundamental problem of constitution-making is to reconcile the rights of _____ with the interests of _____.
12. Contracts which involve either _____ or _____ will not be enforced by the state.
13. The two principal forms in which the Australian ballot exists in the United States are the _____ ballot and the _____ ballot.
14. The _____ primary imposes tests of party allegiance, but the _____ primary preserves the secrecy of the voter's party preference.
15. Deprivation of _____ and of _____ may follow the refusal of a member of Congress to support his party.
16. The term of office of members of a legislative body may be either _____, as in the United States, or _____, as in Great Britain.
17. In a small state with a homogeneous population a _____ legislature is probably superior to a _____ legislature.

EXAMINATION QUESTIONS

18. In practice, proportional representation has encouraged the formation of _____ and has increased the difficulties of obtaining _____ to conduct the government.

19. In Great Britain the _____ is the titular executive and the _____ is the real executive.

20. In Anglo-American judicial procedure, a person may be tried only after indictment by a _____ and may be convicted only by the _____ verdict of a _____.

21. Judges are chosen by _____ in Great Britain and usually by _____ in states of the United States.

22. The operative and auxiliary agencies in the civil service are sometimes called _____ and _____ agencies, respectively.

23. In the United States the merit system has been slowly extended since the passage of the _____ but _____ positions are still subject to political appointment.

24. A tax on the whole estate of a deceased person is called an _____ tax; but a tax on the share which each heir receives is called an _____ tax.

25. Provision for paying off the public debt may be made either through _____ or through _____.

26. French local governments are rigidly supervised by the Ministry of _____, which has an agent called a _____ in every department.

27. The principal unit of local government in New England is the _____; in the Southern states the _____ is the principal unit.

28. Negotiations with foreign states are carried on through the _____ service; business and personal affairs of individuals abroad are handled through the _____ service.

29. In the United States all treaties must be ratified by a _____ vote of the _____ before becoming effective.

30. A merchant vessel suspected of engaging in _____ or _____ may be visited and searched on the open sea.

Association Test

Each word or phrase in the first of each of these pairs of columns is in some way associated with one of the words or phrases in the second of each pair. Fill in each of the blank spaces in column B with the number assigned to its pair in column A; fill in the blank spaces before column D, F, H, and J with the numbers from columns C, E, G, and I, respectively. When you have completed this exercise, compare your answers with those which appear in the key on p. 237.

COLUMN A
1. Religious stage
2. Legislation
3. Governmental contract
4. Chancellor
5. Canadian province
6. Justinian code
7. Damages
8. Metaphysical stage
9. Electorate
10. Jean Bodin

COLUMN B
____ Roman law
____ Sovereignty
____ Plato
____ Common law
____ Political sovereignty
____ Statutes
____ Divine right of kings
____ Declaration of Independence
____ Equity
____ Federal union

COLUMN C
1. Competition
2. Classification of governments
3. League of Nations
4. Labor unions
5. India
6. Aristocracy
7. French Revolution
8. Italy
9. Pure democracy
10. Confederation

COLUMN D
____ Commonwealth status
____ Mandates
____ Liberty, Equality, Fraternity
____ Congress
____ Swiss cantons
____ Individualism
____ Fascism
____ Aristotle
____ Syndicalism
____ Oligarchy

COLUMN E
1. Checks and balances
2. Literacy test
3. *jus soli*
4. Corrupt practice
5. Natural right
6. Bicameralism
7. *Marbury* vs. *Madison*
8. Vote of confidence
9. Electoral college
10. Freedom of speech

COLUMN F
____ Citizenship
____ Indirect election
____ Bill of Rights
____ Judicial review
____ Veto power
____ Suffrage
____ Bribery
____ Cabinet system
____ House of Lords
____ Law of reason

COLUMN G
1. Soviet Russia
2. Negotiation
3. Judicial review
4. Switzerland
5. Grand jury
6. Spoils system
7. Commissions
8. Equity
9. Merit system
10. France

COLUMN H
____ Indictment
____ Quasi-judicial power
____ Strict construction
____ Administrative court
____ Injunction
____ Written examination
____ Collegial executive
____ Ambassadors
____ Presidium
____ Patronage

EXAMINATION QUESTIONS

COLUMN I	COLUMN J
1. Protective tariff	_____ Balance of power
2. Three-mile limit	_____ League of Nations
3. Cession	_____ Fugitive from justice
4. Military Staff Committee	_____ Sinking fund
5. State system	_____ City charter
6. Soviet imperialism	_____ Loss of territory
7. Bond issue	_____ Marginal sea
8. Home rule	_____ Security Council
9. Treaty of Versailles	_____ Customs duties
10. Extradition	_____ Ideological penetration

Key to the Completion Test

1. constitutional . . . international . . . administrative. 2. anarchist . . . socialist. 3. *defacto* . . . *dejure*. 4. Supreme Court . . . judicial review. 5. equity . . . the common law. 6. a necessary evil . . . police protection. 7. New England town meeting. 8. national strength . . . local autonomy. 9. constitutional conventions . . . popular vote. 10. bill of rights . . . existence of the Laender. 11. the individual . . . society as a whole. 12. monopolies . . . personal servitude. 13. Indiana . . . Massachusetts. 14. closed . . . open. 15. seniority on committees . . . party support in elections. 16. a fixed term . . . subject to dissolution. 17. unicamerial . . . bicameral. 18. splinter parties . . . a majority. 19. queen . . . cabinet. 20. grand jury . . . unanimous . . . trial jury. 21. the Lord Chief Justice . . . popular vote. 22. line . . . service. 23. Pendleton Act of 1883 . . . the highest administrative. 24. estate . . . inheritance. 25. a sinking fund . . . serial bonds. 26. Interior . . . prefect. 27. town . . . county. 28. diplomatic . . . consular. 29. two-thirds . . . Senate. 30. piracy . . . the slave trade.

Key to the Association Test

This is the order in which numbers should appear:
COLUMN B: 6, 10, 8, 7, 9, 2, 1, 3, 4, 5.
COLUMN D: 5, 3, 7, 10, 9, 1, 8, 2, 4, 6.
COLUMN F: 3, 9, 10, 7, 1, 2, 4, 8, 6, 5.
COLUMN H: 5, 7, 3, 10, 8, 9, 4, 2, 1, 6.
COLUMN J: 5, 9, 10, 7, 8, 3, 2, 4, 1, 6.

Index

Act of Settlement, 69
Address, 114, 114n.
Administration: and continuous reorganization, 158; and the executive, 125; control of, 113-114; executive control of, 155-156; in the U. S., 154; judicial control of, 156; legislative control of, 155; public, 153-163; relationship to government, 154-156; structure of, 157-158; under unstable governments, 28; and units structures, 158-159; use of, 153, 153n.
Administrators, 158-159
Administrative Procedure Act, 156
Agencies: auxiliary, 158; operative, 157-158; staff, 157
Aliens, 213: and U. S. citizenship, 62n.; defined, 30; duties of, 60
Allegiance: defined, 61; secular, 34
Alliance: defined, 58; terms of, 58
Ambassador extraordinary, 215
American Farm Bureau Federation, 105
American Federation of Labor Organizations, 105
Amendments: Fourteenth, 146; Sixteenth, 171
American party organization, 93-96
Anarchism, 19-20; and syndicalism, 22
Anarchist, 19
Annex to the Convenant, 200
A priori, 14
Arbitration, 151, 152: international, 216; in the U.S., 152
Aristotle, 4, 5, 9, 13, 26
Articles of Confederation (U.S.), 59
Assemblies, in feudal times, 114
Association, freedom of, 65
Associations, 32: international, 187, 199-207; classification of, 199
Atomic Energy Commission, 204
Auditor's office, 168
Austin, John, 37
Australia, 51, 52, 87
Austria-Hungary, and real unions, 52n.
Austro-Hungarian empire, 33n.
Balance of power, maintenance of, 198
Balances, 72, 74
Ballot, 25, 27, 84, 85
Bank deposits, protection of, 18
Belgium, 193: compulsory voting, 87
Bentham, Jeremy, 187
Bible, 46: and natural rights, 63
Bicameralism, 115-116
"Big lie," 103
Bill of Rights (England), 64: and constitutional development, 69
Bill of Rights (U.S.), 66
Bills of rights: in constitution, 64; in preamble, 64
Biparty system, 90-91
Birth, citizenship by, 61-62
Blanket injunctions, 141-142
Bodin, Jean, 35
Bonds: government, 176; serial, 176
Bonn Republic: and federal systems, 51, 52, 54; hierarchies of courts, 146; legislative amendment, 76
Borrowing, government: methods of, 175; reasons for, 175

Bosses, political, 96-98: and control of party organization, 97; corrupt, 97-98; defined, 96-97
Brazil, and federal systems, 52
British Broadcasting Corporation, 110
British Commonwealth, 13: imperial organization, 56-57
British law, 44-45
British party organization, 93
Bryce, Lord, 24, 25
Budget, 166-168: capital outlays, 167; current, 167; defined, 166; executive preparation of, 167, 168, 168n.; legislative action, 168; unbalanced, 166
Business functions, state, 18, 20
Business, regulation of, 18
Bynkershoek, Cornelius van, 212
Byzantine, 10-11
Cabinet, British, 93: accountability of, 131; appointment and tenure of, 131; and Parliament, 133-134
Canada: and federal systems, 51, 52, 54; and federal unions, 31
Candidates: number of, 85; number of in totalitarian states, 84
Cantons, 31
Case: bona fide, 140; civil, 141, 141n.; criminal, 141, 141n.
Caucus American legislative, 96
Central propaganda offices, 111
Citizens, defined, 30, 60
Citizenship, 60-62: by birth, 61-62; by naturalization, 62; conflicts, 62; two principles of, 62
City-States: Greek, 9-10; Italian, 10
Civil liberties, 63-67
Civil rights, 2n., 63-67
Civil Service, 159-163: appointment and promotion, 161-162; defined, 159; discipline and removal, 162-163; European, 161; Great Britain, 162; merit system, 160-161; personnel, 160f; "spoils system," 160; U.S., 161
Civil Service Commission (U.S.), 161
Civil War, 71
Chamber of Commerce (U.S.), 105
Chancellor of the Exchequer, 167
Charles I, 36
Charles II, 69
Charters, municipal: and classification system, 183; and optional system, 183; by legislative act, 183; methods of granting, 183
Checks, 72, 74
Checks and balances, application of Newtonian theory, 5n.
China, 193, 202, 203; communist, 210n.
Church, 11, 35
Clan, 7
Closed primary, defined, 95
Conciliation, 151-152: in U.S., 152
Codes: criminal, 26; Napoleon, 47
Colonial empires, 12-13
Colonialism, 192: defined, 192
Commission for Conventional Armaments, 204
Committee on Accounts, 168
Committee of the Whole, 122
Committee on Rules, 121

238

INDEX

Committee: special, 122; sessional, 122; standing, 122
Committee on Ways and Means, 168
Committees, 122: American political, 96
Communes, 180
Communications, licensing of, 111
Communism, 22
Communist, 19
Comparative method, 6
Compensation, unemployment, 18
Competition, unrestricted, 21
Comptroller General of U. S., 169
Controller's office, 168
Confederation: and sovereignty, 59; and Swiss, 59; and U.S., 59; defined, 58
Congress (U.S.), 37, 46, 77
Congress, Continental, 207
Congressional Campaign Committee, 96
Conservatives, moderate: and Empirical Collectivism, 24
Constitution (U.S.), 37, 71: amendment by constituent assemblies, 77; and popular ratification, 71; loose construction of, 143n.; strict construction of, 143n.
Constitution, Model State, 71, 71n.
Constitution of 1936 (U.S.S.R.), 27: and federal systems, 54
Constitutions, 68-79: amendment by constituent assemblies, 77; and bills of rights, 74; and conventions, 69, 71; and democracy, 26; and judicial review, 78; legislative amendment, 76-77; by royal grant, 71; creation of, 68-71; enforcement of, 78-79; evolutionary development of, 68-69; expansion of, 77; flexible, 74-77; formal amendment of, 76-77; participation of electorate in amendment, 77; requisites of, 71-72, 74; review of, 78-79; rigid, 74-77; unwritten, 68, 69; written, 68, 69, 71, 72
Consul general, 215
Contract, freedom of, 65-66
Council, Economic and Social, 203-205
Council, executive (Swiss): appointment and tenure, 137-138
Council of Republic (France), and legislative amendment, 76
Council (U.S.S.R.), supremacy of, 138f
Councils, judicial, 148
Counties: British, 177; U.S., 181-182
Court of Claims (U.S.), 147n.
Court of Common Pleas, 44
Court of Customs and Patent Appeals (U.S.), 147n.
Court systems, structure of, 144-145
Courts, hierarchies of administrative, 147, 147n.
Courts: hierarchies in federal systems, 145-146; intermediate appellate courts, 145; of general jurisdiction, 145; of summary jurisdiction, 145; specialized, 144; supreme, 145; unification of, 147-148
Courts, U.S.: cases between citizens, 146; cases between states, 146; jurisdiction of federal, 146; state, 146
Convention, 69; defined, 69n.
Conventions, American political, 94
Covenant of the League, 200

Crime, suppression of, 17
Criminals, prosecution of, 17
Crises, internal, 164
Cumulative system, 120
Death rates, 28
Debt, 164
Debts, government, 175
Debts, public, 175-176; methods of borrowing, 175; methods of payment, 176; self-liquidating, 175, 175n.
Decisions: five-to-four, 143; judicial, 216
Declaration of Human Rights, 205
Declaration of the Rights of Man, 64
Deductive logic, 5
De Jure Belli, 208
De Juri Belli ac Pacis, 208
Democracies, 24, 25: and free discussion, 109-110
Democratic states, 12
Democracy, 22, 25-26, 189, 194: direct, 87-89
Departements, 177, 180
Developments: scientific, 24; technological, 24
Dictatorship, 26-27
Dictatorships: and federal systems, 54; pattern of, 27
Diplomats, 215
Direct democracy, in U.S., 87-88
Director of the Budget (U.S.), 167
Discrimination, against Orientals, 55
Disenfranchisement, 80
Disputes, international: adjusting, 214-216; and agents of intercourse, 214-215; and consular service, 215; and diplomatic service, 215; and judicial decisions, 216; and mediation and arbitration, 216; and treaties, 215-216
Disputes, settlement of, 141
Districts, special (U.S.), 182
Docks, construction of, 18
"Dollar diplomacy," 193
Duc de Sully, 187
Dumping, 173n.
Duties, customs, 172-173: defined, 172; discriminatory, 173; protective, 173, 173n.; retaliatory, 173
Election: defined, 83; direct in U.S., 84; indirect in France, 84
Elections, 2n., 83-87: administration 86-87; American administration, 86; American primary, 94-96; centralized administration of, 86; closed primary, 95; compulsory voting, 87; decentralized administration, 86; direct, 83-84; disadvantages of American primary, 95; frequency of, 86; indirect, 83-84; open primary, 95; prevention of corrupt practices, 86; problems of nonvoting, 86-87; time of, 86
Electorate, 37: function of, 80
Empires: ancient, 8-10; and dictators, 26; Austro-Hungarian, 33n., 201; British, 13; colonial, 12-13; Dutch, 13; German, 57; modern, 11-13; Roman, 10, 194; Russian, 193, 201; Turkish, 33n., 57, 201
Empirical collectivism, 23-24
Enforcement, of international law, 209
Enfranchisement, 80

England, 12, 36, 194
Equity, 44, 45
Essential functions, of the state, 17, 20
Executive Acts, review by Supreme Court, 142-143
Executive acts, review of, 142-143
Executive, 124-139: American presidential system, 128-130; and administrative policy, 125; and enforcement of law, 124-125; and foreign relations, 126; and military forces, 125-126; and pardoning power, 126; British cabinet system, 130-134; French cabinet system, 134-137; powers and functions, 124-126; representative systems of, 127-139; Soviet Union, 138-139; Swiss collegial system, 137-138
Executives: and group pressures, 107-108; collegial, 127; real, 127; single, 127; titular, 127
Expatriation, defined, 61n.
Expenditures, considerations: economy, 166; over-all, 165; for governmental enterprises, 166, 166n.; for new services, 165; for public works, 165-166
Expenditures, government, 164-166: and emergency relief, 165; and national defense, 165; and public services, 165; principles of, 165-166; reasons for in U.S., 164-165
Experience, historical, 34
Experimental method, 6
Family, 7
Fascism, 23: defined, 23
Federal Communications Commission, 110
Federation, European, 187
Federal unions, and federalists, 39
Federal Regulation of Lobbying Act, 105-106
Felony, 49
Feudal system, 11
Finance Committee (U.S.), 168
Finance, government: organization of, 166-169; requirements of efficient organization, 166
Finance, public, 164-176: debts, 175-176; taxation, 169-175
Finland, 202
Food and Agriculture Organization, 206
Foreign relations, and executive, 126
Forms of government, municipal: commission, 184-185; council-manager, 185; mayor-council, 184
Fourth French Republic, 120: and legislative amendment, 76
France, 12, 26, 194, 203: and administrative law, 49, 147; and commissions, 122; and League, 202; and perpetual loans, 176; and unitary systems, 31n., 51
Free discussion: and democratic states, 109-110; and means of exercising in U.S.S.R., 110; and totalitarian states, 110-111
Freedom: personal, 66; petition and assembly, 25; speech and press, 25
Functions of state, 16-18: classification of, 17-18; defined, 17; theories of, 19-28
General Assembly, 203, 205, 206

"General recognition," 210, 210n.
General welfare: and empirical collectivism, 23-24; and individualism, 20; promotion of, 16
Geopolitics: and political science, 4; defined, 4
Germany, 12, 33n., 60, 200, 201, 202
Gerrymandering, 118
Glanville, 47
"Good neighbor" policy, 193
Government and business, 2n.
Government, and statehood, 30-31
Government, local, 177-186: and administration, 177n.; and state power, 177, 179; defined, 177; in France, 180; in Great Britain, 180-181; in U.S.S.R., 180n.; in U.S. counties, 181-182; in U.S. towns, 182; in special districts (U.S.), 182; reasons for, 177, 179; rural in U.S., 181-182; systems of, 180-181
Government, municipal: and charters, 183; and home rule, 183-184; forms of, 184-185; in U.S., 182-186; metropolitan areas, 185-186
Government, world, 206-207
Governments, local: creation of, 179; supervision of, 179
Governments, unstable, 28
Governor, office of (U.S.), 130
Grant-in-aid, 179
Great Britain, 69, 203: and broadcasting station, 110; and committees, 122; and constituent functions, 113; and democracy, 26; and unitary states, 31n., 37, 51; and geographical representation, 119; and internal stability, 76; and *jus soli,* 61; and League, 202; and newspapers, 110; and perpetual loans, 176; and personal unions, 52n.; and pressure groups, 108; and unwritten constitutions, 68-69; elective offices in, 84
Great Council, 112n.
Grotius, Hugo, 208
Group pressures: and pressure politics, 106-109; in Great Britain, 108; in U.S., 106-108; on political parties, 106-107
Guild socialism, 23: economic functions of, 23; political functions of, 23
Hegel, G. W. F., 13
Henry IV, 187
Historical method, 6
Hobbes, Thomas, 36
Holding Company Act (1935), 105
Home Owner's Loan Corporation, 159n
Home rule, municipal, 183-184
"Hot pursuit," 212
Houses, membership in lower, 117; membership in upper, 116-117
House of Commons: approval of policy, 69; choice of cabinet, 93
House of Lords, and constitutional development, 69
Human Rights, Declaration of, 205
Impeachment, 114: defined, 114n.
Imperialism, 192-193
Independence, and statehood, 31
India, and British Commonwealth, 56
Indictment, 151

INDEX 241

Individual: and the state, 60-67; subjection of, 195
Individual welfare, establishment, 16, 20
Inductive logic, 5-6
Industry, in U.S.S.R., 28
Industry, self-government in, 24
Inflation, 164
Information, 18, 151, 151n.
Initiative: defined, 88; direct, 88; indirect, 88
Injunctions, 156
Insurance, 18
International Bank for Reconstruction and Development, 206
International Civil Aeronautics Organization, 206
International Court of Justice, 205, 216
International Labor Office, 200
International Labor Organization, 199-200, 206
International law, 48, 208-216
International Monetary Fund, 206
International organization, 2n.
International Refugee Organization, 206
International relations, 2n.: external sovereignty, 38
International Telecommunications Union, 206
International Trade Organization, 206
Invasion, foreign, 17
"Iron Curtain," 193
Italy, 12, 23, 26, 77, 202, 205
James II, 69
Japan, 77, 193, 200, 202, 205
Judges: group pressures, 107-108; making of law, 140n.; and tenure, 149; role of, 150
Judgments, declaratory, 142
Judicial bodies, 30
Judicial, personnel and tenure, 148-149
Judicial review, defined, 78
Judiciary, 140-152: and Anglo-American law, 141; and jury, 151; and non-judicial functions, 144; and procedure, 149-152; and Roman law, 141; and systems of tenure, 149; functions of, 140-144; organization of, 144-148; rules of procedure, 150; selection of personnel, 148-149; separation of, 140; unification of, 147-148
Jurisprudence, 42
Jury, 151
Jury systems, 151
Jus sanguinis, 61
Jus soli, 61-62
Justice: and delays, 149; preventive, 141-142
Justinian Code, 44, 47
Kant, Immanuel, 187
Kingdoms, of Medieval Europe, 10-13
King's Bench, 44
Labor legislation, and Empirical Collectivism, 24
Labor unions, in U.S.S.R., 28
Laender, 54, 76, 146
Language, 33, 33n.
Law: and the executive, 124-125; application of, 141-144; adjective, 41; administrative, 47, 49; and analytical concept, 42-43; and anthropology, 43; and biology, 43; and codifications, 47; and commentaries, 47; and comparative concept, 43; and constitutions, 46-47; and custom, 46; and equity, 44; and ethical belief, 45, 46; and historical concept, 43; and judicial decision, 46; and Justinian Code, 44, 47; and legislation, 46; and "natural law," 46; and philosophical concept, 42; and primitive cultures, 43; and sociological concept, 43; and treaties, 47; basic ssytems of, 43-45; British, 44-45; case, 44; civil, 49; common, 44; constitutional, 48; criminal, 49; decree, 47; definition of, 41; international, 48, 208-216; municipal, 48-49; municipal private, 48-49; municipal public, 48; nature of, 42-43; positive, 42; procedural, 41; Roman, 43-44; sources of, 45-47; substantive, 41; *stare decisis,* 45; statutory, 44
Law, international, 208-216; administrative, 208; and adjusting disputes, 214-216; and individuals, 213; and interstate boundaries, 211-212; and marginal sea, 212-213; and new states, 211; and open sea, 213; and territory, 212; and war, 214; composition of, 208; effectiveness of, 210; obligations under, 210, 211; means of enforcement, 209; nature of, 208-210; private, 208; provisions of, 211-213; rights under, 210-211; sources, 209; validity, 209-210
Law of War, The, 208
Law of War and Peace, On the, 208
Laws, review of (France), 78
League, defined, 58
League of Nations, 200-202, 205: accomplishments and failures, 202; and Great Britain, 200; and mandates, 57, 58; and obligations of member states, 202; and U.S., 200; collapse of, 202-203; organization of, 201; purposes of, 201
Leagues, 7
Lectures on Jurisprudence, 37
Legislation, review of, 143-144
Legislative agent, 105
Legislative bodies, 30
Legislators, and pressure groups, 107
Legislature, 112-113: and bicameral pattern, 114; constituent functions, 113; control of administration, 113-114; electoral functions, 113; internal discipline, 114; powers and functions of, 112-114; statute-making, 113; structure of, 114-117; tenure of, 117
Legislature (Swiss), 138
Legislatures: and committees, 122; and leadership, 122-123; and speaker, 121-122; bases of representation, 118-120; bicameral, 115-116; composition of, 116-117; organization and procedure, 120-123; rules of, 121; unicameral, 115-116
Leviathan, 36
Liberties, 62-67: natural, 63
Liberty: and the individual, 140; defined, 63
Limited vote, 120
Literary Digest, 101

Loans, perpetual, 176
Lobbies, 105-106: defined, 105
Lobbyist, 105-106
Local government, 2n., 177-186
Locke, John, 4, 36
"Long ballot," 84
Machiavelli, Niccolo, 6n., 14
Machines, political, 96-98: corrupt, 97-98; defined, 96-97; use of party organization, 97
Magna Charta, 63: and constitutional development, 69
Mandates, 57: and German empire, 47; and Turkish empire, 57; and World War I, 57
Marbury v. Madison, 78
Marshall, Chief Justice John, 78: and judicial review, 78
Marx, Karl, 22
Massachusetts, and ratification, 71
Mediation, international, 216
Mediterranean, 194
Merchant vessels, 213
Merit system, 160
Method: comparative, 6; experimental, 6; historical, 6; observational, 6; scientific, 6
Metropolitan area, 185-186
Military forces, and executive, 125-126
Military Staff Committee (U.N.), 204
Minister, resident, 215
Ministers (British), duties and powers of, 132-133
Ministers, Council of: appointment and tenure of, 138; election, powers, and tenure of, 136
Minorities, national, 60
Misdemeanor, 49
Modern Democracies, 24
Modern states, 11-13; stages in development of, 7-13
Mohammedanism, 11
Monroe Doctrine, 193
Montesquieu, 72
Morality, promotion of, 16
Multiparty system, 91
Municipal law, 48-49
Mussolini, Benito, 23
Napoleon I, 47
National Assembly, 76, 78, 79
National Association of Manufacturers, 105
National committee, American, 96
National Industrial Recovery Act, 24
Nationalism: and Fascism, 23, 33n., 34; and imperialism, 192; development of, 11; economic, 191-192
National Municipal League, 71, 71n.
National party conference, 93
Nationals, defined, 30
National states, 11-12
Naturalization, 213: collective, 62; individual, 62
"Natural law," 46: conceptions of, 20; principles of, 63
"Natural order," in economics, 21
Near East, 194
Norman Conquest, 47
North Atlantic Treaty Organization, 193

North Korean Police Action, 207
Nuremberg Trials, 211n.
Observational method, 6
Office of Director of the Budget, 157
Officers, consular, 215
Offices, filled by elections, 84
One-party system, 91-92
"Open-door" policy, 193
Open primary, defined, 95
Opinion, meaning of, 100
Opposition bench (British), 93
"Optional clause," 205
Order, establishment of, 15-16
Organization, administrative, 157-159
Organization, government, 72: financial, 166-169
Organizations: imperial, 56-57; types of co-operative, 57-59
Pan American Union, 200
Paper currency, 164
Parliament (British), 37: and Cabinet, 134; and constitutional development, 69; and judicial decision, 46; and legislation, 46; and means of enforcing responsibility, 108; and pressure groups, 108; and unwritten constitutions, 68-69; evolution of, 112, 112n.
Parliament (French), 136-137
Parties, political, 90-98: American committees, 96; American legislative caucus, 96; American organization, 93-96; and democracy, 25; biparty system, 90-91; British organization, 93; convention of American, 94; functions of, 90; multiparty system, 91; one-party system, 91-92; organization of, 2n., 92-96; primary elections of American, 94-96; socialist, 92
Payment, methods of government, 176
Pax Britannica, 198
Pendleton Act, 161
Penn, William, 187
Permanent Court of Arbitration, 152
Permanent Court of International Justice, 201
Personation, defined, 86
Petition of Right, 64: and constitutional development, 69
Pirates, and international law, 213
Plato, 4, 13
Pluralism, 22n.; and syndicalism, 22
Police forces, 17: in U.S.S.R., 27
Politburo, 27
Political philosophy, 6n.
Political science, 1-6: curriculum, 2-3, 2n.; function of, 1; historical background, 7-14; methods of, 5-6; practical applications of, 1; scope of, 2-3; stages in development of, 13-14
Political scientist: and common law, 4; and economist, 3-4, 6; and ethics, 4, 6; and geographer, 4, 6; and historian, 3; and lawyer, 4-5; and philosopher, 4; and psychologist, 4, 6; and science, 5; and scientific methods, 5, 6; and sociologist, 4, 6, 7
Political society, "organismic" theory of, 5n.
Political theory, defined, **2, 6n.**
Polls, 100-101

INDEX

Population, 30, 189: attribute of statehood, 30
Port of New York Authority, 159n.
Postal service, establishment of, 18
Power: political, 19; economic, 19
Powers, separation of, 72, 74
Premier (French), election, 135-136
President: and cabinet, 129; and legislature, 129-130; election, 128-129
President of Republic (French), 78
Pressure groups, 101, 104-109: and executives, 107-108; and judges, 107-108; and legislators, 107; and lobbying, 105-106; and political parties, 107; and U.S.S.R., 108-109; defined, 101n.; nature of, 106
Prime Minister, powers of, 131-132
Primitive social units, 7-8
Procedure, judicial, 149-152
Propaganda, 101-104: defined, 101n.; in Great Britain, 103; official, 103; private, 102-103; techniques of, 103-104; use in dictatorships, 103; use in democracies, 103
Property, private, 22
Protectorates, 31, 57
Protestantism, 11
Psychology, use in dictatorships, 27
Public administration, defined, 3
Public credit, 28
Public health, 18
Public law: administrative, 2; classified, 2; constitutional, 2, 68-79; defined, 2; international, 2, 208-216
Public finance, 2n., 164-176
Public opinion, 2n., 99-111: and free discussion, 109-111; international, 209; means of influencing, 101-109
Public parks, provision for, 18, 24
Pufendorf, Samuel von, 208
Purposes of the state, 15-16
Race, 33, 33n.
Radio stations, operated by state, 18
Railways, operated by state, 18
Rapporteurs, 122
Recall, 88-89: defined, 88; need for, 89
Reconstruction Finance Corporation, 159n.
Record-keeping, 17
Referendum, 88: defined, 88
Reformation, 11
Refunding, 176
Regional corporation, 159n.
Regionalism, 193: American, 193; defined, 193
Relations, international, 187-207
Religion, 34: freedom of, 65
Renaissance, 5, 6n., 11
Repeating, defined, 86
Representation: and cumulative system, 120; and limited vote, 120; bases of, 118-120; functional, 120; geographical, 118-119; origin of, 112, 112n.; proportional, 119-120
Representation, proportional, 119-120: defects of, 120; Hare system, 119-120; list system, 119
Republicanism: and Fascism, 23; and unstable governments, 28
Revenue: external, 172, 172n.; internal, 172, 172n.

Review, judicial, 142, 142n., 143-144: in Great Britain, 142; in U.S., 142-144
Revolution: American, 38, 64, 69, 81, 207; English, 36; French, 25, 81; Puritan, 69
Right, defined, 62-63
Rights, 62-67: individual, 17, 25-28; natural, 63; procedural, 66-67; property, 66
Rights, of individuals, 25-28
Rights of Man, Declaration of, 64
Roman law, 44
Rousseau, Jean Jacques, 187
Royal Grant, and written constitutions, 71
Rules, legislative, 121
Russia, 12: and amendment, 77
Sampling, scientific, 101
Sanctions, 209
Sanitation, maintenance of, 18
Satellite states, 57
Science, defined, 1
Scientific method, 6
Second Treatise of Civil Government, 36
Secretariat, 204
Security Council, 203-204, 206, 216
Senatorial campaign committee, 96
Service: consular, 215; diplomatic, 215
Service functions, of state, 17-18, 20
Sewerage systems, 182
Sinking fund, 179
Socialism, 21-22, 23, 24
Social security, 18, 24
Southern states, and convention, 71
Sovereignty, 35-40; absoluteness, 36; and statehood, 31; characteristics, 36-37; comprehensiveness, 36; *de facto,* 28; defined, 35; *de jure,* 38; development, 35-36; doctrine, 194; external, 31n., 38; indivisibility, 36-37; internal, 31n.; international, 39-40; legal, 35, 37; national, 194; opponents of theory, 38-40; permanence, 36; pluralists, 39; political, 37-38; popular, 38; sociological jurists, 40; types of, 37-38
Soviet Union, 193, 210n.: and hierarchies of courts, 146; and judicial tenure, 149
Speaker, function of, 121
Speech and press, freedom of, 65
Spirit of the Laws, 72
Spoils system, 160
Stage: religious, 13; metaphysical, 13; positive, 13-14
Stare decisis, 45, 141
State: attributes of, 29-31; concepts of, 29-34; cultural groups, 32-34; defined, 29; distinguished from nation, 32-33; federal unions, 31; functions of, 16-18; individual, 60-67; international associations, 32, 199-207; purposes of, 15-16
State, Six Books concerning the, 35
States, 31: ancient, 8-10; and balance of power, 195, 198; and co-operative organizations, 57-59; and dictators, 26; and war, 198; constitutions of

modern, 68; democratic, 12; equality of, 195; federal systems in, 54; maintaining material interests, 191-193; modern, 11-13, 37; national, 11-12
States, power: demographic factors, 189; economic considerations, 188-189; factors underlying, 187-189; geography, 188; politics, 189; psychological considerations, 189; raw materials, 188; technology, 188
"States' Rights," doctrine of, 39
State system, 194-195, 198
"Straw votes," 100
Suffrage, 80-89: age requirements, 82; and citizenship, 80; and education, 81, 82; and "natural rights" theory, 81; a privilege of social status, 80-81; citizenship requirements, 82; defined, 80; equality of, 83; ethical theory of, 81; extension of, 81-82; freedom of, 83; grounds for disqualification, 83; groups defined in constitution, 72; legal theory of, 81; literacy requirements, 82; qualifications for, 81-83; residence requirements, 82; theories of, 80-81; universal, 25
Supreme Court (U.S.), 37, 78
Switzerland, 12: confederations, 59; electoral participation in constitutional amendment, 77; federal systems, 51, 52; federal unions, 31, 31n.; hierarchies of courts, 146
Syndicalism, 22-23: and Fascism, 23
Systems of government, current, 50-59: federal, 54-56; unitary, 50-51
Systems, political party, 90-92
Tariff, 172
Tax-collecting, 17
Tax court (U.S.), 147n.
Tax, defined, 169
Taxation, 169-175: and constitutional provisions, 170-171; essentials of, 174-175; exemptions from, 170; sources of revenue, 169, 169n.
Taxes: customs duties, 172-173; direct, 170; estate, 171-172; excise, 171; general property, 172; gift, 171-172; income, 171, 171n.; indirect, 170; inheritance, 171-172; kinds of, 171-174; land, 172; nuisance, 174; personal property, 172; property, 172; real-estate, 172; shifting of, 169-170; sales, 174; use, 174n.
Telephones, operated by state, 18
Tennessee Valley Authority, 159n.
Tenure, legislative, 117
Terms, length of, 86
Territory: accretion, 212; cession, 212; conquest, 212; discovery, 212; prescription, 212; and statehood, 30
Theory: democratic, 16; totalitarian, 16
Theories of state functions: classification of, 19; contemporary, 24-28; politico-economic, 19-24
Third French Republic, 76
Third German Reich, 120
Tigris-Euphrates, 9
Totalitarianism, 189
Totalitarian states, and free discussion, 110-111

Townships, 31
Towns (U.S.), 182
Treasury notes, 176
Treasury warrants, 176
Treaties: negotiation of, 215-216
Treaty of Versailles, 200
Treaty of Westphalia, 195
Tribes, 7: Teutonic, 10, 11
Trusteeship Council, 205
Trust territories, 57
Turkey, 200, 201, 202, 210n.
Unicameralism, 116-117
Utilitarianism, 43n.
Unions: international administrative, 199-200; personal, 52n.; real, 52n.
United Nations, 199-207: and trust territories, 57; Charter of, 203; specialized agencies, 206
United Nations Educational, Scientific, and Cultural Organization, 206
United States, 193, 194, 203: and administrative law, 49; and application of law, 141-144; and broadcasting stations, 110; and confederations, 59; and constituent functions, 113; and constitutional law, 48; and democracy, 26; and elective offices, 84; and electoral functions, 113; and electoral participation in constitutional amendment, 77; and Empirical Collectivism, 23-24; and federal unions, 31; and federal systems, 50, 54, 55, 56; and geographical representation, 119; and group pressures, 106-108; and hierarchies of courts, 146; and *jus sanguinis*, 61; and *jus soli*, 61; and League, 202; and legislative amendment, 77; and newspapers, 110; and propaganda, 102; and separation of powers, 72, 74; and state courts, 146
Unity: political, 32-33: cultural, 32-33
Universal Declaration of Human Rights (U.N.), 64
Universal Postal Union, 199, 208
U.S.S.R., 200, 203: and communism, 22; and democracy, 26; and dictatorships, 26-28; and group pressures, 108-109; and industry, 28; and labor unions, 28; and wages, 28; and veto, 207; constitution of, 27; elective offices in, 84; police force in, 27
Vattel, Emmerich von, 208
Veto, 204
Violence: domestic, 17; general program of, 20, 22
War, 198: and international law, 214; civil, 71
Waterworks, 182
Whips, British party, 93
Wilson, President Woodrow, 200
Witenagemot, 112n.
Wolff, Christian von, 208
World Health Organization, 206
World Meteorological Organization, 206
World War I, 33n., 194, 200, 210n.
World War II, 33n., 193, 194, 199, 202, 205, 206, 210n.
Writ of certiorari, 145n.
Writs of mandamus, 156: defined, 143